"In this crucial contribution to moral injury research, the authors, diverse in traditions and experience, reveal its powerful spiritual/religious implications—even for atheists—and offer compassionate, effective strategies for alleviating the profound human suffering that moral injury inflicts."

— Rita Nakashima Brock, coauthor of *Soul Repair: Recovering from Moral Injury After War* and Senior Vice President and Director of the Shay Moral Injury Center at Volunteers of America

"The subtitle for this comprehensive collection of essays says it all; as a resource for "Religious Leaders and Professional Caregivers," *Military Moral Injury and Spiritual Care* is a vital and long-needed compendium of thoughtful, well-researched, and relevant essays on the subject of moral injury. Poignant and personal, this volume offers compelling stories revealing the complexity of returning 'home,' and captures the complexity of the dynamics of reentry into families, relationships, and communities. This volume is bold to speak frankly on the inevitable questions of God's love and/or indifference, God's omnipotence and/or God's impotence as the injured (service member, family member, recently returned or elderly war veteran) yearns to make sense of the morally and spiritually unfathomable. Creating a collection of articles that have to this point been available only through professional periodicals, Nancy Ramsay and Carrie Doehring have gifted the caregiving community ready and readable access to both theory and practice in this uncharted field of moral injury. They provide articles that carefully tell the stories of veterans from Korea to Afghanistan and that probe the possibilities for what pastoral care could look like for these survivors. *Military Moral Injury and Spiritual Care* is profound without being prescriptive, sensitive but certain in its commitment to the spiritual healing of those we as caregivers are called to serve."

— Margaret Kibben, Rear Admiral (Ret.), U.S. Navy

"Moral injury affects many service members. Leaders of congregations, healthcare chaplains, and other spiritual care providers need to develop the ability to provide care for service members who experience it, as well as their loved ones and faith communitie~ ~~~ it. This book is an excellent resource for this

— George Fitchett, Rush University Me

D1593253

"This is a profound anthology on moral injury in the military. A must read for soldiers, leaders, and those dedicated to healing the wounds of war and service."
— Cynda Rushton, Johns Hopkins Berman Institute of Bioethics and the School of Nursing

"*Military Moral Injury and Spiritual Care* is a timely theological companion to clinical engagements with moral injury. Steeped in the emerging research in moral injury and forged in close proximity to the lived experiences of veterans, these essays display the power and breadth of pastoral theology to map the moral terrain. The authors scour the depths of their religious traditions, grapple with moral ambiguities, and provide practical advice for spiritual caregivers. If you enter with hopes of finding tips for working with military service members, you exit with a full-throated exploration of moral wounding and repair in the era of America's unending wars."
— Shelly Rambo, Boston University School of Theology

NANCY J. RAMSAY
CARRIE DOEHRING, Editors

MILITARY
MORAL INJURY
——— AND ———
SPIRITUAL CARE

A RESOURCE FOR RELIGIOUS
LEADERS AND PROFESSIONAL
CAREGIVERS

chalice
press

Saint Louis, Missouri

An imprint of Christian Board of Publication

ChalicePress.com

Print: 9780827223783
EPUB: 9780827223790
EPDF: 9780827223806

Printed in the United States of America

*This book is supported in part through
Dianne Shumaker's generosity to
the Soul Repair program
at Brite Divinity School.*

Contents

Contributors

Carrie Doehring is the Clifford Baldridge Professor of Pastoral Care and Director of the Master of Arts in Pastoral and Spiritual Care program at Iliff School of Theology. She is ordained in the Presbyterian Church (USA) and licensed as a psychologist in Colorado and Massachusetts. She is the author of three books, including *The Practice of Pastoral Care: A Postmodern Approach, Revised and Expanded;* and numerous articles and chapters.

Shawn Fawson resides with her family and works in Freeland, Washington, where her passions are in bringing the intersections of poetry and spiritual care to hospital chaplaincy. She is a PhD candidate in the University of Denver/Iliff School of Theology Joint PhD Program. Her book *Giving Way* won the Utah Book Award for Poetry.

Kim S. Geringer, MSW, serves on the faculty at Hebrew Union College-Jewish Institute of Religion in New York City, where she teaches in the rabbinic, cantorial, and Doctor of Ministry programs. She is also rabbi-in-residence at the Chai Center for Jewish Life in New Jersey.

LTCOL **Shareda Hosein,** USA (Ret.) U.S Army, is a community Muslim Chaplain in the greater Boston Area and serves as an educator on Islam in multiple venues across the country. She served active duty and reserves for 34 years, including Kuwait in 2004 during Operation Iraqi Freedom and 6 years as a Muslim educator with Special Operations Command. She holds a MDiv from Hartford Seminary and was the first Muslim Chaplain at Tufts University.

Elizabeth Liebert, SNJM, is Professor of Spiritual Life, Emerita, at San Francisco Theological Seminary/University of Redlands. She is author, coauthor, or coeditor of six books in the areas of spiritual formation, spiritual direction, and discernment, including *Way of Discernment: Spiritual Practices for Decision Making.* She continues teaching at several seminaries and serves on the doctoral faculty of the Graduate Theological Union.

Zachary Moon is Assistant Professor of Practical Theology at Chicago Theological Seminary. He is also a commissioned military chaplain. The author of two books, his most recent is *Warriors between Worlds: Moral Injury and Identities in Crisis.*

Nancy J. Ramsay is Director of the Soul Repair Center at Brite Divinity School, where she is Emerita Professor of Pastoral Theology and Pastoral Care, and served as Executive Vice President and Dean from 2005—2012. Ordained in the Presbyterian Church (USA), Ramsay is the author or editor of four books, including *Pastoral Care and Counseling: Redefining the Paradigms,* as well as numerous articles and chapters.

Nancy H. Wiener, is Founding Director of the Jacob and Hilda Blaustein Center for Pastoral Counseling and holds the Dr. Paul and Trudy Steinberg Chair in Human Relations at Hebrew Union College-Jewish Institute of Religion in New York City, where she teaches in the rabbinic, cantorial, and Doctor of Ministry programs. She recently coauthored *Maps and Meaning: Levitical Models for Contemporary Care.*

Michael Yandell is a PhD candidate at Emory University. Deployed to Iraq as an enlisted soldier in 2004, Yandell now studies moral injury and war through the lenses of theology and ethics.

Introduction

War changes lives forever. This volume offers guidance for spiritual care with those whom war forever changed through wounds of conscience or soul wounds. These wounds may not be easily seen, but they take a costly toll not only on those in or near a war zone, but also on their families, and when not addressed, extend across generations. The Department of Veterans Affairs describes these wounds of conscience as "moral injury." This term describes the consequences of "perpetrating, failing to prevent, or bearing witness to acts that transgress deeply held moral beliefs and expectations…[and may also include] bearing witness to the aftermath of violence and human carnage" (Litz et al. 2009, p.700). Moral injury is a new term for an ancient recognition that war changes us. Moral injury is also identified as one of the primary contributors to a significant increase in suicide among veterans (Kelly et al. 2019). The pain of these wounds of conscience can be intense, and while helpful care can ease the burden, "innocence lost is not innocence regained, it is innocence mourned and moral integrity reestablished" (Graham 2017, p. 78).

Military Moral Injury and Spiritual Care offers resources to inform and support practices of spiritual care for persons affected by moral injury incurred in the context of military service. This book is published with the support of the Soul Repair Center at Brite Divinity School in Fort Worth, Texas. Interreligious in its focus, The Center's mission is to sponsor research and create resources to inform and support religious leaders and communities of faith as they respond to veterans and their families and others affected by military moral injury. A number of the chapters in this volume reflect research recruited and sponsored by the Center in an interreligious research "think tank" 2013–2015.

Contributors to this volume write from their personal and professional location in Jewish, Christian, and Muslim traditions. Each chapter offers theologically reflective and spiritually informed care for veterans and their families as well as others such as nurses and physicians whose service in war zones has rendered them vulnerable to moral injury. These chapters are written to be of use to spiritual care

1

providers serving in faith communities; military chaplains; chaplains in VA hospitals; caregivers in hospice, retirement, and assisted living contexts; and spiritual directors.

The chapters range widely across more clinically informed practices to practices based on spiritual disciplines as well as more innovative practices such as witness poetry intended to facilitate lament in its confessional and ethical modes. Other articles draw explicitly on sacred texts in Jewish and Christian traditions that address moral injury and lament, care for moral injury through the frame of ambiguous loss, and the effective use of ritual practices to support healing. While most of the articles focus on agential moral injury that arises from the exercise of one's agency, several recognize the pain of receptive moral injury, including the experience of a Muslim veteran experiencing religious oppression by her Army comrades on the basis of her Muslim faith. Several articles recognize the importance of faith communities intentionally creating practices to support veterans and their families in their journey of recovery from moral injury. With the encouragement of military chaplains and veterans, several articles address strategies for helping civilians in faith communities become more reflective about how we may be implicated in moral injury when our countries wage war.

We had hoped to include a chapter by Dr. Larry Kent Graham, whose pioneering work in pastoral theology exploring the impact of war on families inspired many of us. Dr. Graham's untimely death prevented him from completing a contribution on lamentation—a generative aspect of recovery that many of our authors referenced in using Dr. Graham's scholarship.

—*Nancy J. Ramsay and Carrie Doehring*

References

Graham, L. K. (2017). *Moral injury: Healing wounded souls*. Nashville: Abingdon.

Kelley, M. L., Bravo, A. J., Davies, R. L., Hamrick, H. C., Vinci, C., & Redman, J. C. (2019). Moral injury and suicidality among combat-wounded veterans: The moderating effects of social connectedness and self-compassion. *Psychological Trauma: Theory, Research, Practice, and Policy*. doi.org/10.1037/tra0000447.

Litz, B. T., Stein, N., Delaney, E., Lebowitz, L., Nash, W. P., Silva, C., & Maguen, S. (2009). Moral injury and moral repair in war veterans: A preliminary model and intervention strategy. *Clinical Psychology Review, 29*(8), 695–706. doi.org/10.1016/j.cpr.2009.07.003

1

Moral Injury and Human Relationship: A Conversation

— Michael Yandell —

Tell me everything that happened / Tell me everything you saw…Did they seem afraid of you?…Was there one you saw too clearly? Did they seem too real to you? / They were kids that I once knew / Now they're all dead hearts to you.
(Millan et al. 2010)

Introductory remarks: Moral injury and human relationship

Moral injury is about human relationship. It is not merely a wound on the inside of a person, belonging solely to an individual. There is a sense in which moral injury exists outside of the individual, belonging to many people at once.

I am a U.S. Army veteran; I was an enlisted soldier from 2002 through 2006, and I was deployed to Iraq as part of "Operation Iraqi Freedom II" for six months in 2004. Those six months in Iraq, and those four years in the army, profoundly shaped who I am and how I think about the world. I self-identify as a person living with moral injury, but this moral injury is not solely my possession. I see it as a scar within me, as well as an untended wound cut deeply into the institutions and conventions that shape social and political life in the United States.

Moral injury is about human relationship. I have never waged a war, but I have fought in one. This is the position in which many military women and men find themselves. Is to say such a thing—that I have never waged a war, but I have fought in one—to shirk responsibility for actions taken during war? One could argue as much—walking a well-trod path shaded by the comfort of binaries. Here on one hand exists the image of the soldier who "follows orders," no matter what the consequences, forfeiting any and all decision making. A comparison to Nazis will inevitably rear its head here. On the other hand, there is the image of the soldier who is free to deliberate over every action taken in war, a sort of moral paragon who can heroically stand in a morally ambiguous and dangerous situation and always do the "right" thing. These images of soldier are false abstractions; the binary ignores the reality in which actual military women and men find themselves. The binary ignores real human relationship.

Moral injury is about human relationship. One will find plenty of company while trafficking in stereotypical images of military women and men, but it will be company gained on a path to nowhere. These images work on the assumption that the only person(s) who matters is the individual warrior—that only the individual carries the meaning of morality and responsibility with her on the battlefield. The lie in this assumption is exposed when the warrior is judged, not by her own moral criteria, but by the moral measuring stick of the society which sent her to the battlefield in the first place. What happened on the battlefield, how it affected the individual, and whether the individual exercised a kind of heroic moral virtue or simply followed orders will tend to matter very little; all that matters is what the individual's community *thinks* of what happened on the battlefield. To say "I never waged a war, but I fought in one" is an attempt to point toward the reality and the complexity of the relationships in which the war fighter finds herself. It is to say simultaneously that I am both far removed from the people and powers who made the decisions necessary to my actually going to war while also being in very close relationship with them—I was one of many who fought the war that others waged. The war is my responsibility at the same time that it is not my responsibility. I cannot absolve myself of the fighting, nor can the nation absolve itself by placing its guilt on the shoulders of military women and men. To do either would be to deny human relationship. The question I am most interested in as I write these introductory remarks is a question that will necessarily remain open: where do *you* find *yourself* in all this, Reader? Do you and I have any relationship other than that of writer and reader? Is the meaning you are looking for in this text a meaning that exists solely outside of yourself? Do you have a relationship to the wars of the twenty-first century—perhaps a first-hand experience, a relationship to those who waged it, a relationship to those who fought it, a relationship to those against whom it was fought? The purpose of this article is to explore these broad questions of moral injury and human relationship. I will explore these questions through engaging scripture, reckoning with the current widely used definitions of moral injury, borrowing some concepts from Dietrich Bonhoeffer, and all while weaving in an account and reflection on personal experience.

You, me, and moral injury: Something in our eyes

Here is an ancient question: "Why do you see the speck in your neighbor's eye, but do not notice the log in your own eye? Or how can you say to your neighbor, 'Let me take the speck out of your eye,' while the log is in your own eye?" (Matt. 7:3–4, NRSV). This passage from Christian scripture is quite germane to discourse on moral injury, but one need not be a Christian to see how. I argue that the site of moral injury is not fixed; moral injury exists at the site of human relationship, and its effects are as diverse as those relationships. I have something in my eye, left over from my war experience, and I suggest that you have something in your eye as well. Moreover, there is a collective obstruction of our vision as a nation. To illustrate this point, I will begin with my own concrete experience and "zoom out," as it were.

An event—something in *my* eye

Where does one begin to write personally about moral injury? For many veterans, there is an acute experience—for instance, profound regret over a pulled trigger—from which all sorts of emotions flow. Others speak of the war(s) generally, or a collection of events and experiences taken together that form moral injury. My own living with moral injury involves more of the latter, though there are indeed events in the war that stand out specifically.

I recall how it felt every time I watched my leader and friend walk down-range to deal with a piece of explosive ordnance or an improvised explosive device—the fear that clenched down in my chest hoping we had made the right decisions. I recall an uneasy feeling while seeing people taken from their homes at night, detained for reasons unknown to me and for lengths of time unknown to me. I remember carrying a shell-full of Sarin, breathing it in and transporting it, feeling betrayed by my own body—and what it felt like to have that moment scrutinized, picked apart, and debated at levels high above me. I was a young explosive ordnance disposal specialist at the time. The encounter with Sarin nerve agent happened in May of 2004, during what seemed to be a routine examination of old, rusted, and obsolete ordnance. The event was anything but routine, and the dissonance between my expectations and my experience that I felt that day have come to characterize the dissonance I feel in regard to the war as a whole (for more information on the Sarin incident, see Chivers 2014).

I remember the shattered confidence in the aftermath, what it felt like to experience such a profound journey of inner personal crisis— questioning *everything*—that one day the mirror showed me a new kind of face, and I realized that I had become, in name and reality, *unfit* for duty. I know what it feels like to look at Facebook in the years after military service to discover one with whom one served has died in a place far away, doing the work one used to do. I remember what it feels like to *become bitter*, to be paradoxically both proud and ashamed of military service—to be paradoxically proud and ashamed of having the good fortune to build a life after military service.

I gesture broadly to these events and feelings, Reader, because any one of them might serve as a starting point for writing about moral injury. Maybe you know and remember these things as well. Perhaps they strike a chord with you. Perhaps you or someone close to you has experienced one or more of these, or something like it. I have no monopoly on moral injury, and I can only speak for myself. However, I hope that I am not merely addressing my keyboard and computer screen, but that I am writing *to someone*. In this way, again, my stories and experiences are not merely my own; on the contrary, they exist in relationship to others.

It will help, for the purposes of this article, to focus in on one experience, acknowledging that it is but one example toward getting at the meaning of moral injury regarding human relationship.

It's April 2004 and I'm in Baghdad, anxiously waiting by our truck as my team leader takes a closer look at some ordnance our robot has deemed relatively safe. As I watch him, some kids approach me. They ask me for candy, as kids here often do. I don't have any candy, but we have some water bottles in the truck, and they're still cool from being in the freezer at the beginning of the morning.

I think: *I'll do a good thing and give these impoverished kids some water.* So I get the water out of the truck and move to hand a couple of bottles to the kid in front. The boy, who's probably about eight, refuses—after all, what he asked for was candy.

Something sparks inside of me. Here I am, risking life and limb, with my team leader downrange checking out an explosive, and this kid won't take something I'm offering out of the goodness of my heart.

I rip the cap off the liter bottle in my hand, dump some of it out on the ground, and throw it at him. An old man, most likely his grandfather, rushes up, grabs the boy, and pulls him away. The old man looks at me, not with anger, hate, or even sadness. His eyes are full of fear. He's afraid of me.

In that moment, I don't recognize that look, because I don't recognize myself. How can he be afraid of me? I'm one of the good guys, after all. (Yandell 2016, p. 52)

Moral injury is about human relationship. Human relationship is happening regardless of any mission or task; relationship exists in the background of missions and tasks. Relationship happens alongside them, above and beyond them, in the midst of them. During this event, I was focused primarily on the task at hand—to have been focused on anything else would have been dangerous. And yet, here alongside this task is a boy and his grandfather. Moreover, there is my team-leader downrange. There are the family and friends of the boy. There is something called the "United States" and something called "Iraq" hovering over us, enveloping us. There are people, powers, and institutions shaping the physical and emotional landscape in which I find myself there with the boy. In the midst of all this, lest it be obscured, there is *me*—my capacity to make choices and shape the landscape a bit myself.

This event has left a speck in my eye. As much as I may write about it, reflect on it, or reinterpret it, there it stubbornly remains. My relationship to the boy was perhaps inconsequential; what makes the event consequential for me is that I dismissed him as something inconsequential. When the stakes were high, and the effort required quite low, I treated human relationship as if it were nothing. To speak here of moral injury as if it were isolated to myself is to rob the term of meaning. *There was a boy.* The story is not about me. This is one way in which moral injury is about human relationship, and it leaves a speck lodged in my eye. Would you be the one to remove it for me, Reader? Are you equipped to do so? *Should it be removed?* Is there something in *your* eye? Beyond this speck in my eye from my own experience, is there a much bigger log which must be addressed? I will return to this question after laying some conceptual groundwork.

Moral injury and conscience

It is my hope, Reader, that I have been able to convey to you some sense of what moral injury is for me—thus far without recourse to specific definitions and research on the topic. However, moral injury is not about *me*; rather, it is about human relationship. In order to get beyond my own experience, it is necessary at this point to "zoom out" and consider broader definitions and concepts. I will explore, in this section, two widely cited definitions of moral injury, and I will reflect on those two definitions both through the gaze of personal experience as well as through theo-ethical terms borrowed from Dietrich Bonhoeffer.

Two definitions of moral injury

Jonathan Shay, M.D., Ph.D., spent years working with Vietnam veterans in a Veterans Affairs Outpatient Clinic in Boston. He develops his own definition of moral injury in two books: *Achilles in Vietnam: Combat Trauma and the Undoing of Character* (1994), and *Odysseus in America: Combat Trauma and the Trials of Homecoming* (2002). Through his years of work with veterans as well as through his own readings of Greek tragedy, Shay arrives finally at a precise, three-point definition of moral injury:

- A betrayal of what's right.

- by someone who holds legitimate authority (e.g., in the military—a leader)

- in a high stakes situation.

All three. (Shay 2014, p. 183)

The question of what constitutes "what's right" is of particular interest to me, theologically and ethically, in my own research. However, for this article that I hope is more of a conversation with you, Reader, my interest lies in the second point of Shay's definition: what constitutes "legitimate authority." In *Achilles in Vietnam*, legitimate authority resides in an officer or other superior in one's chain of command (Shay 1994). Is my personal account of my encounter with the young boy, then, outside that which is considered moral injury? Yes and no. Shay's definition gets at a very specific phenomenon—one involving the human relationship that exists between superior and subordinate within the military. In that sense, my own experience of moral injury does not fit Shay's definition; I was very fortunate that the people directly above me in my chain of command were trustworthy people of integrity. However, if authority is broadened to include those more distant from me—say in the higher echelons of U.S. government—betrayal is a feeling that comes more readily to mind. This adds a complication to the third point, however: can someone like Donald Rumsfeld, for example, be considered present to the "high stakes situations" in which military women and men were finding themselves at the time of my service?

I turn for the moment from Shay's "legitimate authority" to consider the second definition of moral injury. In a landmark 2009 article that prompted the Department of Veterans Affairs to pay closer attention to the phenomenon, Brett Litz, an expert in military trauma and professor at Boston University, along with a team of other expert scholars and clinicians, provided another working definition of moral injury: "perpetrating, failing to prevent, bearing witness to, or learning about acts that transgress deeply held moral beliefs and expectations" (Litz et al. 2009, p. 700) The authors define morals as "the personal and shared familial, cultural, societal, and legal rules for social behavior, either tacit or explicit. Morals are fundamental assumptions about how things should work and how one should behave in the world" (Litz et al. 2009, p. 699). The authors continue to add to their basic definition of moral injury with layers of nuance:

[Moral injury] may entail participating in or witnessing inhumane or cruel actions, failing to prevent the immoral acts of others, as well as engaging in subtle acts or experiencing reactions that, upon reflection, transgress a moral code. We also consider bearing witness to the aftermath of violence and human carnage to be potentially morally injurious. Moral injury requires an act of transgression that severely and abruptly contradicts an individual's personal or shared expectation about the rules or the code of conduct, either during the event or at some point afterwards...The individual must be (or become) aware of the discrepancy between his or her morals and the experience (i.e., moral violation), causing dissonance and inner conflict. In the case of a severe act of transgression, for most service members, the event is, by definition, incongruent and discrepant with fundamental beliefs and assumptions about how the world operates or how an individual or group should be treated (or at odds with military training and rules of engagement). (Litz et al. 2009, p. 700)

The basic distinction between Jonathan Shay's definition and the definition offered by Litz et al. is the question of who does the betraying. In Shay's own words: "In their definition the violator is the self, whereas in mine the violator is a powerholder" (2014, p. 184). If one were to flatten the two definitions, one can argue that the individual self in Litz et al.'s definition simply becomes the legitimate authority from Shay's definition. However, I argue that both of these definitions, taken together with their different emphases, get closer to the reality of moral injury than either can get on its own.

In my introduction, I warn against a binary that sets up a soldier either as an automaton merely following orders or as a paragon of virtue that has the authority and fortitude to always choose rightly in a given situation. Shay's definition, with its emphasis on the betrayal by a legitimate authority, guards against placing undue weight on the soldier's capacity to choose and act freely in a high-stakes situation. Litz et al.'s definition guards against viewing the soldier as a person who can only respond to an authority; in their definition, what the soldier herself believes to be morally right is of critical importance. Consider my own story again: there was no authority that betrayed me by ordering me to yell and curse at a young boy. I did it myself, and I am in fact aware of a discrepancy between the deed and my own morals, which "causes dissonance and inner conflict" (Litz et al. 2009, p. 700). At the same time, I was pursuing a task in a high-stakes situation. I did not encounter the boy in a vacuum; the mission (and with it, authority) permeated the atmosphere. Would a mere rejection of the water I offered him spark such an angry response in me in a "normal," lower-stakes situation? I profoundly hope not. I have never waged a war, but I have fought in one. In the midst of a war waged by others (authority), I acted poorly (self).

Larry Kent Graham (2017) offers another helpful model to dispel the moral binary I warn against that is not limited to a military/battlefield environment. In fact, Graham claims "each of us is a morally injured and morally injuring individual…" (2017, p. 79). Graham distinguishes between "*agential* moral injury brought upon ourselves by our own agency, and *receptive* moral injury caused to us by the agency of others" (2017, p. 13, italics mine). Agential moral injury, in my view, is the sort on which Litz et al. focus, while receptive moral injury more closely aligns with Shay's definition. However, Graham's approach expands the application of moral injury out of the high-stakes situations of the battlefield and military authority and places it within "the context of everyday moral living" (2017, p. 78). We are all moral agents, but we are not *just* moral agents; we also receive the moral actions of others. We give and we receive. We act and we are acted upon.

Dietrich Bonhoeffer on conscience

The importance of both definitions of moral injury cannot be overstated, in my view. These clinical definitions also invite our substantive theological engagement. Dietrich Bonhoeffer (1949/2005) in his *Ethics* develops the concept of "conscience" in a manner that adds layers of theo-ethical depth to the two definitions of moral injury provided by Shay and Litz et al.

Both conscience and shame, according to Bonhoeffer, are signs of a kind of disunion: "*Shame* reminds human beings of their disunion with God and one another; *conscience* is the sign of human beings' disunion within themselves" (1949/2005, p. 307). (I will return to the concept of shame in the next section). In order to put "conscience" in dialogue with the definitions of moral injury already provided, some further excavation of these terms from Bonhoeffer's work is needed. First, Bonhoeffer writes the following regarding conscience:

> Conscience is the call of human existence for unity with itself, voiced from a deep wellspring beyond one's own will and reason. It manifests itself as the indictment of lost unity and as the warning against losing one's self. Its primary focus is not a specific act, but a specific way of being. It protests against activity that threatens this being in unity with one's own self. According to this formal definition, conscience remains an authority the defiance of which is extremely inadvisable; disregarding the call of one's conscience, rather than leading to a meaningful surrender of oneself, must result in the destruction of one's own being, a disintegration of human existence. Acting against one's conscience is similar to suicidal action against one's own life, and it is no accident that both frequently go together. (1949/2005, pp. 276–277)

This account of conscience fits well with the thick account of moral injury given by Litz et al. in the large quote above. "Dissonance and inner conflict" (Litz et al. 2009, p. 700) in extreme form, I suggest, become inner "destruction" and "disintegration" in Bonhoeffer's language. I will leave it to you, Reader, to determine for yourself whether Bonhoeffer is right to suggest the link between a suicide of one's conscience and actual physical suicide. It is important to note that conscience, for Bonhoeffer, is focused on a way of being rather than a specific act. For Litz et al., we recall, "moral injury requires an act of transgression that severely and abruptly contradicts an individual's personal or shared expectation about the rules or the code of conduct…" (2009, p. 700). So, is it the specific act, or the specific way of being? I argue that Bonhoeffer and Litz et al. can both be interpreted in the following way: an act(s) that defies conscience disrupts, destroys, disintegrates, or creates dissonance and inner conflict in one's specific way of being. In other words, act(s) that defy my conscience disrupt or destroy my ability to continue to perceive myself as living in a certain way with myself and others. For example, my encounter with the child in Iraq eroded my perception of myself as a "good guy"— someone whose way of being was defined by helping people. The act, the encounter, disintegrated that perception. What the event revealed to me was not a profound lesson in what it means to be angry with a child; rather, it revealed to me a profound lesson about myself—that I was not who I thought I was.

Bonhoeffer goes on to say that the threatened unity of self that conscience seeks to preserve is "first of all, one's own ego in its demand to be 'like God'...in knowing good and evil...The call of conscience has its origin and goal in the *autonomy* of one's own ego" (1949/2005, p. 277). The only way one can actually find a unity with one's self, a unity that is not threatened, is to surrender one's ego. For Bonhoeffer, this surrender manifests in an explicitly Christian manner: "Jesus Christ has become my conscience. This means that from now on I can only find unity with myself by surrendering my ego to God and others" (1949/2005, p. 278). However, one can take as the foundation of one's self unity various other options, and Bonhoeffer provides an extreme counter-example from his own context:

> When the N.S. [National Socialist] says, 'my conscience is A.H. [Adolf Hitler],' then this is also the attempt to ground the unity of the ego beyond one's own self. The consequence is the surrender of the self's autonomy in favor of an unconditional heteronomy. This, in turn, is possible only if the other human being, in whom I seek the unity of my life, takes on the role of my redeemer. (1949/2005, p. 278)

I warned in my introduction that a comparison with Nazis would inevitably rear its head when dealing with stereotypical images of soldiers; this is certainly not what I wish to do here. What Bonhoeffer offers us here is the image of one's conscience as a type of prison. It is an impossible burden to be fully autonomous—to be the one who determines what is good and what is evil, to deliberate in every moment and try one's best to act accordingly. For Bonhoeffer, "Jesus Christ is the one who sets the conscience free for the service of God and neighbor... Unlike the conscience bound to the law, the freed conscience is not fearful. Instead, it is wide open to the neighbor and the neighbor's concrete distress" (1949/2005, p. 279).

I daresay that military service is an attempt to free the conscience. One wishes to do good, to reject evil, to be a part of something greater than the self. One perhaps even acknowledges that one is not capable oneself of deciding good and evil, and thus takes an oath of enlistment—surrendering one's ego in part to one's superiors. Maybe that is too broad, too general, a statement to make, Reader. Suffice it to say that this is how I thought of my own military service in the midst of it. I wanted to preserve the unity of myself as a "good" person, and thus was eager to join an institution that provided a host of rules, guidelines, and values for how to preserve that unity. The military, in a way, became my conscience, and "conscience divides life into permitted and prohibited" (Bonhoeffer 1949/2005, p. 307). The military's permissions and prohibitions became my justification of myself as a "good person." Bonhoeffer warns, however, that "what conscience cannot grasp is the fact that this unity itself already presupposes disunion from God and from human beings…conscience…is not concerned with a person's relationship to God and other people, but with the relationship to one's own self" (1949/2005, p. 307). I placed my conscience on the foundation of the military because I knew that I was incapable of deciding and dealing with the world's "good and evil"—though I wished to serve the good. The military in turn provided me with a knowledge of good and evil that I could carry into the battlefield, and ultimately: "bearing the knowledge of good and evil within themselves, human beings have now become the judge of God and others, just as they are their own judge." (Bonhoeffer 1949/2005, p. 308).

I cannot justify myself and my actions—I cannot find unity of self—by stereotyping myself as an automaton fulfilling a mission or as a person of conscience perfectly fulfilling the requirements of permission and prohibition. To be wide open to a young boy as a neighbor in a distressing, high-stakes situation, I needed something beyond permission and prohibition—something beyond myself that could liberate my conscience and my desire to justify myself to myself—and no nation or military can provide that. Moral injury, the speck in my eye, is a recognition that human relationship is about so much more than what we think we know about good and evil, what we think we know about permission and prohibition. The speck in my eye is the need to surrender my ego or conscience—my need for self-justification—and thus liberate it, to surrender it to someone/something capable of being my redeemer.

Litz and many of those who contributed to the 2009 article gesture toward this need in a new treatment, "adaptive disclosure," for military trauma including moral injury. In adaptive disclosure, "the service member is asked to have a conversation with a compassionate, forgiving, and benevolent moral authority;" this imagined moral authority speaks "sometimes through the voice of the patient and other times through the voice of the therapist" (Litz et al. 2016, p. 47, 124). The authors go on to acknowledge the importance of the patient's religious beliefs, suggesting "it may be that a discussion with *an actual moral authority figure* is warranted…The hope is that faith, communion with, and empathy from others who share a faith, and messages based on 'good' theology—centered on love and forgiveness—will help heal moral injuries over time" (Litz et al. 2016, p. 126). A fuller exposition of the intersection between adaptive disclosure therapy and "good" theology is warranted but not within the scope of this article. I do argue that Bonhoeffer produced "good" theology that is relevant for discourse on moral injury, for reasons stated above. Conscience is not enough for maintaining or repairing human relationship, because its focus remains on the self. When conscience is betrayed, it becomes a prison of isolation and self- disintegration, and while "conscience claims to be the voice of God and the norm for relating to other people," it remains one's own voice trying unsuccessfully to preserve itself (Bonhoeffer 1949/2005, p. 308).

I remember the boy in Iraq, and I think about him and write about him, and I think about other faces I saw there—soldiers I worked with, civilians we met. I did not wage a war, but I fought in one. Can I be the judge and jury of those faces? Can I be my own judge and jury? I spent some time in such a court in the recesses of my mind and heart, and there is no justice, repair, or reconciliation to be found for anyone there. That mental court of conscience remains focused on the act, on right and wrong, on permission and prohibition: "It was wrong to treat the boy that way, you cannot do that" is the verdict that rings out over and over again. The verdict is necessary but not sufficient. A lesson I learned, and perhaps you have learned as well, Reader, is that war and other high-stakes situations trouble the waters of right and wrong. What I need is not a way to remove the wrong act in my past; the act is done. What I need is a *new way of being*, a way of being unified with God and neighbor.

A focus on doing the right thing, so that we can stand tall in our mental courts, can render invisible the neighbor right in front of us. To be wide open to the neighbor, especially the neighbor in distress, requires an acknowledgement that our private mental courts are insufficient—they must be surrendered to something or someone higher. For Bonhoeffer, that someone higher is Christ the redeemer. I make no prescriptions here for you, Reader. As a reader of *Pastoral Psychology*, I assume you have a human relationship to your clients, patients, those for whom you provide pastoral care. Are you wide open to them as neighbors in distress? Are they looking for something/

someone higher? How might you help them go beyond their interior court and explore who or what that something is for them? I hope this conversation with me has given you some angles toward those questions, but I leave the real work to the experts.

One expert that may be of help to you, Reader, is Larry Kent Graham (2017), who insists that the caregiver must "share the risks" of the care-seeker and embark on a journey of "co-creative discovery," achieved through "attunement and mutual active listening (p. 11). Graham writes from years of experience as a chaplain, pastoral counselor, parish minister, and professor of pastoral theology. In the chapter Graham identifies as the "heart" of his new book, he offers many practical examples of "collaborative conversation" that can be employed in providing care for those suffering from moral wounds (Graham 2017, pp. 109–134).

The National Mall and the log in our eyes

We started with a speck in my eye, but we have left a log unaddressed. Having explored some concepts and definitions, I make a turn now, better equipped to describe what—in my view—constitutes the log in our eyes at a national level.

I first got the chance to visit Washington, D.C., in 2006. I had spent a few days at Walter Reed Army Medical Center (now the Walter Reed National Military Medical Center), dealing with some acute psychiatric problems that would ultimately lead to my medical discharge from the army later that same year. I share that information with you, Reader, because I consider myself in conversation with you. I hope that insight into my mental health does not make it easier to treat my narrative as something objectively distant from you, but rather that you see me more clearly as a person instead of words on a page. Perhaps my narrative gains more credibility in your eyes if I acknowledge that my stay at Walter Reed also involved follow-up examination regarding my exposure to Sarin gas in 2004 (see Chivers 2014). At any rate, I am vulnerable on the page to you now, Reader; all of this is deeply personal to me.

After my stay in the psychiatric ward at Walter Reed, I got the opportunity to spend a day visiting the National Mall with a close friend. I saw all the beautiful monuments that tell a certain story. I remember the pride I felt at being a part of that national story, and I remember the heartache I felt considering the profound *sacrifice* of all those memorialized there.

I stood there proud, and I stood there ashamed. Shame, because I knew the story told of victory through sacrifice leaves out many unattractive details. Shame, because at the time I was given the opportunity to remake for myself a good life, while others had none at all. Shame, because I knew there was a *different* story to tell, or at least a more complete story, and I was afraid to tell it. Shame, most of all, because I knew that what was expected of me in that place was to feel pride and gratitude. This is the worst shame—to feel ashamed for feeling shame.

How can I describe this shame multiplied by itself? I loved (and still love) the people I served with during my deployment to Iraq. I respected (and still respect) the non-commissioned officers and officers who were the superiors I interacted with on a regular basis. Here is the authority and the high-stakes situation: if I begin to feel dissonance about the war in general, and then dissonance with specific leaders who waged that war, at which point in the chain of command does this dissonance separate me from those human beings whom I love and respect? When I stood there at the National Mall, I raged in my heart at Donald Rumsfeld and others who continued to defend the logic of the war. Yet I knew that rage could only partially be directed at Rumsfeld. Rumsfeld was part of a chain—a chain of command that must be taken quite seriously. I was a link in that chain, and so were those people I love and respect. If I feel betrayed by Rumsfeld, do I feel betrayed by them as well? Or, the question really at the heart of this shame over shame, if I stand there at the National Mall hating the war and hating those in authority who waged it, do I by extension hate those whom I love?

Bonhoeffer again provides me with some theo-ethical scaffolding. For Bonhoeffer, shame is a precursor to conscience: "*Shame* reminds human beings of their disunion with God and one another; *conscience* is the sign of human beings' disunion with themselves" (1949/2005, p. 307).

Bonhoeffer (re)tells a story to define shame:

> Instead of seeing God, human beings see themselves. 'Then their eyes were opened' (Gen. 3:7). Human beings recognize themselves in their disunion from God and one another. They recognize themselves as naked. With God and others no longer serving as a protection and covering for them, human beings find themselves exposed. Shame appears. Shame is the irrepressible memory of disunion from their origin. It is the pain of this disunion, and the helpless desire to reverse it… Human beings feel remorse when they have done something wrong, shame when they are missing something…There is something forced about enduring the gaze of another, as is

required when making a personal vow, for example; there is something longing in the love that seeks the gaze of the other. Shame seeks a cover to the estrangement. But at the same time the covering implies an affirmation of the estrangement that has taken place, and is thus unable to repair the damage. Human beings seek cover, they hide from other human beings and from God. (1949/2005, pp. 303-4)

Here conscience and shame come together. I stated above that act(s) that defy my conscience disrupt or destroy my ability to continue to perceive myself as living in a certain way with myself and others. These act(s) reveal to myself my way of being—they leave my disunion with myself uncovered and unveiled, and they expose a deeper disunion between myself, others, and God.

When I put on my first military uniform, I connected with a community and an authority. As I think back to the look of fear in an old man's eyes in Iraq, I wonder now whether he was more afraid of the uniform or the weapon—or what those represented—than he was afraid of me; however, there was a 'me' under the draping of uniform and weapon. There were things germinating within me that a uniform had allowed me to ignore, but I could not continue to hide. I was ultimately hiding from myself: from the "irrepressible memory of disunion from [my] origin" that Bonhoeffer (1949/2005, pp. 303–4) describes using the mythic story of Adam and Eve and the fall.

'Then…they…made loincloths for themselves.' Shame seeks a cover to overcome estrangement…human beings also preserve an ultimate concealment with respect to themselves, they protect their own secret from themselves, by refusing, for example, to become consciously aware of everything that is germinating within them. (Bonhoeffer 1949/2005, pp. 304–5)

With the realization of what my uniform hid, I also began to wonder about other military symbols, like the monuments and memorials at the National Mall: what they represent and what they might conceal. These monuments and memorials are wide open for interpretation. On the one hand, I am glad they stand there so that we do not forget death in our midst. On the other hand, I have heard rhetoric drip from the lips of those in power, imposing meaning on lives and sacrifices that *are not their own*. There is a way in which meaning can be stolen from memorial, to place a grand narrative on top of something like war, forcing it to make sense in its senselessness. This grand narrative is the log in our eyes. The log is a structure of shame that rests heavily on the shoulders of individuals. It is a shame-structure that compels those who feel dissonance with themselves, with others, and with God to remain hidden—to not cast away the clothing of the grand narrative, lest they be cast away.

Deep down I still feel the pull of that national story, that grand narrative, and I know that I *should* feel proud—but I have seen and heard different stories, and perhaps you have as well, Reader.

Consider those events I mentioned, my own individual recollections of war, both broad and specific; these constitute the speck in my eye that allows me to see the log. The speck is aggravating and painful; the speck is the knowledge that war does not really make any damn sense at all. Then there is a log in this nation's eye. There is a log of forced meaning that is being used to bludgeon those who would serve this country and it is used to shame those who have served and feel dissonance over that service. The log is a story we keep telling ourselves that makes a whole lot of sense, a story about threat and defense and necessity and service and sacrifice, a story about glory and pride and honor and gratitude and respect.

We shape that story, and we refine, polish, and admire it. We memorialize it. We tell it over and over; we take it and beat the hell out of the people who have lived a different story. Their memories are bleeding out, wept from eyes that see clearly now the senselessness of war. We let them fall apart, fall through the cracks, fade and slip away, because we cannot bring ourselves to see it! We cannot even see our own wound—our collective moral injury—that is right in our face, in our eyes, the way we have surrendered to a logic of violence. If we cannot see our own woundedness, how can we hope to see a young boy in Iraq as a neighbor in distress?

The nation has a kind of conscience, a way of trying to preserve its self-unity. The meaning of those memorials can be co-opted. I once described moral injury as "the winds that blow when all the laws, all the understood ways of relating to other human beings have been laid flat" (Yandell 2015, p. 12). I was writing about what happens in war, when the enemy is pursued at all costs. A nation cannot exist with this laying flat of morality. Some would take those monuments at the National Mall as a buttress against such winds, a grand patriotic narrative that serves as a *justification* that preserves unity. The greatest memorial cannot restore what has been lost.

A grand patriotic narrative forgets so much. It is a log of insidious necessity that demands all these war memories, all these sacrifices, mean a certain thing. Have you ever heard someone say something like "our women and men in the armed forces are dying for" (fill in the blank)? I invite you to ask the dead what they died for, and to encounter the silence that greets you. I will keep my speck of moral injury, but the log that perpetuates more death by putting words in the mouths of the dead—that log I would have out forever.

Where do *you* find yourself in all this, Reader?

References

Bonhoeffer, D. (1949/2005). *Ethics*. [C. Green (Ed.), *Dietrich Bonhoeffer Works* (vol. 6) (trans: Krauss, R., West, C., and Scott, D.W.)]. Minneapolis: Fortress Press. (Original work published posthumously 1949.)

Chivers, C. J. (2014, October 15). The secret casualties of Iraq's abandoned chemical weapons. *New York Times*, pp. A1, A10–A13. https://www.nytimes.com/interactive/2014/10/14/world/middleeast/us-casualties-of-iraq- chemical-weapons.html.

Graham, L. K. (2017). *Moral injury: Restoring wounded souls*. Nashville: Abingdon Press.

Litz, B. T., Stein, N., Delaney, E., Lebowitz, L., Nash, W. P., Silva, C., & Maguen, S. (2009). Moral injury and moral repair in war veterans: A preliminary model and intervention strategy. *Clinical Psychology Review, 29*(8), 695–706. doi.org/10.1016/j.cpr. 2009.07.003

Litz, B. T., Lebowitz, L., Gray, M. J., & Nash, W. P. (2016). *Adaptive disclosure: A new treatment for military trauma, loss, and moral injury*. New York: The Guilford Press

Millan, A., Seligman, C., Cranley, E., & McGee, P. (2010). Dead hearts. [Recorded by Stars.] On *the five ghosts*. [MP3 file]. Vagrant Records.

Shay, J. (1994). *Achilles in Vietnam: Combat trauma and the undoing of character*. New York: Scribner.

Shay, J. (2002). *Odysseus in America*. New York: Scribner.

Shay, J. (2014). Moral injury. *Psychoanalytic Psychology, 31*(2), 182–191. doi.org/10.1037/a0036090

Yandell, M. (2015). The war within. *Christian Century, 132*(1), 12–13 https://www.christiancentury.org/article/2014-12/war-within.

Yandell, M. (2016). Hope in the void. *Plough Quarterly, 8*, 52–57. http://www.plough.com/en/topics/justice/nonviolence/hope-in-the-void.

2

Military Moral Injury: An Evidence-based and Intercultural Approach to Spiritual Care

— Carrie Doehring—

Introduction

How can spiritual care help veterans struggling with military moral injury? Moral stress and injuries often arise from struggles with God/the divine and from interpersonal struggles with moral and religious authorities and communities (Exline et al. 2014). The key to understanding such struggles lies in a veteran's particular spiritual orienting system "comprised of values, beliefs, practices, emotions, and relationships" that determine whether struggles lead to wholeness or brokenness (Pargament et al. 2016, p. 379). Emerging research on military moral injury and religious struggles in a sample of 155 veterans has demonstrated that religious and spiritual struggles fully mediate the relationship between potentially morally injurious events and anxiety as well as PTSD (Evans et al. 2018). Given the potential for spiritual care to alleviate the religious and spiritual struggles that give rise to moral injury, intercultural spiritual care within a religiously diverse military context helps those struggling with moral injury use the unique and distinctive resources of their religious and spiritual traditions, communities, and practices. Such care is evidence-based when it utilizes current research on military moral injury and religious and spiritual struggles.

In this paper, I draw upon pastoral theologian Larry Graham's work on moral injury and lamentation (2017) to describe two intercultural spiritual strategies—sharing anguish and interrogating suffering—that fully respect the unique existential orienting systems of veterans. Spiritual care begins with lamenting the shared anguish of moral injury using intrinsically meaningful spiritual practices to help veterans compassionately accept the emotions arising from moral injury so intensely felt in their bodies. Once veterans can experience their bodies and emotions as good, then pastoral caregivers can move to the second strategy of care: sharing the lament of suffering through exploring values, beliefs, and coping arising from moral injury. This co-creative process helps veterans find life-giving values, beliefs, spiritual practices, and ways of coping for collectively bearing and sharing the burdens of military moral injury. "Sharing our moral burdens helps us bear them," as Graham (2017, p. xiii) succinctly notes. A literary case study of a young female veteran based on Cara Hoffman's (2014) novel *Be Safe, I Love You* illustrates this evidence-based intercultural approach to spiritual care of military moral injury.

Military moral injury

Military moral injury has been defined diagnostically as "the emotional, spiritual, and psychological wounds that stem from the ethical and moral challenges that warriors face in combat, especially nontraditional forms of combat, such as guerilla war in urban environments" (Drescher et al. 2011, p. 8). Military personnel deployed in war-torn countries often must make quick decisions about using lethal force in encounters with those who may pose a threat. Moral anguish may arise from transgressing "deeply held moral beliefs and expectations" by causing harm to others, especially civilians; failing to prevent harm; or witnessing harm (Litz et al. 2009, p. 700).[1] For example, for some military personnel, witnessing the carnage of war by caring for the bodies of injured or dead military personnel can give rise to moral conflicts.[2] At the heart of military moral injury is guilt, which is a mediating factor between exposure to potentially morally injurious events and distress (Marx et al. 2010). This guilt often prevents many veterans from seeking social and spiritual support. Without such support, veterans will remain stuck in guilt, and less able to co-create more complex meanings about morally injurious events.

Meaning making—the functional interaction between one's values, sense of purpose, and situational appraisal of

---

[1]Hodgson and Carey (2017) review evolving definitions of military moral injury, noting that in Shay's early (2002) definition the moral stressor is betrayal by those in legitimate authority.

[2]Marine veteran Jess Goodell (2011) describes moral injuries arising from her deployment to a military mortuary in Iraq. Her memoir has been referenced recently in several dissertations on war trauma and military moral injury (see, for example, Moon 2016a).

events—is associated with lower levels of psychological distress and higher levels of well-being...and also partially accounts for the relation between PMIE exposure [potentially morally injurious events] and psychological distress. (Evans et al. 2018, p. 361)

The moral anguish experienced by military service members has been historically understood as a dimension of the posttraumatic stress of combat, as religious studies scholars Brock and Lettini (2012) note. Diagnostic criteria for posttraumatic stress disorder (PTSD) formulated in the 1980s included survivor guilt but focused on the fear of life threat rather than the guilt of moral transgressions. The biological sequelae of fear and terror have been researched, measured, and treated by behavioral health providers, but guilt arising from moral struggles was, until recently, considered beyond behavioral health care and more in the realm of spiritual care, as Litz et al. note (2009, p. 696). Although Jonathan Shay (1995) and others have described the ways moral struggles shape the stories of veterans, psychologists have only recently defined moral injury diagnostically, measured it empirically, and treated it in various forms of behavioral health therapy.[3]

Among pastoral theologians, moral injury is defined in personal, interpersonal, and collective ways as "the erosive diminishment of our souls because our moral actions and the actions of others against us sometimes have harmful outcomes" (Graham 2017, p. xi). Deeply held moral values and beliefs threatened or transgressed in moral injury are part of moral orienting systems shaped by many relational networks, as pastoral theologian and Marine Reserve chaplain Zachary Moon (2016a) notes. Family and cultural systems shape childhood values and beliefs that form a bedrock orienting system often re-energized emotionally under stress (Doehring 2015a, b), either by positive relational moral emotions such as love and compassion or by negative moral emotions that make people feel judged (particularly by God) or shunned (Haidt 2002). Depending on one's cultural context, these childhood values and beliefs become differentiated from those of one's family of origin during adolescence and young adulthood. Each branch of the military has its own culture and instills its own values and beliefs during the intensity of basic training, when military service personnel learn to respond

---

[3]Current therapeutic approaches include adaptive disclosure, a six-session individual cognitive behavioral intervention (Litz et al. 2015); building spiritual strength, an eight-session group therapy for use in faith-based settings for military personnel suffering from military moral injury (Harris et al. 2015); and acceptance and commitment therapy (ACT) for moral injury (Nieuwsma et al. 2015).

under high stress as a unit.[4] Moral stress and injury may not become problematic until post-deployment or discharge when "irreconcilable dissonances between military moral orienting systems and the moral worlds of civilian life" emerge in cognitive, emotional, and relational ways (Moon 2016a, p. 3). Civilians often cannot appreciate the complex dynamics of military culture, which is why civilian spiritual caregivers need to develop military cultural competency.[5]

Religious and spiritual struggles

The moral questioning and anguish of moral injury is one of three types of religious and spiritual struggles measured by the Religious and Spiritual Struggles (RSS) Scale (Exline et al. 2014):

- divine struggles with a judging and distant God, anger at God;

- interpersonal struggles (fear of being judged/shunned; anger about religious hypocrisy and moral betrayal); and

- intrapsychic struggles (moral struggles, self-condemnation, feeling unforgivable, doubts about ultimate meanings).

The RSS builds upon extensive research over many decades using Kenneth Pargament's negative religious coping scale (Pargament et al. 1998). Recent research using the RSS has found that religious and spiritual struggles are frequent in many major religious orientations, including atheism (Abu-Raiya, Pargament, Krause, and Ironson 2015; Abu-Raiya et al. 2016; Desai and Pargament 2015). Research demonstrates links between religious struggles and decreased immune functioning, increased emotional distress, depression, and risk of mortality. Research also links religious struggles and growth, notably when people find meaning from struggles, use positive religious coping, and experience religious assimilation (see Abu-Raiya, Pargament, and Exline [2015] for a review of research on risks and potential for growth). Pargament et al. (2016) propose that religious and spiritual orienting systems play a key role in whether struggles lead to wholeness or brokenness.

Ample research has demonstrated how religion and spirituality can support or impede stress-related growth (Abu-Raiya et al. 2015b; Kusner

---

[4]"Military recruit training, by design, destabilizes and diminishes the constancy of a recruit's pre-existing moral orienting system. Having stripped away such moral coding, including embedded values, beliefs, behaviors, and meaningful relationships, military recruit training indoctrinates recruits with a new moral orienting system that supports functioning in military contexts and the high stress environments of combat" (Moon 2016a, p. 2).

[5]Litz et al. (2015), among others, argue for the need for military cultural competency among therapists treating military moral injury and include a helpful appendix on the diversity of military missions, organizations, and relationships (pp. 169–180).

and Pargament 2012; Pargament and Cummings 2010; Pargament et al. 2006; Pargament et al. 2013; Werdel et al. 2014). Recent research on moral injury and religious and spiritual struggles with a sample of 155 veterans has demonstrated that religious and spiritual struggles fully mediate the relationship between potentially morally injurious events and anxiety as well as PTSD (Evans et al. 2018). This research suggests that religious and spiritual struggles are not a symptom of moral injury; rather, they are a predictive factor in the development of anxiety, PTSD, and moral injury following exposure to potentially morally injurious events. This research, the first to link military moral injury with religious and spiritual struggles, highlights the ways that religion and spirituality may help or further harm military personnel and veterans struggling with potentially morally injurious events. Evidence of the mediating role of religious and spiritual struggles in moral injury supports the role of spiritual care in alleviating military moral injury. What is needed within the religiously diverse context of the military is intercultural spiritual care that respects the particularities of each person's orienting system by exploring intrinsically meaningful spiritual practices that mediate complex spiritual orienting systems that include, for example, beliefs in a loving and just God.[6] Without ongoing experiences of the goodness of their bodies, creation, and a creator (for theists), veterans will have difficulty spiritually integrating their experience of moral injury in more flexible and differentiated ways—essential dimensions of life-giving spiritual integration and wholeness, as research has demonstrated (Pargament et al. 2006; Pargament et al. 2016).

This brief review of the research on moral injury and religious and spiritual struggles demonstrates the need for an evidence-based approach to spiritual care of military moral injury. Recent movements in health care chaplaincy are calling for chaplain competency in research literacy[7] but are often short-sighted due to measuring the chaplain's role solely in terms of health care contexts and outcomes instead of within faith traditions and their goals for pastoral or spiritual care. Relying only on psychological research on military moral injury without drawing upon religious and theological studies, especially pastoral theology, runs the risk of medicalizing moral injury, as Graham notes (2017, pp. 15–16). Theologically educated care providers such as chaplains, pastoral counselors, and religious leaders have the expertise to explore the religious and spiritual struggles that are often part of military moral injury (see, for example, Brock and Lettini 2012; Carey

---

[6] See, for example, Graham's (2017) discussion of God as moral conundrum (pp. 43–54).

[7] See Research, HealthCare Chaplaincy Network, https://www.healthcare chaplaincy.org/research.html.

et al. 2016; Graham 2017; Hodgson and Carey 2017; Kinghorn 2012; Moon 2015, 2016a, b; Stallinga 2013). Spiritual care of military moral injury needs to bring evidence from research on military moral injury and religious struggles into an intercultural approach that is exquisitely respectful of the particularities of a veteran's unique religious world and spiritual orienting system.[8] An intercultural approach to spiritual care takes into account the multilayered hybrid spiritual and religious identities common among people today, even among members of the same religious community. This intercultural approach recognizes the unique contextual ways that each service member and veteran may be living out spiritual orienting systems—values, beliefs, and practices— emotionally energized by the anger, guilt, and shame of military moral injury. As Graham (2013) notes,

> Pastors are in a unique position to curiously inquire about the moral weights carried by veterans and their families and to fashion a conversation that may help the veteran bear the moral weight of guilt and shame by sharing it with an emotionally available conversation partner. (p. 71)

Given the intercultural differences between civilian and military life, civilian spiritual caregivers will need to become culturally educated about each veteran they encounter, especially the particular ways veterans internalize their experience of military cultures during basic training and throughout their military service (Moon 2016a). Civilian caregivers might not be able to imagine, for example, the intense relational bonds formed in military service.[9] Some service members differentiate from their initial experience of their military culture by becoming an *unconventional warrior*, a term used by pastoral theologian Ryan LaMothe (2017) for service members who, "after encountering the harsh realities of military life, the horrors and chaos of combat, and the machinations of political leaders,... enter a process of disillusionment and mourning" (p. 834). Whereas some might reject the identity of warrior, others might become unconventional warriors who, while "remaining attached to the warrior ethos, [are] critical toward a government that uses its military to further the aims of political and economic elites"

---

[8]Pastoral theologian Emmanuel Lartey (2003) first proposed the term *intercultural pastoral care* "to capture the complex nature of the interaction between people who have been influenced by different cultures, social contexts and origins, and who themselves are enigmatic composites of various strands of ethnicity, race, geography, culture and socio-economic setting" (p. 13).

[9]"Despite widespread recognition of the strong attachment bonds that develop between service members during war. . ., grief associated with the death of a friend in combat has been surprisingly overlooked in the study of trauma" (Steenkamp et al. 2011, p. 99).

(p. 820). Understanding the unique ways a veteran's moral orienting system is shaped by his or her particular military training, service, and relationships is an important aspect of intercultural spiritual care.[10] The complexities of intercultural spiritual care are compounded by the ways spiritual caregivers have to try to step into the multiple worlds of veterans—the before-basic training world, the military world generated by basic training, the unconventional warrior world arising from moral struggles, and then the re-entry into civilian life world.

Depending on their education and training, pastoral and spiritual care practitioners may be more or less able to combine intercultural and evidence-based approaches in providing spiritual care to veterans with military moral injury. Pastoral caregivers and religious leaders educated exclusively within the beliefs and congregations of their faith traditions will likely use an historical or tradition-specific approach to pastoral care oriented around their tradition's religious goals, sacred texts, doctrines, and religious practices (see, for example, Geringer and Wiener 2019, Hosein 2019, MacDonald 2017, and Wiener and Hirchmann 2014). Many seminaries now teach intercultural approaches that pay attention to how family, culture, and political systems shape religion and spirituality (for example, the ways religion can reinforce oppression—in colonialism and neoliberalism—or confront injustice—in liberation theologies and social justice movements). Contextual education experiences such as clinical pastoral education (CPE) form chaplains and religious leaders who are adept at using intercultural approaches in multifaith contexts.

Those who seek ordination or endorsement as religious leaders or chaplains will often need to use a tradition-specific approach to pastoral and spiritual care within their own faith tradition and then shift to an intercultural approach in multifaith contexts. Chaplains working in research hospitals will often be required to use emerging evidence-based approaches to spiritual care. Chaplains and religious leaders working with veterans in military, health care, and veteran administrative contexts will need to be competent in both evidence-based and intercultural spiritual care. What would such care look like? How can such care help veterans struggling with military moral injury? I will begin to answer these questions through a case study in order to illustrate the ways that the intercultural dynamics of military moral injury are expressed within a particular veteran's story.

Intercultural spiritual care always begins with the stories of care seekers. My description of intercultural evidence-based care begins, then, with a lived experience of military moral injury artistically

[10]See, for example, Yandell's (2019) and Hosein's (2019) reflections on their moral injuries from military service.

portrayed in Hoffman's (2014) novel, *Be Safe I Love You*. This literary work depicts the transition from military to civilian life of Lauren Clay, a recently discharged, young, White female Army sergeant struggling with traumatic memories and moral injury. Hoffman writes as a civilian who extensively researched accounts of women in combat in order to realistically portray a woman's experience of military moral injury. I found her account credible as the basis for a case study in which *religion is both helpful and harmful* in the aftermath of military moral injury.[11] After I summarize the story of this veteran's first week at home, I use her story to imagine strategies for evidence-based intercultural care that utilize lament, drawing upon the work of Graham (2017).

Be Safe I Love You: A literary case study

When Lauren Clay graduated from high school, she could have accepted a music scholarship to study vocal performance. Instead, she enlisted in the Army to prevent a looming foreclosure on the home where she, her younger brother Danny, and their depressed, unemployed father lived in upstate New York. Throughout her deployment, Danny's letters to her always closed with the words, "Be safe I love you," conveying the bonds of love and survival fused through coping with their father's psychological struggles and their mother's departure many years ago. At first while she was deployed, Lauren worried about Danny's safety. Over time, she began to emotionally detach, a strategy in her "new war economy, the new austerity plan she instituted in her soul" (Hoffman 2014, p. 12).

The novel opens on Christmas Day when Lauren returns home unannounced, having been honorably discharged after her tour of duty as a sergeant in Iraq at a forward operating base (FOB) outside of an oil field. The novel tells the story of her escalating stress in her first week stateside as she struggles with morally haunting memories and nightmares about a traumatic event that she has trouble fully recalling. Readers are given narrative fragments here and there of a ten-minute episode when, as Sergeant Clay, Lauren was in charge on sentry duty outside the FOB with her closest Army buddy Daryl. The full details of what happened are not disclosed until the end of the novel, when Lauren puts the fragmented trauma memories together and faces the reality that Daryl was killed under her watch. An Army psychiatrist who had initially determined Lauren to be a model soldier, based solely on the online Post Deployment Health Assessment forms Lauren filled out, realizes belatedly that something Lauren had reported was a red

---

[11]Although literary critics have paid attention to the ways that Hoffman portrays a woman veteran's return home (Goodman 2017; Hosey and Hoffman 2014), none have commented on the role of religion in this story.

flag. Lauren had shared that she wanted to "reconnect" with Daryl, implying that she was thinking of killing herself in order to reunite with her deceased friend. Throughout the novel, the psychiatrist repeatedly tries to contact Lauren, but to no avail; Lauren refuses to return her calls.

In the week following her return home, Lauren struggles to adjust to civilian life, often feeling angry with family and friends who now seem so different from her. She misses Daryl and thinks of him often. They had become close when they realized they had shared values and were different from the other soldiers in their unit in terms of not complaining about the hardships of deployment, seeking out educational courses to supplement their military training, and reading about politics and culture. Daryl and she became critical observers of Army culture, questioning many of its ideals and seeing the oil field they were protecting as the reason for their military presence.

Lauren's disillusionment both with military and civilian life surfaces repeatedly in her first week home, especially in her responses to questions and comments about her military service. When a friend asks whether she had saved anybody's life, she replies sarcastically that she "saved" people from the "inconvenience of taking public transportation" while also saving enough money to cover her brother's college tuition (Hoffman 2014, p. 71).[12] She scorns her military medal as a fake, cheap trinket (p. 35). Her hometown feels like a movie set of facades viewed through a rifle scope that removes "surprise or empathy" (p. 74). She suspects people of watching her for signs that her training in using lethal force will make her do something wrong (p. 73).

Lauren has a hunch that Troy, her music mentor and organist at her church who returned from military service in 1990 to study music, may understand her anger, guilt, and cynicism. She senses his "reconciled sorrow. . . . self-mocking abnegation [and the] weight of [his] being alive, being a victim of the killing [he might have] done" (p. 60). Though tempted to talk with him about their military experiences, she fears that a gulf will open between them or that his traumatic memories are too terrible to mourn together (p. 60).

Lauren can no longer find solace in the classical sacred music she once sung. She visits the church where she had spent every afternoon from the age of 14 until she joined the Army practicing her singing in the resonant space surrounded by stained glass windows she loved (p. 52). Now, she cynically sees the stations of the cross as yet another

---

[12]As literary critic Goodman (2017) notes, "For Hoffman, the end of war and the exit from the field of war mean the extension of the war front into every aspect of civilian life. The war is called upon to heal the economic violence that violates, damages, and disbands the family" (p. 34).

war story. She is reminded of the hypocrisy of soldiers in her unit who became religious, demanding battlefield baptisms in order to secure God's reward through forgiveness and absolution for unforgivable acts of war (pp. 51–52). She now likens the mystery of religion to the senselessness of war: "that impenetrable false logic was necessary to make people do stupid things" (p. 52). The sanctuary's smells and sights that once combined with music to instill a sense of mystery now represent "fixed melancholic nostalgia, hopeful birthday cries of 'make a wish' and the faint odor of wreckage" (p. 53). A few days after Christmas, Lauren comes upon a children's choir singing "O Holy Night" at the mall. She remembers the physical experience of singing the solo as she hears the girl whose voice is "a golden bell" beckoning Lauren out of her guilt-filled memories (p. 149). As soon as Lauren feels a yearning to sing, her vocal chords constrict and close (p. 63).

The week culminates in her making a kind of sacred pilgrimage to Daryl's home in Canada. Pretending to pack for a car trip to visit their mother, she takes her brother Danny into the far north of Canada, to an old hunting lodge near the home of Daryl's wife. The arctic landscape has a breathtaking beauty that reminds Lauren of the minimalist sacred music of Arvo Pärt that she used to sing. Struck by such beauty, she momentarily transcends her body, with its "instinctual chemical flood of being [a] hunted, hunting animal," and remembers the "grounded yet soaring feeling that comes from using your body to sing" (p. 201). This self-transcendence reveals to her how much military experience has changed her world—like the shattering of a mirror (p. 207). In turn, the image of a broken mirror reminds her of a childhood story she and Danny loved—"The Snow Queen"—in which a piece from the devil's distorting mirror turns everything bad, then lodges in a boy's eye until his sister rescues him and cries over him, washing the fragment out (pp. 127–129).

Lauren's journey north is her own way of reconnecting with Daryl and rescuing Danny from his continual escapism into social media. In the bitter cold of the abandoned hunting lodge, she initiates Danny into her own version of boot camp with exercise drills and survivalist training but without military ideals. She drives him to look at an enormous oil rig rising from the floor of the ocean—a symbol of the god of capitalism and the war she fought: "busily sucking the past up from the ground and melting the future, burning [peoples'] lives before they could live them" (p. 251).

In the complete darkness and freezing cold of the night, Lauren finds her voice and begins to sing, at Danny's anxious urging, a song about homecoming: "My Heart's in the Highlands, Wherever I Go." To Danny, her voice conveys a reality of goodness "filled with friendship and older than memories," and now he realizes their common existential bond in "some code that was twisted beyond repair. . . . a new way of being [which] even if it killed them . . . was impossibly, imponderably right" (pp. 254–255).

Lauren drives from the hunting lodge to Daryl's home to meet his wife Camille. When Lauren asks after Daryl, Camille explodes with anger at Lauren's willful denial of her husband's death. This is the moment when Lauren is forced to face the traumatic memory of Daryl's death in its entirety. Now she fully recalls how their encounter with the car speeding toward them at the FOB ended in her killing a driver trying to get medical care for his pregnant wife in labor and how the pregnant woman grabbed Daryl's weapon and killed him as he reached down to help her (pp. 259–262). The suicidal nature of this pilgrimage to pay for Daryl's death is now explicit as a plan to join Daryl beyond the grave (p. 269). After leaving Danny at a hotel in a nearby town, Lauren heads back to the oil rig to lie down in the snow and freeze to death. Danny finds her just as the sun rises, and she is rescued.

Lamenting military moral injury

Let us imagine that we are chaplains on a behavioral health team offering spiritual care to Lauren during her subsequent hospitalization. We will be doing evidenced-based spiritual care by employing research on military moral injury and religious struggles. We will be drawing upon our theological education and training in intercultural spiritual care as we prepare to step into Lauren's moral orienting system with its particular values, beliefs, and ways of coping and connecting with the sacred, shaped by family, religious, and military cultures and now reshaped by moral injury amidst her return to civilian life. Where would such care begin?

Intercultural, evidence-based care of military moral injury needs to begin with spiritual practices that foster self-compassion. Veterans experiencing military moral injury will often have a hard time revisiting memories or exploring meanings until they can tolerate the intense emotions—typically anger and guilt—at the heart of military moral injury.[13] Mindfulness practices and yoga have been used extensively with both trauma survivors and veterans to help them experience and not dissociate from or avoid emotions arising from painful memories

---

[13]Bessel van der Kolk (2014), a preeminent trauma researcher and psychiatrist, began his research and clinical practice in the U.S. Department of Veterans Affairs with veterans experiencing both PTSD and military moral injury. Research with this population demonstrates the need for establishing a sense of safety and emotional containment at the outset of care. In her seminal work *Trauma and Recovery* (1992), Judith Herman's three-part process of recovery begins with survivors experiencing safety before they can explore memories without re-traumatization.

(see, for example, van der Kolk 2014). Liebert (2019) details the ways specific practices can inform spiritual care to veterans experiencing military moral injury.

As research on religious struggles (reviewed above) suggests, explicitly religious practices may not be initially helpful for veterans like Lauren who are struggling with anger at God and their religious communities and are experiencing religious doubts, especially when their moral orienting systems have been radically reconstructed by military training (Moon 2016a) and moral injury. In Lauren's case, her religious struggles with God, along with her interpersonal religious and moral struggles, have generated a life-limiting, potentially fatal spiritual orientation to her moral injury that is rigid, inflexible, and cut off from God's benevolence and the goodness of humanity and creation. Life-giving aspects of her formative religious experiences are no longer resources. This toxic religious orientation to her moral injury is similar to what suicidologist Shneidman (1993, 1996) identifies as tunnel vision created by a suicidal constriction of the mind. Ryan Hall (2017) found evidence for this tunnel vision in her research on participants' stories of how positive religious resources became unavailable in the final stages of their near-lethal suicide attempts. For Lauren, religious and spiritual practices and meanings that once had fostered wholeness became harmful when her tunnel vision enlisted religious meanings in support of suicide as a way of "coping" with moral injury.

How can spiritual practices be reconstructed when religious and spiritual struggles invalidate them, as happened to Lauren? One possible route through such struggles toward wholeness is to give voice to anger, protest, and disillusionment through lamentation. Graham's research on the impact of war on families convinced him that lamentation is "a strong personal and communal spiritual and ritual resource for reclaiming lives from war, including healing moral injury" (personal communication, July 26, 2017). Graham (2017) identifies "three interacting poles of lamentation—sharing anguish, interrogating causes, and reinvesting hope" (p. 139)—that are similar to Herman's (1992) three phases—establishing safety, mourning memories and exploring meanings, and reconnecting with ordinary good-ness. I will now apply Graham's spiritual care strategies in imagining intercultural and evidence-based care for Lauren.

The lament of sharing anguish

Sharing anguish must begin in veterans' bodies with spiritual practices that foster compassion while allowing their bodies to experience the angry grief arising from spiritual orienting systems broken by war, especially for "unconventional warriors" such as

Lauren. Using an intercultural approach, chaplains and religious leaders can help veterans explore and possibly reclaim spiritual practices that lovingly hold the emotional energy of guilt, anger, and shame. An intercultural spiritual caregiver, for example, would be able to appreciate Lauren's ability to sing a lament of shared anguish in the song "My Heart's in the Highlands" that she sang to Danny in the arctic night. Knowing how church choral music used to connect Lauren with sacred beauty and a loving God, a spiritual caregiver might suggest that she and Lauren listen together in a meditative way to Pärt's setting of "My Heart's in the Highlands"[14] and pay attention to what it feels like in Lauren's body. Lauren could then focus compassionately on how her body responds to this music. In a welcoming prayer (Vennard 2013) led by her spiritual caregiver, Lauren could invite this constriction and its related emotions to communicate its bodily wisdom to her. If these emotions involve the anger, guilt, and shame of moral injury, then she would try listening again and allowing the lament of the music to hold her feelings with compassion and so hold the Lauren whose body witnesses "the suffering that remains . . . the ways in which death pervades life" (Rambo 2010, p. 15).

Given Lauren's artistic sensibilities, she may find poetry a meaningful way to share anguish. Fawson (2016, 2019) demonstrates how the witness poetry of veterans laments the grievous losses of moral injury in ways no other genre of literature can. She describes and illustrates how spiritual caregivers and religious leaders can "facilitate lamentation in processing moral injury in the context of small groups of military service members, veterans and/or their families" (Fawson 2019, p. 31) by studying poems by veterans who have experienced military moral injury. Fawson uses poetic studies to explore how Walt Whitman's poetry has "wrestled with experience, ideas, history, the speaker's own psychic drama in a way that transforms it, and utters the complex and varying emotional responses we have" (2019, pp. 34-35). Fawson suggests ways that a spiritual caregiver could share the anguish of war through reading Whitman's poetry. Musical settings of Whitman's poems by Ned Rorem and Ralph Vaughan Williams, for example, could be especially evocative for a singer like Lauren.

---

[14]Pärt's unique musical style seems particularly conducive for the lament of sharing anguish. Unlike traditional classical music, Pärt's music does not move from tension to resolution. It has been likened to contemplative prayer: "meditative, repetitive, filled with silences, using simple combinations of notes. The effect is a feeling of being suspended in time" (Heffern 2002, p. 27). Many listeners experience a physiological sense of comfort from his music. Musicologist Robert Sholl (2012) wonders, could "the spirituality of Pärt's music can be located in the body itself? Through its delicacy, and its sensitivity to the preciousness and freshness of organized sound itself, his music could be understood and experienced as embodied" (p. 154).

In fact, Vaughan Williams himself could be described as an unconventional warrior. He enlisted in the British army at the age of 42 during the First World War and was part of an ambulance team that brought the wounded out of the Third Battle of Ypres at Flanders, which went on for months, with one and a quarter million British, French, and German soldiers killed and many wounded. He wrote *Dona Nobis Pacem: Sancta Civitas* in 1936 as a way of sharing the anguish of lamentation for the suffering of the First World War amidst the threatening atmosphere of further war. The movement "Reconciliation" is like a lullaby sung by a soprano using a text from Whitman:

> Word over all, beautiful as the sky,
> Beautiful that war and all its deeds of carnage must in time be utterly lost,
> That the hands of the sisters Death and Night incessantly softly wash again and ever again, this soiled world;
> For my enemy is dead, a man divine as myself is dead,
> I look where he lies white-faced and still in the coffin—I draw near,
> Bend down and touch lightly with my lips the white face in the coffin. (Whitman 1855, p. 521)

Lauren is an artist who knows what it is like to perform beautiful sacred music. Her suicidal mission was going to be a way to experience fragments of her military moral injury in the midst of the beauty of the arctic, reminding her of the music of Pärt. In a spiritual care context, she might well experience shared anguish in the artistic witness of Whitman and Vaughan Williams. The poetry of the music she listens to and sings might open ways for her to use art to share the anguish of lament.

The lament of interrogating causes

If Lauren is able to use music and poetry to experience the goodness of shared lament in her body and within trusted relationships, then her embodied, relational experience of compassion could reveal the role of guilt or anger in her life-limiting spiritual orientation to her moral injury. For example, Lauren's embedded theology of feeling solely responsible for her brother's survival has likely been shaped by intersecting sexism and classism (Ramsay 2013) in ways that have now cut her off from the interconnected responsibility shared with God and others in her relational webs of life. It is possible that Lauren's socialization as a girl and young woman in a vulnerable economic or precarious economic situation shaped the drastic ways she tries to take care of her younger brother. Parsing out the complex interacting aspects of a person's social identity is difficult, and research is not helpful here. Research on military moral injury has not yet fully taken into account the role of gender, let alone social class, sexual orientation, and other formative aspects of social identity.[15] Exploring the ways Lauren's values, beliefs, and ways of coping have been shaped by her gender and social class would be part of intercultural spiritual care, especially the ways she experiences her female body as she uses spiritual practices to stay connected with a loving God when she experiences anger, guilt, and grief.

Lauren's religious doubts and struggles have been a private lament that needs to be shared through spiritual care that helps her and others "question, complain, protest, and assess responsibility for what happened . . . [so that] we devise ways to name and frame what happened so that we might bear the costs and heal from the consequences of the wounds to our souls and communities" (Graham 2017, p. 142). Lauren's unconventional warriorism expresses her anger about the capitalistic nature of militarism and her disillusionment with naive patriotism. Intercultural spiritual caregivers will need to be theologically empathic to the narrative truth of Lauren's angry interrogation of religious symbols such as the stations of the cross and the crucified Christ. Music from Holy Week commemorating the gospel stories of the Passion narratives could help her theologically interrogate her suffering. The gospel narratives recounted on Maundy Thursday of Jesus tenderly washing the feet of his disciples even though he knew the ways they would betray him and experience their own moral injuries could provide a kind of meditation for Lauren in which she imagines Jesus' compassionate presence with her throughout her military service, homecoming, and suicide attempt. Commentaries on the Passion narratives (e.g., Borg and Crossan 2008)[16] might help her experience the crucified Jesus used by Roman authorities for military purposes. She might experience a sense of reconciliation with Jesus and God as "our co-creative partner in healing, sustaining, and guiding

---

[15]Although there is research on gender and military sexual trauma, the relationship of gender to military moral stress has been understudied except in recent doctoral dissertations such as Moon's (2016a). Other publications have missed the opportunity to explore this issue. For instance, Gray et al.'s (2012) initial testing of a treatment approach to military moral injury called "adaptive disclosure" makes no mention of gender differences, though it included 2 female and 40 male Marine Corps and Navy personnel. Litz et al.'s (2015) book *Adaptive Disclosure: A New Treatment for Military Trauma, Loss, and Moral Injury* uses male and female pronouns when referring to service members but has no case studies about women.

[16]A recently published New Testament biblical study uses moral injury as a hermeneutical lens for considering the construction of Peter as a character in the Gospels of Matthew and John (Carter 2017).

the shaken, shattered, exploded, bombed, bulleted, and drowning human community" (Graham 2017, p. 144). Reconciliation may, in turn, lead to ritual ways of experiencing forgiveness. Meditative use of religious images, music, and poetry could spiritually engage Lauren imaginatively with the dead in ways similar to counseling strategies for military moral injury described by Litz et al. (2015) and spiritual care strategies elaborated in Fawson (2019), Geringer and Wiener (2019), and Moon (2019).

Reinvesting hope

In an intercultural spiritual care encounter, Lauren would likely experience hope when the beauty of music and poetry or other life-giving spiritual resources that come to light help her share anguish about and meanings of suffering. The hope glimpsed in moments of beauty on her journey north could now point to life and not death.

As these strategies for intercultural spiritual care suggest, spiritual care of military moral injury is distinct from behavioral health care in its engendering hope through

- the use of spiritual practices to somatically foster lament, self-compassion, and the capacity for relational connection in ways that reveal life-limiting spiritual orienting systems energized by the guilt, anger, and grief of military moral injury and

- the co-creating of intentional values, beliefs, and ways of coping that foster spiritual integration and wholeness (Doehring 2015b).

Lauren seems particularly ready for spiritual care that helps her use religious practices and meanings to share anguish, interrogate suffering, and reinvest hope. At the conclusion of the novel, Lauren is recovering in the hospital and constructing her own stations of the cross out of the vivid sequence of events in her traumatic memory, peopled by

the still bodies and the falling bodies; the mother the son and the weight of the never born all pulling, blood pooling, toward the earth where Lauren stood armored, the color of desert dust, holding tight the same kind of instrument that had cut them down. The cathedral in her head shone with this iconography. What sacred song could pass through her lips now? (Hoffman 2014, p. 286)

In this imagery and her confession to her music mentor Troy that she did terrible things, we sense the movement through lament made possible by spiritual practices and meanings that Troy, as a religiously committed unconventional warrior, along with intercultural spiritual caregivers could facilitate.

If Lauren is able to use intrinsically meaningful spiritual practices to sustain lamentation and interrogate her suffering, she is more likely to reconnect with her childhood experience of God and her Roman Catholic religious tradition, now with a second naïveté (Ricouer 1967).[17] She may now be able to experience the ordinary goodness of life through her childhood Roman Catholic sacraments. Religious rituals offer a sensory, communal way of tangibly experiencing transcendence and goodness, especially within the beauty of sacred spaces and music.

Conclusion

The poignant literary case study based on Hoffman's (2014) novel illustrates how a chaplain or religious leader could combine evidence-based and intercultural spiritual care to understand the unique religious and spiritual features of a veteran's spiritual orienting system energized by the angry guilt of military moral injury. The chaplain's and religious leader's own process of spiritual integration will help them stand with veterans in the shared anguish of their lamentation. Chaplains and religious leaders may become unconventional representatives of their faith tradition if they go through their own process of what Carlin (2014) calls 'religious mourning' that parallels, as LaMothe (2017) notes, the process of becoming an unconventional warrior. Indeed, the religious mourning of religious leaders and chaplains may bring them face to face with their religious, spiritual, and moral struggles. Like the veterans to whom they minister, they may need to find their own spiritual and religious practices to share the anguish of lament while seeking partners and communities for interrogating suffering.

The chaplain's and religious leader's theological education and intercultural training and personal journeys toward spiritual wholeness will help them explore with veterans how intrinsically meaningful beliefs, values, and practices can bear the weight of their moral injury in a lifelong process of spiritual integration. Providing spiritual care to those who are morally wounded is challenging, as research and case studies tell us. Chaplains and religious leaders have a unique role to play in the search for spiritual practices and meanings that can help them collectively share with veterans the burdens of military moral injury through lament and hope.

---

[17]Religious struggles lead many people to reject their childhood religious faith and traditions and become spiritual seekers who turn to nontheistic spiritual practices such as Buddhism that do not engage childhood experiences of a punitive God. Although for many this can be a path to spiritual wholeness, for Lauren this would mean leaving behind the sacred religious music at the core of her childhood experiences of beauty and holiness.

References

Abu-Raiya, H., Pargament, K., & Exline, J. J. (2015a). Understanding and addressing religious and spiritual struggles in health care. *Health & Social Work, 40*(4), 126–134. https://doi.org/10.1093/hsw/hlv055.

Abu-Raiya, H., Pargament, K., & Krause, N. (2015b). Religion as problem, religion as solution: Religious buffers of the links between religious/spiritual struggles and well-being/mental health. *Quality of Life Research, 25*(5), 1265–1274. https://doi.org/10.1007/s11136-015-1163-8.

Abu-Raiya, H., Pargament, K., Krause, N., & Ironson, G. (2015c). Robust links between religious/spiritual struggles, psychological distress, and well-being in a national sample of American adults. *American Journal of Orthopsychiatry, 85*(6), 565–575. https://doi.org/10.1037/ort0000084.

Abu-Raiya, H., Pargament, K., Weissberger, A., & Exline, J. (2016). An empirical examination of religious/spiritual struggle among Israeli Jews. *International Journal for the Psychology of Religion, 26*(1), 61–79. https://doi.org/10.1080/10508619.2014.1003519.

Borg, M. J., & Crossan, J. D. (2008). *The last week: What the gospels really teach about Jesus' final days in Jerusalem.* London: SPCK.

Brock, R. N., & Lettini, G. (2012). *Soul repair: Recovering from moral injury after war.* Boston: Beacon Press.

Carey, L. B., Hodgson, T. J., Krikheli, L., Soh, R. Y., Armour, A.-R., Singh, T. K., & Impiombato, C. G. (2016). Moral injury, spiritual care and the role of chaplains: An exploratory scoping review of literature and resources. *Journal of Religion and Health, 55*(4), 1218–1245. https://doi.org/10.1007/s10943-016-0231-x.

Carlin, N. (2014). *Religious mourning: Reversals and restorations in psychological portraits of religious leaders.* Eugene: Wipf & Stock.

Carter, W. (2017). Peter and Judas: Moral injury and repair. In J. MacDonald (Ed.), *Exploring moral injury in sacred texts* (pp. 151–168). Philadelphia: Jessica Kingsley.

Desai, K. M., & Pargament, K. (2015). Predictors of growth and decline following spiritual struggles. *International Journal for the Psychology of Religion, 25*(1), 42–56. https://doi.org/10.1080/10508619.2013.847697.

Doehring, C. (2015a). *The practice of pastoral care: A postmodern approach* (rev. and expanded ed.). Louisville: Westminster John Knox.

Doehring, C. (2015b). Resilience as the relational ability to spiritually integrate moral stress. *Pastoral Psychology, 64*(5), 635–649. https://doi.org/10.1007/s11089-015-0643-7.

Drescher, K. D., Foy, D. W., Kelly, C., Leshner, A., Schutz, K., & Litz, B. (2011). An exploration of the usefulness of the construct of moral injury in war veterans. *Traumatology, 17*(8), 8–13. https://doi.org/10.1177/1534765610395615.

Evans, W. R., Stanley, M. A., Barrera, T. L., Exline, J. J., Pargament, K., & Teng, E. J. (2018). Morally injurious events and psychological distress among veterans: Examining the mediating role of religious and spiritual struggles. *Psychological Trauma, 10*(3), 360–367. https://doi.org/10.1037/tra0000347.

Exline, J. J., Pargament, K., Grubbs, J. B., & Yali, A. M. (2014). The Religious and Spiritual Struggles Scale: Development and initial validation. *Psychology of Religion and Spirituality, 6*(3), 208–222. https://doi.org/10.1037/a0036465.supp.

Fawson, S. (2016). The contemporary elegy and the poetics of grief: Sustaining lamentation. Presentation at the 2016 American Academy of Religion. San Antonio: American Academy of Religion.

Fawson, S. (2019). Sustaining lamentation for military moral injury: Witness poetry and naming the traces of extremity. *Pastoral Psychology, 68*(1), 31–40. doi.org/10.1007/s11089-018-0855-8.

Geringer, K. S., & Wiener, N. H. (2019). Insights into moral injury and soul repair from classical Jewish texts. *Pastoral Psychology, 68*(1), 59–75. doi.org/10.1007/s11089-018-0848-7.

Goodell, J. (2011). *Shade it black: Death and after in Iraq.* Philadelphia: Casemate Publishers.

Goodman, R. T. (2017). *Gender for the warfare state: Literature of women in combat.* New York: Routledge.

Graham, L. K. (2013). Exploring forgiveness of veteran guilt through collaborative pastoral conversation. *Sacred Spaces: The E-Journal of the American Association of Pastoral Counselors, 5*, 146–171.

Graham, L. K. (2017). *Moral injury: Restoring wounded souls.* Nashville: Abingdon.

Gray, M. J., Schorr, Y., Nash, W., Lebowitz, L., Amidon, A., Lansing, A., et al. (2012). Adaptive disclosure: An open trial of a novel exposure-based intervention for service members with combat-related psychological stress injuries. *Behavior Therapy, 43*(2), 407–415. https://doi.org/10.1016/j.beth.2011.09.001.

Haidt, J. (2002). The moral emotions. In R. J. Davidson, K. R. Scherer, & H. H. Goldsmith (Eds.), *Handbook of affective sciences* (pp. 852–870). New York: Oxford University Press.

Hall, E. R. (2017). "Maybe Jesus was suicidal too": A qualitative inquiry into religion and spirituality in suicide attempts. (Doctoral dissertation). Retrieved from ProQuest Dissertations and Theses database.

Harris, J. I., Park, C. L., Currier, J. M., Usset, T. J., & Voecks, C. D. (2015). Moral injury and psycho-spiritual development: Considering the developmental context. *Spirituality in Clinical Practice, 2*(4), 256–266. https://doi.org/10.1037/scp0000045.

Heffern, R. (2002). Spirit in sound: New sacred music. *National Catholic Reporter, 39*(7), 25–29.

Herman, J. (1992). *Trauma and recovery.* New York: Basic Books.

Hodgson, T. J., & Carey, L. B. (2017). Moral injury and definitional clarity: Betrayal, spirituality and the role of chaplains. *Journal of Religion and Health, 56*(4), 1212–1228. https://doi.org/10.1007/s10943-017-0407-z.

Hoffman, C. (2014). *Be safe I love you.* Simon & Schuster: New York.

Hosein, S. (2019). Muslims in the U.S. military: Eroding rights and moral injury. *Pastoral Psychology, 68*(1), 77–92. doi.org/10.1007/s11089-018-0839-8.

Hosey, S., & Hoffman, C. (2014). "Hiding in plain sight": An interview with Cara Hoffman. *Feminist Teacher, 24*(1), 32–42.

Kinghorn, W. (2012). Combat trauma and moral fragmentation: A theological account of moral injury. *Journal of the Society of Christian Ethics, 32*(2), 57–74.

van der Kolk, B. A. (2014). *The body keeps the score: Brain, mind, and body in the healing of trauma.* New York: Viking.

Kusner, K. G., & Pargament, K. (2012). Shaken to the core: Understanding and addressing the spiritual dimension of trauma. In R. A. McMackin, E. Newman, J. M. Fogler, & T. M. Keane (Eds.), *Trauma therapy in context: The science and craft of evidence-based practice* (pp. 211–230). Washington, DC: American Psychological Association.

LaMothe, R. (2017). Men, warriorism, and mourning: The development of unconventional warriors. *Pastoral Psychology, 66*(6), 819–836. https://doi.org/10.1007/s11089-017-0756-2.

Lartey, E. Y. (2003). *In living color: An intercultural approach to pastoral care and counseling* (2nd ed.). London: Jessica Kingsley.

Liebert, E. (2019). Accessible spiritual practices to aid in recovery from moral injury. *Pastoral Psychology, 68*(1), 41–57. doi.org/10.1007/s11089-018-0825-1.

Litz, B., Stein, N., Delaney, E., Lebowitz, L., Nash, W. P., Silva, C., & Maguen, S. (2009). Moral injury and moral repair in war veterans: A preliminary model and intervention strategy. *Clinical Psychological Review, 29*(8), 695–706. https://doi.org/10.1016/j.cpr.2009.07.003.

Litz, B. T., Lebowitz, L., Gray, M. J., & Nash, W. P. (2015). *Adaptive disclosure: A new treatment for military trauma, loss.* New York: Guilford.

MacDonald, J. (2017). *Exploring moral injury in sacred texts.* Philadelphia: Jessica Kingsley.

Marx, B. P., Foley, K. M., Feinstein, B. A., Wolf, E. J., Kaloupek, D. G., & Keane, T. M. (2010). Combat-related guilt mediates the relations between exposure to combat-related abusive violence and psychiatric diagnoses. *Depression and Anxiety, 27*(3), 287–293. https://doi.org/10.1002/da.2065.

Moon, Z. (2015). *Coming home: Military service, reintegration, and the role of the church.* St. Louis: Chalice Press.

Moon, Z. (2016a). *(Re)turning warriors: A practical theology of military moral stress* (Doctoral dissertation). Retrieved from ProQuest Dissertations and Theses database. (UMI No. 10133601).

Moon, Z. (2016b). Pastoral care and counseling with military families. *Journal of Pastoral Care & Counseling, 70*(2), 128–135. https://doi.org/10.1177/1542305016633663.

Moon, Z. (2019). "Turn now, my vindication is at stake": Military moral injury and communities of faith. *Pastoral Psychology, 68*(1), 93–105. doi.org/10.1007/s11089-017-0795-8.

Nieuwsma, J., Walser, R., Farnsworth, J., Drescher, K., Meador, K., & Nash, W. (2015). Possibilities within acceptance and commitment therapy for approaching moral injury. *Current Psychiatry Reviews, 11*, 193–206. https://doi.org/10.2174/1573400511666150629105234.

Pargament, K., & Cummings, J. (2010). Anchored by faith: Religion as a resilience factor. In J. W. Reich, A. J. Zautra, & J. S. Hall (Eds.), *Handbook of adult resilience* (pp. 193–210). New York: Guilford Press.

Pargament, K., Smith, B. W., Koenig, H. G., & Perez, L. (1998). Patterns of positive and negative religious coping with major life stressors. *Journal for the Scientific Study of Religion, 37*(4), 710–724. https://doi.org/10.2307/138815.

Pargament, K., Desai, K. M., & McConnell, K. M. (2006). Spirituality: A pathway to posttraumatic growth or decline? In L. G. Calhoun & R. G. Tedeschi (Eds.), *Handbook of posttraumatic growth: Research and practice* (pp. 121–135). Mahwah: Erlbaum.

Pargament, K., Mahoney, A., Exline, J., Jones Jr., J., & Shafranske, E. (2013). Envisioning an integrative paradigm for the psychology of religion and spirituality: An introduction to the *APA Handbook of Psychology, Religion and Spirituality*. In K. Pargament, A. Mahoney, J. Exline, J. Jones Jr., & E. Shafranske (Eds.), *APA handbook of psychology, religion and spirituality* (Vol. 1, pp. 3–19). Washington, DC: American Psychological Association.

Pargament, K., Wong, S., & Exline, J. (2016). Wholeness and holiness: The spiritual dimension of eudaimonics. In J. Vittersø (Ed.), *The handbook of eudaimonic wellbeing* (pp. 379–394). Switzerland: Springer International.

Rambo, S. (2010). *Spirit and trauma: A theology of remaining.* Louisville: Westminster John Knox Press.

Ramsay, N. J. (2013). Intersectionality: A model for addressing the complexity of oppression and privilege. *Pastoral Psychology, 63*(4), 453–469. https://doi.org/10.1007/s11089-013-0570-4.

Ricouer, P. (1967). *The symbolism of evil* (E. Buchanan, Trans.). New York: Harper & Row.

Shay, J. (1995). *Achilles in Vietnam: Combat trauma and the undoing of character.* New York: Simon & Schuster.

Shay, J. (2002). *Odysseus in America: Combat trauma and the trials of homecoming.* New York: Scribner.

Shneidman, E. S. (1993). *Suicide as psychache: A clinical approach to self-destructive behavior.* Northvale: Jason Aronson.

Shneidman, E. S. (1996). *The suicidal mind.* New York: Oxford University Press.

Sholl, R. (2012). Arvo Pärt and spirituality. In A. Shenton (Ed.), *The Cambridge companion to Arvo Pärt* (pp. 140–158). New York: Cambridge University Press.

Stallinga, B. A. (2013). What spills blood wounds spirit: Chaplains, spiritual care, and operational stress injury. *Reflective Practice: Formation and Supervision in Ministry, 33*, 13–30.

Steenkamp, M. M., Litz, B. T., Gray, M. J., Lebowitz, L., Nash, W., Conoscenti, L., Lang, A. (2011). A brief exposure-based intervention for service members with PTSD. *Cognitive and Behavioral Practice, 18*(1), 98–107. https://doi.org/10.1016/j.cbpra.2009.08.006.

Vennard, J. E. (2013). *Fully awake and truly alive: Spiritual practices to nurture your soul.* Woodstock: SkyLight Paths.

Werdel, M. B., Dy-Liacco, G. S., Ciarrocchi, J. W., Wicks, R. J., & Breslford, G. M. (2014). The unique role of spirituality in the process of growth following stress and trauma. *Pastoral Psychology, 63*(1), 57–71. https://doi.org/10.1007/s11089-013-0538-4.

Whitman, W. (1855). *Leaves of grass.* Auckland, New Zealand: The Floating Press.

Wiener, N., & Hirchmann, J. (2014). *Maps and meaning: Levitical models for contemporary care.* Minneapolis: Fortress.

Yandell, M. (2019). Moral injury and human relationship: A conversation. *Pastoral Psychology. 68*(1), 3–14. doi.org/10.1007/s11089-018-0800-x.

3

Sustaining Lamentation for Military Moral Injury: Witness Poetry That Bears the Traces of Extremity

— Shawn Fawson —

Over the last decade in North America, one way the concept of military moral injury has been entering the public arena is through poetry performed in the following contexts: the medical humanities including narrative medicine,[1] writing groups held at moral injury training seminars at the Braxton Institute, and literary magazines,[2] among other venues.[3] Whereas some poetry-performance groups, such as Theater of War,[4] are more recent arrivals to the veteran poetry scene, other groups have been emphasizing poetry to articulate veterans' war experiences for decades.[5] Despite all these successful contributions,

---

[1]Medical practice has increasingly recognized the importance of "narrative medicine" to the patient's healing. For an in-depth discussion, see Rita Charon's (2017) *The Principles and Practice of Narrative Medicine* and Arthur Frank's (1995) *The Wounded Storyteller: Body, Illness, and Ethics.*

[2]Each year, *The Iowa Review* holds a creative writing contest, the Jeff Sharlet Memorial Award for Veterans, for veterans writing in any genre.

[3]Examples are the Soul Repair Center at Brite Divinity School and the nonprofit organization entitled Military Experience and the Arts at Longwood University.

[4]Visit the website of *The New York Times* to hear U.S. veterans read the words of the Greek hero Ajax and his wife Tecmessa as he contemplates suicide. The article's author, Bruce Headlam, remarks, "So instead of getting insights into themselves by listening to Greek poetry, these veterans are using the poetry to give us insight into their own experience." "U.S. Veterans Use Greek Tragedy to Tell Us About War," *The New York Times*, May 26, 2017, https://www.nytimes.com/2017/05/26/opinion/us-veterans-use-greek-tragedy-to-tell-us-about-war.html.

[5]In 1993, poet Maxine Hong Kingston began one of the first veterans' writing projects in the Bay Area, and she and others fostered the healing power of writing in community about war experiences. Her book *Veterans of War, Veterans of Peace* (2016) resulted from that project.

poetry as a resource is not widely known in the practice of spiritual care for moral injury. Leaders in faith communities can draw upon poetry in the context of small groups of military service members, veterans, and/or their families.[6] I propose that witness poetry helps to recognize the tragic, traumatic, and violent experiences of war-related losses and to sustain lamentation for these losses with the expectation of finding ways to live with moral injury.[7]

Sustaining lamentation

In this article, military moral injury is defined as "not merely a state of cognitive dissonance, but a *state of loss of trust* in previously deeply held beliefs about one's own or others' ability to keep our shared moral covenant" (Nash and Litz 2013, p. 368). "A state of loss of trust" may have long-lasting impacts on how veterans[8] and their families grieve combat experiences. Pastoral theologian Larry K. Graham (2011) defines the war-related concept of "sustaining lamentation" as (1) "a means of living as well as possible in spite of what is forever lost and using what remains to rebuild a life worth having in the future" (p. 9) and (2) "a means of enduring irrevocable gaps" (p. 9). Graham elaborates on what he means by gaps:

> War regularly creates irrevocable gaps or cut-off places within persons and within families. These gaps between what is desired and what now actually exists are often unnamed and hidden. Frequently they are more than "gaps;" they are "unbridgeable gulfs." They may even be "fatal disconnects," inasmuch as they actually kill the capacity for life and love that existed before war. (2011, p. 8)

Fatal disconnects, unbridgeable gulfs, and irrevocable gaps are examples of states of loss that could impact a veteran's life in very

---

[6]See Doehring (2019) for ways that music and poetry can lament shared anguish. She emphasizes the need for laments that "begin in veterans' bodies with spiritual practices that foster compassion while allowing their bodies to experience the angry grief arising from spiritual orienting systems broken by war" (p. 24).

[7]My exploration of the use of poetic language in a process of lament may resonate with pastoral theologians such as Christie Neuger (2001) and Karen Scheib (2016), who use narrative therapy in regard to witnessing suffering rooted in social oppression. The poetic approach described in this article and the approach of narrative therapists pay close attention to how words can be used to describe complex life experiences. My approach pays close attention to the poetic use of language. Narrative therapists pay close attention to how the articulation of narrative themes can become strategies for counteracting the internalization of social oppression that causes psychological struggles.

[8]Pastoral theologian Zachary Moon (2016a) notes that "moral injury is not a certain and universal outcome of particular events, just as post-traumatic stress symptoms may be experienced differently by different persons, or not experienced at all" (p. 17).

profound and unresolvable ways. Veterans make a long journey home and often struggle to understand that the person who traveled to Iraq or Afghanistan or Vietnam—the young person they had been—did not come back.

In a faith community of veterans, a spiritual caregiver might acknowledge how much war often separates one from the person one had been. A spiritual caregiver might also consider how families are impacted by separations and other disconnects that war brings (Moon 2016b). War leads to unrecognized knowledge and gaps between people who otherwise expect to be close and to understand one another. These gaps, gulfs, and disconnects are not necessarily nameable, and even when they are, they may not be closeable, despite efforts to find techniques to close them. Is there a way to recognize these gaps exist and help both veterans and their families live better with them? The witness poems discussed below invite readers[9] into new worlds of language that help us express gaps, gulfs, and disconnects and encourage us to "find a different way of speaking from the depths" (Rambo 2010, p. 164). Moreover, witness poetry can help sustain lamentation for what has been lost because witness poetry does not foreclose unresolved grief.

Witness poetry

Poet Carolyn Forché (1993) defines poems of witness as those that "bear the trace of extremity within them, and they are, as such, evidence of what occurred" (p. 30). For Forché, extremity (utmost suffering and intense struggle) arises from historical events and social conditions such as "exile, state censorship, political persecution, house arrest, torture, imprisonment, military occupation, warfare, and assassination" (p. 29). The poets of witness have *been there*, and they write to tell the truth of their experience. Poems of witness do not close wounds or answer questions; they break open the silence of pain.

In *Spirit and Trauma*, one of theologian Shelly Rambo's (2010) key insights is that the unspeakable dimension of traumatic events cannot be fully voiced or integrated into a narrative account. Rambo writes, "Language falters in the abyss; it fractures at the site of trauma" (p. 164). Certain events are unspeakable. Nevertheless, they shape our destinies. What witness poems make clear is that even though words

---

[9]There is currently interest among practical theologians such as Heather Walton (2014) in writing poetry as a source for doing contextual practical theology. I do not want to conflate reading poetry with writing poetry. Although writing poetry could be part of a veterans' group, I would first suggest reading poetry together; the writing would come later.

are always an approximation,[10] the poems keep searching for avenues of connection. Thus, witness poems offer "a means of enduring" (Graham 2011, p. 8) by showing that we readers need not be so invested in our dominant stories that we cannot discover an understory, see different slants of light, or see the shadow of emotion that a surface narrative tends to mute. Witness poems about war do not simply represent the losses incurred by war; they also weep, interrogate, admit complicity, embrace, lament, and bear out on the page traces of extremity.

In a faith community of veterans and their families, a spiritual caregiver might wonder about the ways in which "the trace of extremity" is borne by the speakers[11] in poems of witness, and together we readers might come closer to discovering new ways of recognizing the impacts of moral injury on lives in ways that help us maintain our humanity, dignity, and sense of belonging. The reading and writing of witness poetry in community is a social process that cuts against the privatization and self-enclosure that moral injury's shame, secrecy, and feelings of failure often lock veterans and their families in.

In the poems that follow, North American poets—Walt Whitman, Khadijah Queen, Yusef Komunyakaa, and Brian Turner—show that war is never over. War creates orientations, mindsets, and identities that shape the speakers' consciousness in ways that the speakers themselves are not always aware of. Moreover, the poems contain a complex array of features characteristic to moral injury and war-zone loss such as "conflicting feelings," "broken continuity" (Litz et al. 2016, pp. 102–105), "irrevocable gaps" (Graham 2011, p. 8), and "a questing body" (Graham 2017, p. 85). These elements of moral injury are expressed in the structure of a poem at the level of syntax and line through unresolved tensions, gaps, and fragmentation. By learning new ways of expression, we may move to a place of greater integration and strength.

Walt Whitman: The moral injury of irrevocable gaps

During the Civil War, poet Walt Whitman (1819–1892) performed the office of "wound dresser" in Washington, D.C., where he visited wounded soldiers in makeshift hospitals and wrote poems about his experiences. From the book *Drum-Taps: The Complete 1865 Edition*

---

[10]For further discussion, see Gray and Keniston (2012), who speak about "the gap between the need to tell and the limitations of the language" (p. 2).

[11]When poems are discussed in community, they create a safe space to name and address emotions because it is customary not to assume that the poet writing the poem is the "I" in the poem. That person is "the speaker." When reading and discussing a poem, our attention is directed away from speculating what the writer intended and toward what is directly conveyed by the actual words on the page. This establishes distance between the poet, the event, the writer, and the reader but does not prevent trust.

(2015), the poem "A March in the Ranks Hard-Prest, and the Road Unknown" (pp. 55–56) illustrates Whitman's contact with combat soldiers. Here is the poem's middle section:

> Shadows of deepest, deepest black, just lit by moving candles and lamps,
> And by one great pitchy torch stationary with wild red flame, and clouds of smoke;
> By these, crowds, groups of forms, vaguely I see, on the floor, some in the pews laid down;
> At my feet more distinctly, a soldier, a mere lad, in danger of bleeding to death, (he is shot in the abdomen;)
> I stanch the blood temporarily, (the youngster's face is white as a lily;)
> Then before I depart I sweep my eyes o'er the scene, fain to absorb it all; . . . (p. 55)

The sentences "He is shot in the abdomen" and "the youngster's face is white as a lily" are in parentheses. Parentheses in Whitman often signify moments when the speaker's emotional response erupts and suggest the speaker is describing an inner dialogue he is having with himself, as though showing us how the event of tending to a wounded soldier is working on him. Whitman creates an interior state as well as describing an exterior experience and illustrates the kinds of "irrevocable gaps" (Graham 2011, p. 8) that war creates. Whitman feels no need to tie things up neatly. This part of the poem could be used to begin a collaborative conversation[12] about what it means to live with the tension between (1) the actions one has had to take in war alongside (2) how one feels about those actions. Are there "irrevocable gaps" within one's memories of war? Other collaborative conversation questions that might come up are: Is the speaker of the poem the cause of someone's death? How does the speaker face this guilt? Whitman's poem witnesses these kinds of gaps and invites veterans and their families to use poetic language to speak to their own experiences of gaps.

In order to witness the gaps created by moral injury, poetry cannot simply comfort or fascinate, nor can it give way too quickly to a summarizing impulse. We want poems that have wrestled with experience, ideas, history, and the speaker's own psychic drama in a way

---

[12]A collaborative conversation is not a matter of two known entities disclosing what is known to each other but two in-process entities discovering and becoming who they are in the conversation itself. One of the hallmarks of collaborative conversation is not being the expert but letting others tell about their experience as experts of it. For further discussion, see Graham (2017, pp. 33–35).

that transforms the drama and utters the complex, varying emotional responses we have.[13] Whitman's (2015) poem ends:

> These I resume as I chant—I see again the forms, I smell the
> odor;
> Then hear outside the orders given, *Fall in, my men, Fall in;*
> But first I bend to the dying lad—his eyes open—a half-smile
> gives he me;
> Then the eyes close, calmly close, and I speed forth to
> the darkness,
> Resuming, marching, ever in darkness marching, on in the
> ranks,
> The unknown road still marching. (p. 56)

The speaker closes the dying young man's eyes and must leave the young man's corpse and continue on. The speaker now resumes the march, which is continuous, not to be completed. "The unknown road, still marching" sounds as though the self were still marching, which could be the way a soldier fraught with anguish might feel.

If "a pervasive consequence of war is the creation of permanent gaps" (Graham 2011, p. 8), then, in the context of a caregiving relationship, a communal reading of this poem could open up a conversation about naming what it means for each veteran to live with unresolved tensions and gaps. "And while these gaps or abysses may never be named fully or removed, they must at least be acknowledged as real if there is to be the hope of reclaiming life from their devastating consequences" (Graham 2011, p. 9). Whitman's poem is not just a recording of experience but also a brooding and conjuring of it. Whitman creates an interior state as well as describing an exterior experience. There is no commentary, no need to explain.

The poem's end is open in its closure. Nothing has been fully ended, as is reflected in the participles ("resuming" and "marching") and the unknown and the darkness. The speaker feels no need to package things up or contain them. The speaker's chanting brings experience, not categories of experience or interpretations of experience. A discussion of how this poem remains open in its closure might foster new expectations of "blending into a dynamic whole the brokenness and resiliency that enables us to bear the pain of our moral injuries and live vitally with what remains available to us" (Graham 2017, p. 99). Furthermore, it could be a relief to a veteran that this story is no longer just one person's story.

---

[13] I first heard the concept of what we want from poetry from the poet Betsy Sholl in the summer of 2013.

Khadijah Queen: The moral injury of a questing body

Of her poems about war, poet and former Navy sonar technician Khadijah Queen writes, "I felt that the complexities surrounding the events made poetry a necessary reaction" (Cain and Bowden 2008, p.138). Her book *Fearful Beloved* (2015) addresses what it is like to hold unresolved tensions in one's body, which for Queen is a female body. Graham writes, "Trauma always involves the body, both in terms of its effect on bodily health and on subsequent body-based emotional processes" (2017, p. 85). Graham uses the term "questing body" to describe a man who has experienced killing in combat and who now for himself "seeks a body that will be worthy of touch" (2017, p. 85) by a beloved other.

Fearful Beloved insists that we not look away from a body and how it is shaped by fear when one "strikes at movements invisible to those accustomed to the light" (p. 19). Furthermore, this book shows how a woman veteran's body processes moral revulsions that go along with the quest for healing. Her body holds the tensions of war: the anguish and the grace, the worthiness and the shame, the beauty and the dark. One does not expunge the other.

Among the most powerful poems in the book are the first-person narratives touching on Queen's service in the Navy, such as this section from "Bodies of Water":

> Because of our son, we were not in Yemen
> when the tug pulled up—men smiling
> as they waved, then exploding—
> turning 39 people to steel-grey
> ash and more into zombies, the lucky ones
> only breathing in the midship blast
> flattening their lungs, or losing their feet
> to the crumbling deck below them. (p. 60)

Reading this poem in a faith community, we might discuss how the poem looks. Visually, the dashes acknowledge the loss of bodily wholeness that resulted from an explosion. We might talk about the speaker's guilt and self-blame for not being "in Yemen / when the tug pulled up."

In his very popular but still useful definition, poet W. H. Auden defined poetry as a "clear expression of mixed feelings" (1941, p. 119). And that mixture of clarity and complexity is an element of poetry that would not foreclose "intense feelings of grief [that] are incompatible with the warrior identity of feeling strong" (Litz et al. 2016, p. 103). Later in the book, Queen's poems do not show us images of massive violence but instead depict the residue of war as small scenes of interpersonal abuse that affect the speaker's weakening body. We might discuss the many ways a woman veteran expresses a *questing body*. One might ask: What might be permanently absent from the speaker's body, and what might not be?

Yusef Komunyakaa: The moral injury of broken continuity

Litz et al. (2016) describe broken continuity as the impact on a soldier's conscience from "witnessing the destruction of life" (p. 105). In regard to his own poetry, poet and Vietnam veteran Yusef Komunyakaa wrote, "The mood I desire in my poetry is one in which the truth can survive" (Buckley and Merrill 1997, p. 80). His book *Dien Cai Dau*, a chronologically arranged selection of poems about the Vietnam War, takes the reader on a confused and painful journey through the past and into the present. Throughout these poems, the speaker wrestles with his conscience for the egregious acts committed in combat. If the speaker is responsible for one death, is it possible he is somehow responsible for more, even for them all?

In the poem "Starlight Scope Myopia" (Komunyakaa 1988), the broken continuity the speaker feels in the aftermath of fighting in Vietnam is expressed in fragments: "Smoke-colored / Viet Cong / move under our eyelids, / lords over loneliness / winding like coral vine through / sandalwood & lotus / inside our lowered heads / years after this scene ends" (p. 8). Komunyakaa writes about his poetic process, "This is how poems happen for me. Bits and pieces, glimpses and strokes, hints and imagistic nudges, and at some almost-accidental moment it all flies together—not to make sense but to induce a feeling" (Kuusisto et al. 1995, p. 136). Fragments remain fragments rather than being translated into an illusion of a seamless narrative. They hold together, at least in terms of mood and feeling—the longing for intimacy, the longing for relationship, and the imagining of home. Reading this poem in community, a spiritual caregiver might discuss how Komunyakaa expresses broken continuity by not filling in details or by not making the book's meaning fluent. Encouraging veterans to write in fragments might be a useful invitation that could raise the possibility of a different approach to narrative, one that is more aware of the gaps, the memory holes, the many versions, and the inconsistencies and that doesn't try to explain them or cover them up.

Brian Turner: The moral injury of conflicting feelings

Litz et al. (2016) discuss conflicting feelings in terms of experiencing "what the abstract concepts such as 'sacrifice,' actually look like . . .

in the aftermath of absolute loss" (p. 104). Clearly, the sensory costs of war (some veterans come home maimed physically, morally, and/or psychologically with little resources) lead to inner conflicts because abstract concepts such as "sacrifice" come into question. Is war worth it? Who's it for? How can we bear it?[14] Conflicting feelings "raise questions about the legitimacy of authority, the war, and the value of the enormous sacrifices being made" (Litz et al. 2016, p. 104). Poet Brian Turner served as a U.S. infantryman in both Iraq and Bosnia-Herzegovina. His first book, *Here, Bullet* (2005), chronicles his time in Iraq and meditates on the incongruities of war. Some poems raise conflicting feelings of betrayal as the speaker wonders what he has really been a part of. Other poems address shocking topics such as a veteran's ambiguous relationship with weapons and ammunition. In the poem "Here, Bullet," the speaker addresses the bullet as "you" and ends with these words:

> And I dare you to finish
> what you've started. Because here, Bullet,
> here is where I complete the word you bring
> hissing through the air, here is where I moan
> the barrel's cold esophagus, triggering
> my tongue's explosives for the rifling I have
> inside of me, each twist of the round
> spun deeper, because here, Bullet,
> here is where the world ends, every time. (p. 13)

A spiritual caregiver[15] might ask a small group of veterans to notice the form of the poem. Unlike in prose, line breaks shift the words' rhythm, thereby communicating a break in the poem's message. In this poem, the words "Bullet" and "I" are separated by line breaks. That is, these two words do not appear in the same line anywhere in the poem. This suggests a physical distance between the "I" and the "Bullet." The bullet does not reach the target. This gives the sense of a haunting bullet, one that keeps moving even after the poem ends. This poem could be used to open a dialogue about feelings that are hard to put into words, such as what a weapon means to veterans and how a weapon can represent two conflicting things: (1) a way to protect themselves and their units and (2) a way to exit the world.

---

[14]See, for example, Yandell's (2019) reflections on his moral injuries from military service.

[15]See Ramsay (2019) for ritual resources of care that illustrate how veterans from several combat locations over several decades have found witness poems helpful when sharing across differences.

Although much more could be said about the relationship between the speaker and the bullet, perhaps this is enough to convey how a poem goes more deeply than conventional language and more expansively than other forms of expression normally take us. Simply put, a poem's form produces a certain rhythm of language that can get us closer to naming our experiences in different ways. In this instance, the line breaks intensify the complex, ambiguous relationship and conflicting feelings that a veteran might have toward weapons and ammunition.

In closing

This article has argued for poems of witness as resources for veterans and their families in processing moral injury in community because such poems acknowledge traces of extremity, help us bear them, and bond us together. After reading each of the poems, we could also explore how our understandings of God have been challenged and/or clarified. We humans are made for loving connection in those places where the life of God and the world interconnect in the here and now; grief from moral injury severs that connection and forces us to bond together even more deeply to accommodate and further our connectedness and preserve its gifts to us.

U.S. Poet Laureate Tracy K. Smith said in an interview that "poetry gives us a vocabulary for the feelings that don't easily fit into language and it's not a static vocabulary because we as beings are constantly changing and contradicting ourselves and growing and coming up against problems that feel completely new" (Martin 2017). Witness poems invite us to process grief-related aspects of moral injury because they evoke complex ways to recognize and lament "non-linear and non-narrative dimensions of human suffering" (Rambo 2013, p. 448) and to convey the complexity of emotions in ways other modes of language cannot.

In the context of spiritual caregiving, "Careful attention to language is arguably the most essential practice for effective counseling amid any kind of difference and a primary factor that makes it possible to engender meaningful care and counseling in relationships characterized by religious difference" (Greider 2015, p. 236). On the one hand, to be human is to create language and to create worlds from language; on the other hand, some experiences that contain horror and awe alike leave us speechless; words can only at best approximate these experiences. Words always seem to be an approximation; they disclose and they hide all at the same time. But they are the avenue for connection, transcendence, and freedom, so we keep searching.

Although the witness poems discussed in this article represent a very small slice of poetry that could be used in spiritual care settings focusing on moral injury, they show that we can form deeper connections to others by acknowledging the impacts of war on social, historical, and cultural forces beyond the individual. For example, we might read Yusef Komunyakaa as a poet who engages his experiences within African American culture as well as his experiences in the Vietnam War. Many speakers within Komunyakaa's poems discuss not only the conflict and struggle with racism but also, especially in his collection *Dien Cai Dau*, what it means to be an African American soldier in combat. Similarly, Queen's poems discuss being an embodied African American female in a male-dominated military culture. Furthermore, across the distance of time, culture, and extremity, witness poets such as Osip Mandelstam, Anna Akhmatova, Marina Tsvetaeva, Paul Celan, Miklos Radnoti, Yannis Ritsos, and others are reminders of the impacts of war, dislocation, censorship, and totalitarian regimes on larger world cultures. Intersectionality (Ramsay 2013) helps us gain some insight into how identities are multiple, not singular or narrowly circumscribed by one factor such as race, gender, orientation, nationality, or religion. In witness poetry, the historical context of siege, deprivation, and exile provides an intersectional background for the many contexts for framing the features of moral injury, while slivers of poems provide hints of lived experiences and different ways of naming them.

Witness poetry helps to lament the grief that both separates and bonds us in memory and affection, which, theologically speaking, could be seen as shedding light on the meaning of human community and spiritual communion. The ability of witness poetry to create connections between those who have lived through egregious violent actions and/or have been implicated in the cause of those actions and their journey through sustaining lamentation seems crucial at the present moment, a moment holding the dynamic capacities either to open a new epoch of relational possibilities for restoring humanity or to close us into diminished selves by tying up neatly those experiences that threaten to overwhelm our capacities. What does that mean, though? Should we revise our limits? Be more patient with our art of curiosity? Not rush to the latest technique? I don't know, really, but it strikes me that we have to be willing to ask these questions and to take our time answering them rather than simply use conventional language to name things.

References

Auden, W. H. (1941). *New Year letter*. London: Faber.

Buckley, C., & Merrill, C. (Eds.). (1997). *What will suffice: Contemporary American poets on the art of poetry*. Salt Lake City: Gibbs-Smith.

Cain, S., & Bowden, L. (2008). *Powder: Writing by women in the ranks, from Vietnam to Iraq*. Tucson: Kore Press.

Charon, R. (2017). *The principles and practice of narrative medicine*. New York: Oxford University Press.

Doehring, C. (2019). Military moral injury: An evidence-based and intercultural approach to spiritual care. *Pastoral Psychology, 68*(1), 15–30. doi.org/10.1007/s11089-018-0813-5.

Forché, C. (Ed.). (1993). *Against forgetting: Twentieth-century poetry of witness*. New York: W. W. Norton.

Frank, A. (1995). *The wounded storyteller: Body, illness, and ethics*. Chicago: University of Chicago Press.

Graham, L. K. (2011). Narratives of families, faith, and nations: Insights from research. *Journal of Pastoral Theology, 21*(2), 1–18. doi.org/10.1179/jpt.2011.21.2.005.

Graham, L. K. (2017). *Moral injury: Restoring wounded souls*. Nashville: Abingdon.

Gray, J., & Keniston, A. (2012). *The new American poetry of engagement: A 21st century anthology*. Ann Arbor: University of Michigan Press.

Greider, K. (2015). Religious location and counseling: Engaging diversity and difference in views of religion. In E. A. Maynard & J. L. Snodgrass (Eds.), *Understanding Pastoral Counseling* (pp. 235–257). New York: Springer.

Kingston, M. H. (2006). *Veterans of war, veterans of peace*. Kihei: Koa Books.

Komunyakaa, Y. (1988). *Dien Cai Dau*. Hanover: Wesleyan University Press.

Kuusisto, S., Tall, D., & Weiss, D. (Eds.). (1995). *The poet's notebook: Excerpts from the notebooks of contemporary American poets*. New York: Norton.

Litz, B. T., Lebowitz, L., Gray, M. J., & Nash, W. P. (2016). *Adaptive disclosure: A new treatment for trauma, loss, and moral injury*. New York: Guilford.

Martin, M. (Narrator). (2017, June 17). Capitol Hill to undergo changing of the guard with new poet laureate [Radio broadcast episode]. In E. McDonnell (Producer), *All Things Considered*. Washington, DC: National Public Radio.

Moon, Z. (2016a). *(Re)turning warriors: A practical theology of military moral stress.* (Unpublished doctoral dissertation). Iliff School of Theology/Denver University. Denver.

Moon, Z. (2016b). Pastoral care and counseling with military families. *Journal of Pastoral Care & Counseling, 70*(2), 128–135. doi.org/10.1177/1542305016633663.

Nash, W. P., & Litz, B. (2013). Moral injury: A mechanism for war-related psychological trauma in military family members. *Clinical Child and Family Psychology Review, 16,* 365–375. doi.org/10.1007/s10567-013-0146-y.

Neuger, C. C. (2001). *Counseling women: A narrative, pastoral approach.* Minneapolis: Augsburg Fortress Press.

Queen, K. (2015). *Fearful beloved.* Litchfield: Argos Books.

Rambo, S. (2010). *Spirit and trauma: A theology of remaining.* Louisville: Westminster John Knox Press.

Rambo, S. (2013). Changing the conversation: Theologizing war in the twenty-first century. *Theology Today, 69*(4), 441–462. doi.org/10.1177/0040573612463035.

Ramsay, N. J. (2013). Intersectionality: A model for addressing the complexity of oppression and privilege. *Pastoral Psychology, 63*(4), 453–469. doi.org/10.1007/s11089-013-0570-4.

Ramsay, N. J. (2019). Moral injury as loss and grief with attention to ritual resources for care. *Pastoral Psychology, 68*(1), 107–125. doi.org/10.1007/s11089-018-0854-9.

Scheib, K. (2016). *Pastoral care: Telling the stories of our lives.* Nashville: Abingdon Press.

Turner, B. (2005). *Here, bullet.* Farmington: Alice James Books.

Walton, H. (2014). *Writing methods in theological reflection.* London: SCM Press.

Whitman, W. (2015). In L. Kramer (Ed.), *Drum-taps: The complete 1865 edition.* New York: New York Review of Books.

Yandell, M. (2019). Moral injury and human relationship: A conversation. *Pastoral Psychology, 68*(1), 3–14. doi.org/10.1007/s11089-018-0800-x.

4

Accessible Spiritual Practices to Aid in Recovery from Moral Injury

— Elizabeth A. Liebert —

Introduction

When I first met Joel (not his real name), he had just returned from his third tour of duty, fine on the outside but crumbled on the inside. He reports, "I've seen too much. I can't unsee what I have seen. I can't undo, what I have done. I can't do the things that I wish I had done. It's too late for that. I'm not the man I was when I left, and I am disgusted with the man I have become. I don't think I can ever be forgiven. In fact, I can't imagine any kind of God who would love me now."

Joel is not alone. His situation is mirrored in many combat veterans but also in others who have lost their moral bearings, a condition now called moral injury.

Michael Yandell (2015) describes his own experience this way:

Moral injury describes my disillusionment, the erosion of my sense of place in the world. The spiritual and emotional foundations of the world disappeared and made it impossible for me to sleep the sleep of the just. Even though I was part of a war that was much bigger than me, I still feel personally responsible for its consequences. I have a feeling of intense betrayal, and the betrayer and betrayed are the same person: my very self. (p. 12)

This essay is based on the claim that spiritual practices can help sustain and rebuild even deeply wounded human spirits. It introduces simple spiritual practices, two of which originated within the Christian tradition but are adaptable to other traditions or no specific tradition. It is addressed primarily to those in recovery from the deep spiritual wound described as military moral injury, as well as their families, spiritual caregivers, congregations, and other supporters, in the hope that these practices can provide concrete ways to participate actively in spiritual healing, whether for oneself or for a loved one or community member.

The discussion proceeds as follows. The first section briefly describes moral injury from the perspective of its spiritual impact not only on the individual sufferer but also on his or her surrounding support community. The second section clarifies the use of contested terms such as 'spirit' and 'spirituality' in order to provide the foundation for the practices that follow since, at first glance, the first two practices, deep listening and the circle process, may not appear to be spiritual practices. The third section is devoted to these two listening processes, not only introducing the processes but also noting a variety of potential applications and some cautions. The final section turns to the Judeo–Christian tradition to present two "classic" spiritual practices, namely, using the psalms of lament as a resource for reflecting on and writing one's own lament and the awareness examen, based on the reflective process articulated by Ignatius of Loyola. All four practices are set in the context of healing from moral injury. Throughout, I offer reflections on an extended series of conversations with Joel, whose words opened this essay.

The spiritual situation of moral injury

In a now-classic work entitled *Trauma and Recovery: The Aftermath of Violence—From Domestic Abuse to Political Terror*, Herman (1992/2015) surveys the variety of deep spiritual wounds and their similarities and the commonalities in healing processes across various kinds of traumas. Herman demonstrates that these various traumas share some strikingly similar metadynamics: they all provoke terror that is deep or prolonged (or both), hyperarousal, intruding images and thoughts, and the contradictory manifestations of constriction and numbness. Ordinary processes by which we weave our experiences together and learn from them become frozen into a cycle of reliving the trauma, continued arousal, vulnerability, and a lack of resilience, both in the individual and in the surrounding relational systems (p. 86).

Moral injury is a name given to a particular form of spiritual wound. Moral injury describes a trauma to the moral sensibility grounding our personhood, a trauma in which one's moral moorings are so challenged that it is experienced as a wound to the very spirit.

This wound comes from having transgressed one's basic moral identity by violating a core moral belief or from having failed to do something that one's conscience demands be done, or from having sustained blows to one's spirit from another person or from the context in which one is living such that one's moral compass is shattered (Graham 2017, pp. 82, 92). Its symptoms include profound shame; judging oneself as worthless or as guilty of having committed violations that are unforgiveable by oneself, others, and even God; the inability to trust other people; isolation from support communities; and abandoning the values and beliefs that have guided one's behavior and moral choices. Consequences of this constellation can include overwhelming depression, self-medication, feelings of worthlessness, remorse, and despair, the inability to connect emotionally to others, and suicidal ideation.

Moral injury and posttraumatic stress disorder (PTSD) may coexist in the same person, but they are not the same. In fact, when PTSD diagnoses did not adequately explain a spike in suicides by returning veterans, Litz et al. (2009) studied the extant research and pointed out the key role that conscience plays in moral injury. They describe the dynamic: "Moral injury requires an act of aggression that severely and abruptly contradicts an individual's personal or shared expectation about the rules or the code of conduct, either during the event or at some point afterwards" (p. 700). Doehring's (2019) literary case study, for example, describes a situation in which military personnel had to make split-second decisions about matters of life and death in an encounter that included civilians. Modern guerilla war presents numerous occasions for such moral ruptures, which extend beyond what one does to what is done to one and even to what one has witnessed. This essay focuses on moral injury that occurs as a consequence of war and allied military service, though its conclusions and suggested practices also apply to moral injury more widely conceived.

Brock, Lettini, Graham, and Litz and his colleagues all note that the suffering of moral injury is grounded in the basic humanity of the one suffering a crisis of moral personhood. Paradoxically, persons with a developed moral sense can be more vulnerable to moral injury, but they also may have reserves of moral strength that can be activated in the course of reconstructing their moral compass (Brock and Lettini 2012, pp. xiv–xvi; Graham 2017, p. 82; Lettini 2013, p. 43; and Litz et al. 2009, p. 701). Moral injury, and military moral injury in particular, is a spiritual wound, and its healing needs to touch the spirits of wounded persons in order for them to reconstruct a moral compass out of the shards of their moral life.

Graham also points out that whereas war often inflicts extreme trauma to one's moral self, moral injury actually happens to many persons simply trying to navigate the moral dissonances occurring in everyday life. By widening the category of moral injury beyond those suffering acute moral shattering in the context of war, Graham (2017) does not intend to dilute the meaning and significance of the moral wound that may happen as a result of war. Rather, he intends to help us understand that we all find ourselves in the same boat to some degree (pp. 78–79).

Using the case of modern warfare, Graham (2017) also demonstrates that moral injury is not adequately understood as something that happens strictly within the individual; rather, the wider culture is inescapably implicated in the complex moral questions around war itself and how modern war is conducted. These are questions for all of us (p. 40). Individual stories are inevitably embedded in these system stories of family, ethnicity, politics, and culture itself. Reconstruction of a moral self is inevitably a system process (Lester 1995, pp. 37–39).

Recognizing that combat-induced moral injury may be a difference in degree but not in kind, then, can allow us both to empathize with those who suffer from military moral injury and to join in the healing process alongside persons with a fractured moral compass. It also invites these persons to join us in our own moral wrestling and search for healing and restoration. Additionally, the settings for the healing and reintegrating of those suffering military moral injury spill over from the treatment room or the spiritual caregiver's office to the ordinary spaces where life goes on day by day: conversations with friends, colleagues, and family members at church, in the grocery store, at the bus stop, around the dinner table—any place that people gather without judgment, with respect for and curiosity about others' experiences (Graham 2017, pp. xi, 103, 109, 155).

This widening of the healing context opens many spaces for spiritual practices. Furthermore, spiritual practices, even if done by an individual, inevitably reverberate between members of a community of support and can simultaneously affect the very structure of the community. Likewise, communal spiritual practices reverberate within and between the individuals who participate together in the practice. In this sense, too, we are all in this together. Given this reverberation, I, as Joel's primary spiritual caregiver, need to be prepared to hear about all sorts of gratuitous violence and to hold such violence without any sign of condemnation (Litz et al. 2009, p. 702). I also need to be committed to my own process of healing, consciousness-raising, and social action as I accompany him in the twists and turns of his journey.

Spirit, spirituality, and spiritual practices

To anchor this discussion, it will be helpful to clarify some of the language. When describing a human person, 'spirit' names that unique core of one's humanness that integrates the biological and psychic aspects of self, all one has become as one navigates the givenness of life and the fruit of one's choices. 'Spirituality' describes the various ways that humans connect with their spirit and God's Spirit. Spirituality is that dynamic process in which humans seek the divine and live in the presence and guidance and care of the divine.

Spirituality has multiple, almost endless, expressions throughout human communities. These expressions are set within varying philosophical and theological assumptions about what it means to live well. These assumptions could include notions of freedom, hope, vulnerability, responsibility to others and to oneself, conscience, and moral integrity. Likewise, these expressions grow out of communities holding varying understandings of the divine, the divine-human relationship, ritual practices, and ethical commitments. Certain of these spiritual expressions have proven fruitful enough to be passed on through generations.

The Christian tradition, for example, offers a plethora of ways of praying, worshipping, and living to ground individuals in their search for meaning, for wholesome ways of living together in human communities, and for reaching out toward the transcendent. Indeed, it has done so for millennia in the face of the wounds of war (Verkamp 2006, pp. 1–8, as cited in Brock and Lettini 2012, p. 136, n. 7). Corporate practices within the Christian tradition include Eucharist/Communion/Lord's Supper, confession/reconciliation, funerals, and memorial services. Because these practices are generally well known, I will focus attention on other less obvious spiritual practices, chosen in light of the particular situations of those suffering moral injury. These practices also have both individual and corporate dimensions. Other practices, of course, may also prove fruitful.

In light of this immense variation, it is incumbent on spiritual caregivers to be clear about their beliefs and commitments and to be accountable within their communities for these commitments. It is equally incumbent on them that they attend to the assumptions and commitments of the persons they accompany. As Doehring (2019) points out, competent intercultural counseling includes attending sensitively to differences in religious beliefs, spiritual sensibilities, and ethical practices while supporting the individual's work with her or his own religious and spiritual assumptions and practices. Those healing from moral injury may eventually find themselves in a different tradition or no tradition, believing in God or not. The spiritual caregiver's role is to help them find the most fruitful path forward.

Without claiming that moral injury can be healed exclusively through prayer and other spiritual practices (though I do not want to deny that this could happen), I do claim that spiritual practices can support and nourish a person's spirit and thereby help sustain and rebuild even a deeply wounded spirit. I make a further claim: the four spiritual practices that I present below, namely, contemplative listening, circle processes, lamentation, and examen, can also serve the persons surrounding the suffering person. They too need sustenance for their spirits. They too need communities of support. They too need comfort and strength for the long haul. These same spiritual practices, then, can be part of nourishing the whole system surrounding individual soul repair: friends, family, pastor, church community, and beyond.

Which practices are embraced should be the decision of the one who is doing the practice. How long the practice is sustained should be determined by the fruits of the practice and the individual's own choice to continue. Family members and spiritual care providers may be in a privileged position to introduce one or more spiritual practices, support the individual in growing in these practices, help regulate and process feelings and thoughts stirred up in the course of spiritual practices, and hold a safe space during the sometimes lengthy process of repairing a person's moral compass.

These and other spiritual practices should be seen as adjunct to appropriate therapies, medication, spiritual direction, and counseling. Once internalized, they can play a key role in living toward the future. Individual spiritual practices can come and go, be appropriate for one season and then outgrown. But the need for *some* spiritual practice is never outgrown. They are intentional actions by which we reach out toward the transcendent, the divine, however we have come to know and experience the divine.

Herman (1992/2015) provides a simple trajectory for healing from soul wounds: "The fundamental stages of recovery are establishing safety, reconstructing the trauma story, and restoring the connection between survivors and their community" (p. 3). Although many others have built on Herman's work, taking it into the territory now called moral injury, this three-phase trajectory still helpfully illumines a healing and restoring trajectory (Stallinga 2013, p. 21). I note it here to alert the spiritual caregiver that the same practice may have a very different valence depending on where persons are in this healing trajectory.

Foundational practices of deep listening

Listening and being deeply heard create the foundation for other spiritual practices and, indeed, for multiple healing modalities with respect to moral injury. The most basic need at the beginning of the healing process, gaining a sense of safety, can be profoundly facilitated as trustworthy persons come alongside. Nothing conveys trustworthiness as directly as being deeply heard. In a lovely dynamic of grace, the more one is heard, the more one can trust hearing for oneself. The more wounded persons are responded to in ways that invite the telling of their stories however they wish, controlling both what is said and how it is said, the more they can connect with others in a similar fashion (Stallinga 2013, p. 24).

The first listening practice can be called by various names; deep listening, contemplative listening, mindful listening, and empathic listening are the most common. In this practice, the roles of narrator and responder can be taken by anyone in the system; indeed, as the practice becomes habitual, it can suffuse everyday responses in the family and church community. However, the role of the listener is key in the support system that surrounds the individual who has sustained moral injury, particularly in the early stages of recovery, so the spiritual support person will usually occupy the listening role. In support groups and faith-sharing groups, however, all persons assume both roles. Indeed, it may be through practicing deep listening to another's suffering that an individual begins to listen deeply to his or her own wounded self.

To understand the power of being heard, imagine yourself first in the role of the storyteller or narrator. The first thing you as narrator do is pay attention to an aspect of your own experience, either as it is presently happening or from memory. Shifting to the metaphor of seeing, as you engage your present experience or remember a past experience, you want to "gaze" at it with a "long, loving look at the real," as Jesuit Walter Burghardt (1989) described the process of contemplation. If you cannot achieve a loving look, try at least to look without judging yourself and maybe even with a kind of gentle or slightly quizzical curiosity about what is happening. Write down what you notice, again without judgment, just describing it to yourself in words. These couple of paragraphs are what you will share with the one listening to you. As your listening partner responds to you (more of this in a moment), take what is offered into yourself with the same contemplative stance of a long loving look at the real. See what that response evokes in you. At your own pace and being only as transparent as you feel you wish to be (remember that safety is the primary issue early in the healing process), respond to your conversation partner. If your conversation partner doesn't quite "get" what you said, you are free to clarify if you wish. As you do so, you will, in fact, become clearer about the shades of meaning in your own experience and how it is affecting you. You will be able to own it more and name it with increasing accuracy. It becomes, in a sense, more "you" and less dependent on being named by another. Being heard by another confirms you, the narrator, in your own story.

This process, repeated over and over, allows those suffering moral injury to explore bits and pieces of their experience at a pace that they control. Vary the process according to what is helpful. For example, writing may aid clarity or block it; omit writing if it blocks the process. One story or several stories may come at the same time, chained together in a kind of memory thread. Stories may focus on the locus of the moral injury or may focus on everything but the trauma. Launching into a story may cause a flood of memories and emotions and bodily sensations; be prepared to step out of the story if the experience begins to feel overwhelming. Spiritual caregivers, for their part, need to monitor the narrator's level of anxiety in order to stay in the range that is productive and respects the teller's preferred level of self-revelation. Persons do not have to narrate deeply wounding experiences unless and until they are ready. Deep listening still frees, even if revealing the wound is not the object of the conversation at the moment.

Now switch to the role of the responder. As responder, you will be hearing from the narrator something that she or he wishes to share with you. You take it in with the same quality of a long, loving look at the real; this is your primary stance. But now things get rapidly more complex.

Being able to hear clearly means being able to rise above your own "static" for the moment to avoid the risk of mishearing. So your first asceticism, your first renunciation, is to put aside—for the moment— all interpretations ("That's a sign that . . ."), all judgments ("He surely should be able to . . ."), all desires to fix ("If you would just. . ."), all impulses to give advice ("You should . . ."), all subtle or not so subtle co-opting of the teller's story into your own story ("You know, that same thing happened to me, and I . . ."), and any assumption that you get the full range of the experience you are hearing about ("Oh, I understand completely . . ."). Out of that asceticism and hospitality, frame a first response that says back to the narrator what you heard or a portion that stands out to you. You may reflect the content or the feeling tone or both the content and feelings. Become, at this early moment in the conversation, like a sounding board, magnifying the person's story so that they can hear it better themselves.

If you are even partially accurate, the effect on the narrator is that of feeling heard, or, at least, of knowing that you are *trying* to hear and that you *want* to hear accurately. The narrator's response is almost always to go further into the experience, either by going back inside and revisiting the event again or by engaging you in conversation about it. Either way, the story gets woven between you. As the narrator responds back, you again listen in this softly curious yet self-restrained posture, trying to welcome and understand the other's experience more accurately. These exchanges go on for some moments until the reality that the narrator wants to communicate is sufficiently expressed and heard that the conversation can proceed in some kind of direction.

Now the role that the listener holds comes into play. Therapist, pastor, family members, and friends all have different role-based relationships to the narrator. Once you have established trust that you have really heard the person's experience, further responses do take into account your role with respect to the narrator. Therapists do not step out of the therapist role if the narration takes place within a therapy context. Pastors and chaplains and spiritual directors still hold their roles, responsibilities, and covenants with the narrator. Friends and spouses remain, first of all, friends and spouses. But if you have deeply heard the person in front of you and deeply respect their ownership of their story, you will have a greater chance of fulfilling your relationship and becoming one of those safe persons surrounding the survivor, patient, parishioner, family member, or friend.

This spiritual practice encourages the narrator to attend reflectively and contemplatively to her own personal experience, listening deeply to it in all its fullness. But when that experience is full of shame, guilt, self-loathing, or other painful emotions, the teller may be either unable or unwilling to enter into the experience contemplatively. Contemplative listening can occur nonetheless. Indeed, the faithful listening and nonjudgmental responding of the listener, repeated over and over, may provide the first hope that the teller could also eventually listen in this way to her own experience.

Persons seeking healing from moral injury can turn contemplative listening toward themselves, wounds and all, asking to see themselves with the same loving gaze with which God looks upon them. This kind of deep listening, I believe, can be profoundly self-calming, especially if it is combined with deep breathing. If necessary, begin the self-listening by recalling incidents that help to lower anxiety and bring calmness.

Only later, and at a pace and to a degree controlled by the necessary sense of safety, invite experiences that might evoke greater anxiety, stress, or shame. Persons seeking moral healing can lower their own anxiety by telling their story to themselves and not (yet) to another. They can write it in a journal and close the journal until they are ready to return to it. They can ritualize their progress by burning a journal or memoir at a significant transition. Creativity and personalization are the keys here. At an appropriate moment, they may choose to tell their story in the presence of a respected moral authority, either in person or in their imagination. They may wish to express sorrow for what they have done or failed to do, offer what they would like to do to make amends, and receive (or verbalize) the reply of that moral authority (Litz et al. 2009, p. 704). Again, they should never force self-revelation that violates their sense of safety. Such self-compassion can serve as a crucial element in healing from moral injury and moving forward as a moral, if wounded, person.

Therapists, chaplains, and pastoral counselors will likely name the process I have just described at length as empathic listening. It has a long and distinguished history within these pastoral helping modalities. Following Carl Rogers's client-centered therapy (1961) as well as, from among many possible examples, the work of Gerard Egan (1975/2018), John Patton (1990), Charles Taylor (1991), Michael Nichols (1995), and John Savage (1996), generations of pastors have been taught the skill of empathic listening. Why then do I call it 'contemplative listening' and consider it a spiritual practice? Listening becomes a spiritual practice when the root meaning of contemplation is embraced, that is, when the intention of the parties is to see and hear the other as God sees and hears that person. Because God indwells each part of creation, listeners desire to see and hear God as God is manifested in that other person. Gazing with gentle curiosity and love and attempting to see and hold that other as a unique aspect of God's creation is, in fact, gazing at a "face" of God. Returning to Burghardt's felicitous definition, "Contemplation is a long, loving look at the real," I ask, What is more real than God?

Joel and I moved all around this spiritual practice. In our early meetings, Joel's story came out in bits and pieces. Sometimes he spoke of things happening in the present and sometimes of things that had happened in the past, both during and prior to his deployment. In the beginning, it was extremely difficult for Joel to have any compassion for himself or to receive compassion from me, let alone from a God whom Joel was convinced could not love him. Joel, and I accompanying him, was trying to reconstruct the thread of a life severed by his time in combat. Was he the same person? How could he be? Did he want to be?

(As the one experiencing and telling)	(As the one responding)
I. "Listen to" an aspect of your experience: i.e. remember or attend with a contemplative attitude, a "long, loving look at the real."* Write your experience down in one or two paragraphs.	

II. Read your experience to another or to a group, without trying to interpret it orally to your listener. Let your writing speak for itself.	A. Listen contemplatively to what is said, that is, in an attitude of a "long, loving look at the real."
	 B. Attend to your inner responses to what you hear:
	   a. Bracket out all interpretations, especially judgments, desires to fix, give advice, and so on.
	   b. Resist the temptation to take the teller's experience as a springboard back into your own experience.
	   c. Become, as far as possible, a "sounding box" to magnify the person's experience back to him or her.
	 C. Frame a response: what you noticed as you heard the teller. You may reflect back to the teller the content, the feelings, or both.

III. Listen contemplatively to the responses from the person or group to what you have shared. Respond as you feel led.	
	D. Continue responding, gradually removing the brackets in your response, always taking your lead from the teller about what is appropriate. As you move further into the conversation, and as the original experience "lives" between you, more focused and directive responses are appropriate, depending on the relationship you have to the speaker.
IV. Respond to your experience of what has been shared with you, if you desire to do so. V. Continue your dialog as long as you wish.	

*For this definition of contemplation, see Walter Burghardt, "Contemplation: a long, loving look at the real," in *Church* 5 (4) 1989, 14–18.

© 2017 by Elizabeth Liebert. Process based on John Patton (1990), *From Ministry to Theology* (Nashville: Abingdon, 1990).

Often it was the same song, next verse. Bit by bit, he brought out the experiences he had for so long avoided. Bit by bit, he faced his guilt over things he had done and shame over who he had become. Bit by bit, however, he was also experimenting with putting the shattered pieces of his life in some kind of moral frame that he had to discover as he went along. It was long. It was messy. It was often discouraging to Joel as well as to his wife, with whom he sometimes shared the ups and downs he was experiencing.

At first, Joel talked about whatever he was experiencing in the moment, and I listened with as much contemplative heart as I could muster. Eventually, he began to bring excerpts from his journal for us to listen to together. Joel began to sense that, within the very experiences that had left him shattered, he would find the way forward to a reconstructed sense of self. God he was not so sure about, however. But Joel was ever so slowly learning to treat his own life with some of the presence and gentle curiosity of contemplative listening. My role was to be his primary listener, reframing and giving back to Joel the story he was narrating, holding the space nonjudgmentally, helping Joel to believe that he could say anything—to me or to God—and the world would not crash down upon his head. Often, as Joel questioned who he was before God, I quietly held his faith for him since he couldn't quite find a viable faith or express it himself. Once, though, Joel caught a glimpse of how God gazed on him as he reflected on the profound love he had for his own daughter. The glimpse lasted but an instant, but the very fact that it happened shifted the spiritual ground under Joel's feet and gave him hope to continue.

Listening together: Circle processes

The basic process of contemplative listening, one person with another, can be magnified powerfully when brought carefully into group settings. Iterations of circle processes offer one way to do so.

Circle processes bring people together in a way in which everyone is respected, everyone gets to speak without interruption, participants may explain themselves, all persons are equal, and the spiritual and emotional, as well as the behavioral, aspects of experience are welcomed into the dialogue. All the listening skills developed in contemplative listening come to bear in circle processes except that there is no direct response from another circle member to what a speaker shares until the turn of the person wishing to respond comes around again. Carefully crafted and led circles can safely contain anger, frustration, joy, pain, truth, conflict, diverse worldviews, intense feelings, silence, and paradox (Pranis 2005, p. 9). Such circles can strengthen the foundations on which communities can flourish and wounded persons can be reintegrated into them.

The elements of circles are straightforward. They begin with ceremony, a ritual to mark the opening and closing in such a way as to involve the whole person, including spiritual aspects. Ceremony marks off the space and time as sacred and invites the participants to be present to themselves as well as to each other. The opening ritual says that this is not an ordinary meeting. In an overtly religious setting, this opening ceremony can be or include prayer, but in a secular setting, the planners will need to find creative ways of bringing people together and marking off the space as sacred in such a way that all feel included and honored.

A talking piece, any easily held and passed object, signals that the person holding the piece may speak. This rule gives the one holding the talking piece the freedom to take the time needed, to have as many false starts as necessary to get the right words, or even to refrain from any words while holding the piece. The pace slows as the piece moves around the group. The participants have time to take in what is said and all the resonances that it sets off in the speaker, themselves, and the group as a whole.

The facilitator, who is often called the circle keeper, introduces the process, leads the opening ritual, and maintains the groups boundaries. The circle keeper intervenes only if the circle veers off course. The participants take a major role in designing the guidelines, which are promises about how they will relate to each other in the circle. Participants can request guidelines that will make it safe for them to speak their truth. If any decisions come out of a circle, they are arrived at by consensus decision-making. Consensus does not require enthusiasm from all parties, but it does require the willingness to live with and cooperate with the decision that emerges from the group. Thus, no passes are permitted when coming to a decision.

The dynamic power of circle processes comes through the relationships that are built through the interaction. The usual means is storytelling, describing one's own experience and listening to the experience of others. This basic process has morphed into a variety of types. Some orientations lend themselves particularly well to certain aspects of healing from military moral injury. For example, talking circles assist in exploring a particular topic or issue. There is no attempt to reach a consensus; participants simply try to hear diverse perspectives and be heard themselves. A talking circle might gather divergent voices to explore the morality of a particular war, for example. A circle of understanding is a talking circle focused on understanding some aspect of a conflict or difficult situation. A group of veterans suffering from moral injury could employ a circle of understanding to address the struggles of conscience that have occurred as a result of their individual actions (Ramsay 2019). Not usually a decision-making circle, the goal is simply to develop a more complete picture of what is happening or how a person is behaving. Support circles come together to support a person through a particular difficulty or major change in life. Support circles can be particularly appropriate for people when the healing may take months or years, as could be the case when moral injury is involved. Usually, support circles meet regularly over some time. These circles may develop agreements or not, as they choose, and may develop multiple agreements over time. Family and church community members might participate in a support circle to surround and uphold one of their members through a particularly rough patch. Healing circles share the pain of a person who has experienced trauma or loss; there may be a plan for further support, or not, as the participants desire. A person suffering from moral injury may welcome a healing circle as a context for apology and restoration among those she wounded as she struggled with her own woundedness (Pranis 2005, pp. 11–17).

Circles, however, are not magic, nor, as simple as they are to describe, are they necessarily easy to implement. They are frequently multistage processes that extend over a period of time, sometimes months. They may require trained facilitators to ensure the safety of all gathered. Distinct stages characterize the circle process, its lead-up, and its follow-through. These stages may be simple and straightforward in many situations but delicate and complex in others.

1. Determining suitability: Is a circle appropriate for this situation? What kind of circle? Are trained facilitators needed here? Can safety be maintained? Do the participants have sufficient resources to engage constructively in the process? Is there sufficient time to follow up with the dynamics that may be uncovered?

2. Preparation: Who needs to be there? Are they willing? Who can facilitate? What preparation needs to occur before the parties are ready to freely participate?

3. Beginning well: Convening the parties begins with some kind of ritual that builds a base of shared values and a common set of guidelines created within the circle so that all participants are involved in setting conditions that will work for them.

4. Storytelling, the heart of the process: These stories include the participants' concerns and hopes and feelings. Together, they probe underlying causes of the situation and identify next steps, if any. They develop agreements and clarify responsibilities. Obviously, doing all this may take more than one meeting. The circle process is central to this step, though circles can be used at other stages as well, such as determining who needs to be present.

5. Follow-up, the key to long-term effectiveness: Accountability is often fragile among some of the participants, so commitments need to be clear and followed up on. Are all parties fulfilling their obligations? If not, why not, and what will be the remedy? It may be necessary to adjust the agreements. It is also important to celebrate successes (Pranis 2005, pp. 49–55).

Joel's first forays into this spiritual practice were indirect. He did participate in something akin to a circle process as he was transitioning from military to civilian life. The next time was not until he returned to the VA for a vets' sharing group. Again, this was not exactly a circle process, but the deep listening among the participants approached the deep listening of a circle process. Joel's third step was to participate in a men's sharing group through his church, his first, and so far only, venture into a church setting, which occurred months after we began meeting. In both the vets' group and the men's group, Joel practiced being the listener himself and began to recognize that all that had happened to him could allow him to serve as a resource for others. About the time that Joel began attending the men's group, he discovered the restorative justice program in his local school district. He is now looking into serving as a community member for these restorative justice circle processes. He is planning to take the training when it is offered again, and then he will see if he is ready to make the necessary commitment, knowing that doing so may bring up his own struggles with guilt and shame when he least expects it. "All this work to get my own life in some working shape maybe can help some kid step back from the brink and not have to reconstruct his life after such a deep facture," he told me recently. "I want this to work—if not now, later. It's one small way I can pay it forward."

Lamentation: Writing your own psalm

Moral injury's insidious effects too often include the rupture of any personal connection to the divine, anger at God, anger at oneself for one's moral disintegration, and isolation from faith communities that have previously fostered a connection to the larger story of faith. I turn now to the spiritual practice of lament, which invites direct engagement with God despite—and indeed through—a whole range of negative emotional responses toward the divine. The classic model for this spiritual practice is the psalms.

The psalms are ancient biblical prayers in the form of poetry. They cover an amazing variety of subjects. Poetry defies neat and simple language but somehow expresses our human experiences in words via the medium of the images that the words create (Endres and Liebert 2001, pp. 8–15; Fawson 2019). Linear language may come later or may not come at all.

For persons who have trouble engaging God, the psalms give plenty of practice in approaching God no matter how one feels. There are praise psalms, thanksgiving psalms, worship psalms, psalms asking for forgiveness, psalms celebrating victory; there are war-like psalms and peaceful psalms. Most important for our purposes, there are psalms in which the psalmist is figuratively shaking a fist at God. Those who do not feel, deep down, that they can rage at God will have plenty of encouragement to express exactly how they feel directly to God if they model themselves on the psalmists.

The psalms literally cry out for bodily expression: "Give praise with tambourines and dance," says Psalm 150:4. "I bow low towards your holy temple," we intone in Psalm 138. "By the rivers of Babylon we sat mourning and weeping," says Psalm 137. "I lie prostrate in the dust" (Psalm 119:25) and "Enter, let us bow down in worship, let us kneel before the Lord who made us" (Psalm 95:6) give some hint of the bodily postures that the psalmist invokes as part of our prayer. Given this physicality in the poetry, one spiritual practice is simply to pray psalms in a whole-bodied way, aloud and in motion, enacting the psalm as it is read or, even better, sung. Such bodily prayer can awaken something in us that our minds have not yet recognized and may be particularly helpful to those suffering from military moral injury as they try to reconnect to their bodies and connect their bodies to their spiritual lives.

However, the spiritual practice that I want to highlight involves creating one's own lament psalm. Almost one-third of the psalms are psalms of lament; together, they give us a rich model for praying in times of estrangement or anger at God. Lament psalms almost always share the following structure, which provide the outline of the spiritual practice of lament:

- Addressing God: "O Lord!"

- Complaining/lamenting the distress: "How long will my enemy be exalted over me?" One can complain about the situation, about human enemies, about God, or even about oneself. All are there in the psalms.

- Beyond the complaint, though, is professing innocence—or, as the situation warrants, confessing one's own complicity and failure. Both occur in the psalms.

- Petition for what one desires generally follows: "Consider and answer me, O Lord, my God! Give light to my eyes or I will sleep the sleep of death."

- Many lament psalms shift toward the end to confessing hope and trust in God, and occasionally thanksgiving returns at the end as the psalmist recognizes what God has and is doing.

- Many conclude with the psalmist vowing to praise God in the future (Endres and Liebert 2001, pp. 52–53).

If you prefer, you may use the following format for prayerfully creating your own lament psalm:

Practice: Creating your own lament psalm

1. Formulate the issue and identify with the oppressed (who may be yourself):

Begin by recalling a painful situation or a situation of injustice. Let God speak deeply within you to surface a condition, in you or beyond you personally, that needs to be rectified and for which you will intercede.

Be in touch with the variety and depth of the woundedness and estrangement evoked by the situation.

Name the situation aloud.

2. Address God in whatever way seems fitting, calling God to hear you. Articulate your complaint forcefully, repeatedly, as strongly as you can.

3. Confess your trust in God in whatever words come to you. Place your petitions and, yes, even your demands, before this God.

4. Hear God speak words of assurance to you. Address words of assurance to yourself and to the community. Offer God your promise of praise in the face of this stubborn situation.

5. Bring your prayer to a conclusion in some appropriate way, perhaps with a bow or some other gesture of reverence.

© Elizabeth Liebert. Based on Endres and Liebert (2001, pp. 80–81).

Joel had to work up to this practice because of his ambivalence toward God; his first instinct was simply to turn away from a God he assumed could never love him again. But when he finally realized that tactic was getting him nowhere, he decided that he and God would have to have it out. That's when this practice finally made sense to Joel. He began to address entries in his journal to God, and he is now becoming more comfortable saying whatever he is thinking about God to God directly. Joel would be the first to tell you that his ambivalence around God is far from gone. Maybe it never will be gone entirely. "But now I tell Him directly," he says.

Public services of lament take the intensely personal spiritual practice of creating one's own lament psalm to the corporate level through public ritual. Often done on Memorial Day, Fourth of July, Canada Day, or Veterans Day, these services can be a powerful witness to individuals and communities about the complexities of moral living in a complex world. As Graham (2017) notes, "Corporate ritual processes such as lamentations and memorialization also help the body politic itself to mourn its losses, share its anguish, confront its failings, honor or modify its values and reinvest its hopes in a transformed future" (p. 137). Among the many resources available online, the Institute for Congregational Trauma and Growth offers a useful template for preparing such a service for use in the congregational setting. It will guide a planning group in creating a service that fits the religious tradition, the context, and the occasion eliciting the lament prayer.

Examen: Restoring and maintaining connection with God, self, and community

The final practice is variously called awareness examination, consciousness examen ("examen" being the Spanish for "examination"), or some combination of those phrases. The point of this exercise in its many variations is to see our lives just as they are, the very place where God is already present and active and inviting us to greater life. The examen is not only for those who suffer from moral injury but for all of us. The fruit of a regular, honest practice of the examen is deeper self-knowledge and a deeper connection to the presence of the divine in one's daily life. Examen can be fruitful, although in different ways, at any stage of healing from moral injury.

Once again, the basic practice is very simple. Simply reflect prayerfully on small bits of your life, but do so with regularity. The most common practice is to reflect each evening on that day, looking for how God was at work and how you responded. Done regularly, threads and themes become evident, self-knowledge deepens, and the facets of daily life appear in relation to God. Usually, the practice proceeds in five steps: ask God for light, give thanks, review the day, face shortcomings, and look forward to the day to come (Maney 2011, p. 1). There are many variations of this practice. In addition to Maney, useful resources include Aschenbrenner (2007) and Thibodeaux (2015); the latter calls this spiritual practice "the most amazing prayer you have never heard of" (p. v).

The version here is designed for small group practice but can just as easily serve individuals in their own deepening awareness of how God continually permeates and guides them in their daily lives. It was developed by a ministry team as a way to bring the grace and insight of the examen to their team's work (Linn et al. 1995). The beauty of this version is its flexibility. Parents can use it with small children as part of a bedtime ritual. Spouses can pray it with each other. Families can engage this examen conversationally around the dinner table. Groups of all kinds can use it to review their shared work.

Practice: The examen for a small group

This practice is suitable for the end of the day or at the conclusion of an activity such as a family vacation, a holiday, a project, a class, or a workshop.

- Light a candle or devise some other simple ritual to mark the time as prayer.

- Take about 5 minutes of quiet to reflect on two questions:

For what moment today am I most grateful?

For what moment today am I least grateful?

- Share these two moments with the others in the group.

- Conclude the time with a simple ritual and expression of gratitude, as appropriate.

Many other pairs of questions may be suitable, depending upon the group and circumstances. For example:

- When did I give and receive the most love today? When did I give and receive the least love today?

- When did I feel most alive today? When did I feel life draining out of me?

- When did I feel closest to God? When did I feel most distant from God?

- When was I happiest today? When was I saddest?
- What was today's high point? What was today's low point?

Adapted from Linn et al. (1995, pp. 5–6)

Actually, although presented last, this practice became important to Joel's family almost two years ago. Even though Joel was not comfortable going to church other than, eventually, to connect with the men's group, he did want to help his children begin to relate to God in their own way, without their relationships being colored by his struggles. Because it is so easy to involve children in this practice, he and his wife made a very simple version of the awareness examen part of the bedtime ritual, first with their daughter and then with their younger son as soon as he was old enough to talk. The children adapted readily to this ritual, and now they ask for it whenever the parent who is tucking them into bed forgets it.

As for the individual form of the awareness examen, at present Joel uses it simply to notice moments of beauty, calm, and love, usually in relation to his family. That seems enough for now. "Maybe sometime I will feel ready to engage directly with God in looking at my day," he remarked recently. "But right now it's enough to realize that my relationship with God, while battered, is actually operational—sort of. I couldn't have imagined even this much several years ago."

Conclusion

Spiritual practices are human attempts to forge and strengthen bonds with the transcendent. When responsibly introduced, willingly entered into, and sensitively followed up on, spiritual practices can be powerful aids in the healing of moral injury precisely because they act in direct opposition to any severing of relationship with the divine and with representatives of the divine that is caused or exacerbated by moral injury.

The first challenge for the spiritual caregiver, then, is to approach the topic of the relationship with the divine (and/or the current or former faith community) with exquisite sensitivity. What are the currently operative concepts of the divine? How does the individual address the divine? What emotions swirl around the thought of any relationship with the divine? How does the individual feel about attending to the divine at all? About engaging with a faith community? What spiritual practices proved nourishing in the past? Do they serve now? What yearning (if any) arises when this topic comes up? What resistances? (Spiritual caregivers should also answer these questions for themselves as part of responsible caregiving in order to be clear about what is their own and what belongs to those accompanied.)

What, indeed, counts as a spiritual practice? I have taken a broad understanding of spiritual practice as any intentionally chosen attempt to connect with or remain in relationship with the transcendent. This wide understanding allows one to consider even very common human activities such as listening to another, walking and running, dancing, journal writing, poetry reading and writing, photography, art, playing a musical instrument, singing, gardening, walking a dog, swimming, or even cooking and cleaning as spiritual practices under appropriate circumstances. Begin where there is a draw, some energy, or some fruit, even if it does not match common definitions of a spiritual practice. When resistance to anything approaching religion is high, such indirect approaches may be the only viable way to begin.

Ideally, some spiritual practices connect directly to the individual's current or former faith community. But, particularly in an age when so many claim to be spiritual but not religious, the connection to viable faith communities, even through spiritual practices, may be impossible or, at best, tenuous. Yet there may be other communities of practice, such as Quaker meetings open to persons of any or no faith tradition, centering prayer and meditation groups of various kinds, or AA groups, that could provide communal support for continuing and deepening spiritual practices. Such communities serve as a support during the sometimes long and arduous process of reconnecting the threads of one's moral self and reintegrating into life-giving communities.

How can spouses and families also be nourished during this period of recovery? Perhaps spouses could learn and practice the same exercises together. Perhaps spouses could address together the spiritual lives of their children rather than focus on the spiritual life of the one suffering from moral injury. Perhaps it works best for spouses to practice whatever spiritual exercises each finds most nourishing and simply share the fruit with the other spouse on occasion. There is no one rule that fits all with respect to families. Nor is there one rule when it comes to faith communities. If the spiritual caregiver has appropriate access to the careseeker's family and other support communities, they should consider if and how they could share these practices with the persons in the wounded person's support system.

I selected the four spiritual practices presented here because they have the potential to speak to a wide swath of persons suffering from moral injury. They may also aid in the growth of those in the surrounding care system as they do their own work around soul care. I have chosen these practices because of their simplicity and their adaptability to a variety of persons and religious or spiritual contexts, because they lend themselves to individual and corporate practice, and because they can support both those seeking healing and their entire circle of support.

Joel's journey illustrates one person's ongoing attempt to use these spiritual practices in healing from moral injury. Listening undergirds all stages of healing, with the spiritual caregiver's intense holding the safety of the exchange gradually yielding to collaborative conversation around reconstructing and implementing a new moral identity (Graham 2017, p. 33). Over time, Joel learned to use storytelling to connect himself first with himself but then later connect himself to his wife and small children. Eventually, Joel began to sense that he could channel that storytelling into restorative justice circles with troubled kids. Because it took Joel a long time to admit his anger at God, the practice of lament only became salient when Joel realized that hiding from God was keeping him stuck. He now regularly uses his journal as a place to record whatever he wants to say to God, and usually no one but him sees the written record of their disputes. As the long Jewish tradition attests, fighting with God actually indicates a relationship, contentious though it may be. The awareness examen provided a way to allow Joel's children to form their own relationships with God without being unduly influenced by his struggles. Both Joel and his wife cherish these moments with their children. Joel has adapted the awareness examen as an ongoing tool to observe and be grateful for little moments of beauty and love. Each time Joel does notice these moments, it allows grace a bit more room in his spirit. In the end, finding and holding spaces for grace is what healing is all about.

May these and other spiritual practices provide peace, sustenance, and appropriate challenge in the arduous task of regaining or repairing a viable moral narrative for both careseekers and those who surround them.

References

Aschenbrenner, G. (2007). *Consciousness examen.* Chicago: Loyola Press.

Brock, R., & Lettini, G. (2012). *Soul repair: Recovering from moral injury after war.* Boston: Beacon Press.

Burghardt, W. (1989). Contemplation: A long, loving look at the real. *Church, 5*(4), 14–18.

Doehring, C. (2019). Military moral injury: An evidence-based intercultural approach to spiritual care. *Pastoral Psychology, 68*(1), 15–30. doi.org/10.1007/s11089-018-0813-5.

Egan, G. (2018). *The skilled helper: A problem management and opportunity development approach to helping.* Pacific Grove: Brooks Cole. (Originally published in 1975).

Endres, J., & Liebert, E. (2001). *A retreat with the psalms: Resources for personal and communal prayer.* New York: Paulist Press.

Fawson, S. (2019). Sustaining lamentation for military moral injury: Witness poetry and naming the traces of extremity. *Pastoral Psychology 68*(1), 31–40. doi.org/10.1007/s11089-018-0855-8.

Graham, L. (2017). *Moral injury: Restoring wounded souls.* Nashville: Abingdon Press.

Herman, J. (2015). *Trauma and recovery: The aftermath of violence, from domestic abuse to political terror.* New York: Basic Books. (Originally published in 1992).

Institute for Congregational Trauma and Growth. A guide to planning a service of lament. http://www.ictg.org/uploads/1/2/9/5/12954435/ictg_guide_to_planning_a_service_of_lament.pdf.

Lester, A. (1995). *Hope in pastoral care and counseling.* Louisville: Westminster John Knox.

Lettini, G. (2013). Engaging the moral injuries of war: A call to spiritual leaders. *Reflective Practice: Formation and Supervision in Ministry, 33*, 37–46.

Linn, D., Linn, S., & Linn, M. (1995). *Sleeping with bread: Holding what gives you life.* Mahwah: Paulist Press.

Litz, B., Stein, N., Delaney, E., Liebowitz, L., Nash, W. P., Silva, C., & Maugen, S. (2009). Moral injury and moral repair in war veterans: A preliminary model and intervention strategy. *Clinical Psychology Review, 29*(8), 695–706. doi.org/10.1016/j.cpr.2009.07.003.

Maney, J. (2011). *A simple life-giving prayer: Discovering the power of St. Ignatius Loyola's examen.* Chicago: Loyola Press.

Nichols, M. (1995). *The lost art of listening: How learning to listen can improve relationships.* New York: Guilford Press.

Patton, J. (1990). *From ministry to theology.* Nashville: Abingdon Press.

Pranis, K. (2005). *The little book of circle processes: A new/old approach to peacemaking.* Intercourse: Good Books.

Ramsay, N. (2019). Moral injury as grief and loss: Ritual resources for care. *Pastoral Psychology 68*, 107–125. doi.org/10.1007/s/11089-018-0854-9.

Rogers, C. (1961). *On becoming a person.* Boston: Houghton Mifflin.

Savage, J. (1996). *Listening and caring skills: A guide for groups and leaders.* Nashville: Abingdon Press.

Stallinga, B. (2013). What spills blood wounds the spirit: Chaplains, spiritual care and operational stress injury. *Reflective Practice, 33,* 13–31.

Taylor, C. (1991). *The skilled pastor: Counseling as the practice of theology.* Minneapolis: Fortress Press.

Thibodeaux, M. (2015). *Reimagining the Ignatian examen: Fresh ways to pray from your day.* Chicago: Loyola Press.

Verkamp, B. (2006). *The moral treatment of returning warriors in early and modern times.* Scranton: University of Scranton Press.

Yandell, M. (2015). The war within: A veteran's moral injury. *The Christian Century, 132*(1), 12–13.

5

Insights into Moral Injury and Soul Repair from Classical Jewish Texts

— Kim S. Geringer & Nancy H. Wiener —

Core Jewish teachings

Every weekday morning, praying Jews sing or recite:
Elohai, n'shamah sh'natata bi t'horah hi.
Atah b'ratah, atah y'tzartah, atah n'fachtah bi.
V'atah m'shamrah b'kirbi.
My God, the soul you have given me is pure.
You created it, You shaped it, You breathed it into me.
And You protect it within me.

The Hebrew word *n'shamah*[1] is usually translated as 'soul,' but it also can mean 'breath.' In Judaism, our souls—the breath of God—come to us in purity, and every human being has been created in the image and likeness of God, *b'tzelem Elohim* (Gen. 1:26–28, 5:1–3, 9:6). However, because we live in a world filled with pain and brokenness, the original purity of our souls is not enough to protect us from error. Judaism teaches that each human being has a *yetzer tov* (an inclination toward goodness) and a *yetzer ra* (an inclination toward evil). Goodness and evil, thus, are ever-present possibilities, and they become reality when human beings enact them. We lie, steal, cheat, fight, covet. Sometimes we cause grievous harm—even loss of life. In Judaism, life is lived in relationship and in the responsibilities that undergird those bonds. Every individual is, at all times, in concurrent relationships

---

[1]Other common Hebrew words for 'soul' are *nefesh* and *ruach*. In this article, the English word will be offered as their translations.

79

with self, community, the world, and God. Judaism conceives of the relationship between God and the human being as a covenant, that is, a bond of mutuality in which each partner has obligations to the other. God offered the first covenant to all of humanity via Noah following the flood, and God and humanity committed themselves to not destroying the world again (Gen. 8:21). Beginning with Abraham and fulfilled with Moses, the God of the *Tanakh*[2] forged a covenant with the Jewish people to create a just and peaceful world. God promised divine love, care, and security and presented the Torah ('instruction' in Hebrew) to the people as a sign of that love. For their part, the Jewish people promised to fulfill God's word. Each generation discerns meaningful ways to act on the essence and values of the Torah. To be in relationship is to take on responsibilities for oneself and others. God and all of creation exist with an inherent tension between two attributes—justice (*din*) and mercy (*rachamim*). This tension, according to *midrash*,[3] goes back to the Creation:

> Thus said the Holy One, blessed be God's name! 'If I create the world with the Attribute of Mercy, sin will abound; and if I create it with the Attribute of Justice, how can the world exist? Therefore I create it with attributes, mercy and justice, and may it thus endure.' (Genesis Rabbah 12:15)

Both attributes, then, are woven into the essential essence of the world, and both must inform our actions and our reactions. Endowed with the gift of free will, human beings will invariably err, sometimes grievously. Judaism teaches that human errors disrupt the balance of creation—disrupting relationships among human beings, disrupting personal relationships with God, and disrupting the entire people's relationship with God. In order to "get right" with God and to restore the balance (Wiener and Hirschmann 2014, Chapter 2), Judaism prescribes a system both just *and* merciful known as *teshuvah* (return), comprised of recognition, acknowledgment, contrition, and responsibility for mistakes. This path ultimately restores the person to a compassionate and forgiving God, returns the person to life in community, and reconciles individuals with each other, resulting in the erasure of sin and guilt.

---

[2] TaNaKH is an acronym based on the words Torah (Instruction), Nevi'vim (Prophets) and Ketuvim (Writings), the three sections comprising the Hebrew Bible.

[3] Midrash (pl. midrashim) is the Hebrew word for interpretive stories and explanations of biblical texts, a process that began in the rabbinic period and continues to the present. Each source following a midrashic citation is for a specific midrashic collection.

'As I live,' says the Eternal God, 'it is not My desire that the wicked shall die, but that they turn from their [evil] ways and live. Return, return from your [evil] ways that you may not die, O House of Israel!' (Ezek. 33:11)

A *midrash* teaches, "The Holy One declares no creature unfit—God receives all. The gates of repentance are always open, and one who wishes to enter may enter" (Exodus *Rabbah* 19:4). *Teshuvah* has internal elements, but it is ultimately an interpersonal process. And because it is, we are responsible to both seek forgiveness and offer it. "Human beings are godlike when they approximate the prophetic ideal of goodness, one that is stern in the grandeur of its vision and still forgiving of the flaws in humanity" (Wolpe 1990, p. 73).

Rabbinic Judaism identified three means for humans to communicate with God, retain the world's balance, and uphold the covenant: return (*teshuvah*), prayer (*tefilah*), and righteous acts (*tzedakah*). All of these require action and engagement; beliefs may inform actions, but beliefs alone never suffice.

It was with these fundamental Jewish understandings that we joined a think tank of religious leaders and faculty organized by the Soul Repair Center at Brite Divinity School on the campus of Texas Christian University, Fort Worth, Texas, to enrich the literature and resources for communities of faith in addressing moral injury and begin to explore moral injury from a Jewish perspective. We studied traditional Jewish texts from the *Tanakh* through the great legal compendia as well as contemporary literature. We sought to find in Jewish sacred text, liturgy, and legal codes sources of wisdom that could provide Jewish language and concepts to understand moral injury, enhance Jewish pastoral work with those who suffer from it, and help non-Jewish caregivers appreciate the unique cultural and religious context in which Jews might experience and understand their own moral injuries. As teachers of rabbinic and cantorial students, we also wanted to find new ways to prepare our future clergy to function as witnesses and healers for those suffering moral injury, however derived.

Hebrew Bible (*Tanakh*) and Jewish midrashic understandings of soul wounds

The *Tanakh* and later rabbinic commentaries and *midrashim* reflect a profound sensitivity to and awareness of the existence of wounds that are neither physical nor psychological but, rather, spiritual. These texts identify a spiritual brokenness resulting from perpetrating, witnessing, or failing to stop acts that "transgressed one's basic moral identity and violated core moral beliefs" (Nakashima Brock and Lettini 2012, xiv). The following selections are emblematic of the messages and concerns about this particular type of wound and their broader ramifications for individuals and collectives.

The nature of soul wounds in the *Tanakh*

While the modern terms 'soul wounds,' 'moral injury,' 'moral distress,' and 'moral stress' appear in contemporary psychological and pastoral literature, their precursor can be found in the *Tanakh* in the original Hebrew. The biblical text recognizes a unique condition that affects the soul. However, it does not reflect the contemporary distinctions that Doehring (2015) discerns.

The phrase "his soul's distress," (*tzarat nafsho*) makes its first appearance in Genesis 42:21–22:

> They said to one another, "Alas, we are being punished on account of our brother, because we looked on at *tzarat nafsho*, his soul's distress, yet paid no heed as he pleaded with us. That is why this distress (*tzarah hazot*) has come upon us." Then Reuben spoke up and said to them, "Did I not tell you, 'Do no wrong to the boy'? 'But you paid no heed. Now his blood requires explanation."

In this brief exchange, a group of brothers recalled a time when they had conspired to kill their brother Joseph. Upon the advice of one of them, they had agreed to strip Joseph of his treasured garment and throw him in a pit. Following this violent and angry action, the text states, "They sat down and ate." Their focus shifted from Joseph to their own bodily needs. The brothers then sold Joseph to a passing caravan and feigned his death when they reported his absence to their father (Gen. 37:17–33). At a time of famine, more than a decade later, the brothers found themselves standing before their former victim, although they did not recognize him. For the first time, the brothers had a chance to acknowledge the spiritual wounds of the past and to consider ways to work together toward healing. In Chapter 42, Reuben, a leader among the brothers, attributed their current distress and hardship to those prior actions and referred to a quality in Joseph's cry while he was in the pit that had informed them that the wounds he suffered were in his soul. For the biblical brothers, as with many suffering from moral injuries, detailed memories arose after a great time lapse, and their appearance led the brothers to acknowledge the past, a first step toward repairing their own and their victim's wounded souls (Litz et al. 2009, p. 701).

Rather than protect their kin, these brothers ignored their familial obligations and attacked Joseph, sold him, and planned to feign his death and report his demise to their father. The moral order was breached, and Joseph was left pleading to deaf ears; the very ears that were supposed to hear his cries and soothe him instead heard him and ignored him. In this second scene, the brothers identified themselves as being wounded, suffering. The moral conundrum in which they found themselves—to decide if they themselves, their families, or their father would experience irreparable pain and suffering—is a clear example of a case of soul wounds (Doehring 2015; Nakashima Brock and Lettini 2012). The impact of the original breach of the moral code that bound the brothers still rocked the lives of the entire family decades later, a common experience of veterans (Boudreau 2010).

Earlier in Genesis, when Jacob and Esau were about to encounter each other for the first time since Jacob's flight after his brother threatened to kill him, we find a phrase that resonates with the phrase *tzarat nafsho* and parallels Joseph's brothers' description of their state. As Jacob divided his family and possessions into two camps while watching 400 men approach him, Genesis 32:8 states, "*Vayitzar meod Yaakov vayira.*"—"And Jacob was in great fear and distress." Rashi,[4] Judaism's most famous medieval exegete, explained this phrase in the following way, "He was afraid lest he be killed, and he was distressed that he might kill others" (s.v. Genesis 32:8). Nachmanides[5] expanded on Rashi and explained, "He feared for his soul because he concluded that what he saw before him was only done to wage war against him" (s.v. Genesis 32:8). Nachmanides identified Jacob's fear as mortal fear resulting from his dread that his brother's legion was set to attack him—a breach of the moral order.

This moment relates to larger questions about the emotional and soul responses of engaging in war as a combatant. The emotional response is fear. The soul response is one of distress and woundedness when faced with the untenable moral quandary of either facing one's own death or killing someone else in order to remain alive. This distress is heightened when combatants recognize each other as kin.

The distinctiveness of a soul wound from other wounds and illnesses suffered by individuals is underscored in Rabbi David Kimchi's[6]

---

[4]Rabbi Solomon ben Isaac of Troyes (1040–1105), known by the acronym RaSHI, wrote commentaries to the Talmud and *Tanakh*.

[5]Rabbi Moses ben Nahman (1194–1270), known as Nachmanides or by the acronym RaMbaN, was a scholar, philosopher, kabbalist, and biblical commentator who spent most of his life in Girona, Catalonia.

[6]Rabbi David Kimchi (1160–1235), born in Narbonne, Provence, was a rabbi, biblical commentator, grammarian, and philosopher.

commentary on Psalm 58. He wrote that this psalm "remind[s] those who suffer from illness or a wounded soul to pray the words of this psalm." Soul wounds may respond positively to the same balms as other illnesses and wounds. Nonetheless, trying to understand them as part of other types of suffering is to diminish their importance and fail to honor their uniqueness.

Ancient Jewish responses to suffering souls

Recitation of psalms is one of a number of options available to those with wounded souls. In Psalm 23, we learn that the ultimate goal for a wounded soul is the restoration of that soul. Enemies, danger, and pain—"deepest darkness"—are present even in the lush and pastoral setting described in Psalm 23. Yet the psalmist painted a picture of perfect security and safety in God's nurturing presence. As a shepherd protects a flock with rod and staff, so God guides the people. In this scenario, they lack for nothing; food, drink, oil, goodness, and love are theirs not only in the present but in the future too. This is the true relationship of the human being to God; fear and brokenness do not preclude finding the peace that comes from living in God's house, a possibility available to all. Psalm 23 suggests to the reader that nothing is required of the person and that one's very humanity is sufficient for God's protection and love because each individual is made in the image of God, *b'tzelem Elohim*.

Even a soul that has been in the valley of the shadow of death can return to its former state. First Kings 17:17–25 provides an example of how turning to God and human contact can be a means to bringing one's soul back, even when one is seemingly dead: "…and the soul of the child came back into him, and he lived" (…*v'tashov nefesh-hayeled al kirbo, vayechi*). One's soul can be wounded, distressed, depleted; one can even appear to be dead. But one need not remain in the depths of despair. The suffering speaker of Psalm 130 called to God "out of the depths" of despair or estrangement. God was beseeched to notice the one who suffered, and God was challenged to remember that no one could ever survive if God "[kept] account of sins." Implied is the speaker's trust and belief that after a long period of darkness, God would indeed be revealed in "the morning." At the conclusion of the psalm, the speaker had become more than just an individual. The isolation experienced in the depths was replaced by the supplicant's becoming part of a community that waited together for God's deliverance.

Connection with community is essential in times of joy as well as times of distress. In the *Mishnah*,[7] *Pirkei Avot* 2:4, the great first-century

---

[7]The first compilation of rabbinic laws dating from 200 BCE—200 CE.

sage, Hillel, is quoted as saying, "Do not separate yourself from the community." As the Babylonian Talmud (*Ta'anit* 11a) teaches, "A person should share in the distress of the community." Similarly, Rabbi Abraham Isaac Kook (1865–1935) taught, "No Jew . . . should be torn from the community because one's soul and self-perfection require it." Active engagement in community, then, is an essential component of recovery from grave emotional wounds (Sippola et al. 2009, p. 65).

Psalm 30 teaches that even in the direst of circumstances, reversal is possible. The psalmist turned to God, crying from a pit in *Sheol*.[8] The image of the pit harkens back to Joseph, who experienced two pits: the first the one into which his brothers threw him and the second the one into which he was thrown in an Egyptian prison. Joseph's story is one of deepest despair that ultimately reverses and becomes one of triumph, love, and reconciliation. Joseph was no innocent victim of fate. His bragging and insensitivity to his brothers' envy paved the way for their harsh treatment of him, and twice death came close. Still, as the psalm says, God did not "let [his] enemies rejoice." God can bring a person "up from *Sheol*." Spiritual healing, joy, dancing, and singing remain within reach of even those whose soul wounds have brought them to despair (Currier et al. 2015, pp. 13–17).

Leviticus offers yet another means to address the deep wounds that a soul can experience— the necessity of bringing offerings. In the Levitical worldview, every member of society, from the High Priest to the average Israelite, was fully human and, therefore, susceptible to transgressing laws. Leviticus categorized transgressions as intentional (*yecheta*) and unintentional (*yecheta vishgaga*). Lack of intent did not free one from the responsibility of acknowledging what had happened and taking responsibility for making appropriate offerings or setting things right. The process had multiple stages. (See Leviticus 4 and 5.) The external process began either when another member of the community brought a transgression to the individual's attention or when individuals themselves realized what they had done. The next step was internal; one was obligated to realize one's guilt, and that realization led back to the external process. Individuals were required to make their guilt known to others; merely knowing of it in their own hearts did not suffice. Then they were required to bring the necessary offerings, for the sin and for restitution, to the priest. Through these acts, individuals reconnected with the community, its religious leaders, and God. All three needed to be engaged in order for balance to be restored and for the individual to be reintegrated into the community.

---

[8]While many translations render this as "the underworld," biblical scholar Herbert Brichto (1973) suggests it was where a family's or tribe's dead souls resided together.

From the High Priest to the individual Israelite, each individual and the entire collective had the obligation and the possibility of returning to a state of integrity and wholeness.

Justice and mercy are ever-present and necessary, even in the case of the most egregious unintentional sin, the slaying of another human being. Brother against brother, a repeated biblical theme, goes back to the first fraternal pair, Cain and Abel (Gen. 4:1–18). There, we find that Cain's distress at his offering not finding God's favor led him to lash out and fail to treat his brother as kin. It would seem that this rejection of his offering ran counter to his understanding of how the world worked; it was his moral injury. He expressed his unnamed and unaddressed soul wound through indiscriminate rage, a pattern noted in contemporary soul repair literature (Nakashima Brock and Lettini 2012). Murder does not appear to have been Cain's goal. As the narrative continues, God offered Cain an opportunity to take responsibility by inquiring about Abel's whereabouts. Cain's first response was ignorance. Yet, when Cain heard the punishment he was to receive, he did not argue about his guilt. Rather, he pleaded with God to recognize that his crime was not worthy of God's harsh punishment, the death sentence. God meted out justice and tempered it with mercy, allowing Cain to live and ensuring that he would not be killed because of his transgression.

Numbers 25 addresses the importance of the appropriate punishment for unintentional killers. Like Cain, unintentional killers were allowed to flee without fear of revenge. Six of the cities set aside for the Levites (Num. 35:1–6) were known as Cities of Refuge, safe havens where an unintentional killer might live. Though these were cities of the Levites, the Levites were not the cities' only inhabitants. The entire Israelite community, not just those among whom unintentional killers lived, was responsible for the care and safety of those who had found refuge there.

According to the rabbis of the *Mishnah*, these were to be medium-sized towns in places that had water (or to which water could be brought), with markets and diverse populations. They were places where weapons of war and weapons of hunting were not sold. Therefore, the blood avenger would have no means to do harm there. The community at large was responsible for maintaining direct roads with clear signage, enabling all to know how to find a city of refuge and ensuring it remained connected to other population centers (*Makkot* 2:4–5). For safety's sake, unintentional killers did not travel to a city of refuge alone; instead, community members always accompanied them on this journey. Unintentional killers had access to scholars and priests, engaged in the activities of daily life, and had the chance to reestablish themselves as full members of a new community. Some interpretations suggest that this new life was built with family by one's side since keeping the family intact was understood as beneficial for both the individual and the family unit as a whole.

Preventing moral injury when possible

The Babylonian Talmud teaches,

> Whoever is able to protest against the wrongdoings of his family and fails to do so is punished for the family's wrongdoings. Whoever is able to protest against the wrong- doings of his fellow citizens and does not do so is punished for the wrongdoings of the people of his city. Whoever is able to protest against the wrongdoings of the world and does not do so is punished for the wrongdoings of the world. (*Shabbat* 54b)

Core to the Jewish understanding of what it means to be human are responsibility and interdependence. Being human is taking responsibility for one's self and, when appropriate, reminding others of their responsibilities as well. The failure to intervene is a punishable offense. Witnesses who suffer from moral injury know all too well the guilt of an offense of omission (Nakashima Brock and Lettini 2012, p. xxi).

Although Jacob's soul wound occurred when he contemplated armed battle, the need for special attention to the souls of actual soldiers is treated in detail in both Deuteronomy 20 and Numbers 31. Everyone was called to report for duty. Once assembled, religious leaders underscored the warriors' relationship to God (Deut. 20:4) as well as to the social and political entities of which they were a part. Then the military leaders addressed the troops with words of encouragement and support—support for those who would serve as well as those who would not (Deut. 20:5–7). Contemporary exemptions from military service focus heavily on physical well-being or diagnosed mental illness. The biblical list of exemptions (recent marriage, newly planted vineyards, etc.), in contrast, demonstrated an awareness that normative life transitions related to domestic and professional commitments could inhibit one's ability to be fully committed, to be present in body and soul, to the shared goals that bind and guide those who are in battle. While the desire to see initiatives through and to enjoy what they produced was valued, it was also understood to be a potential distraction. Victory required warriors to honestly assess their nonphysical readiness because distractions, "fears," or "faintheartedness" would not only impact their own participation but negatively impact others in their company as well (Deut. 20:8). No shame or blame was attached to these exemptions. All met their obligation by responding to the initial call to present themselves for service. And those who went into battle did so accompanied by God and with the words and well-wishes of communal leaders. Today's service members could benefit from this model.

Providing space and time to heal

In the *Tanakh*, no one returned home from the battlefield without four essential supports: community leaders to welcome them, a chance to acknowledge what they had done, rituals to address the impact of time in a battle zone, and transitional time in a transitional space that was neither the war zone nor the main Israelite camp. All of this prepared them for the transition back to civilian life. Reentry was a matter of attending to one's own soul to restore balance.

As an Israelite battalion returned from a war zone, Moses, Eleazar the priest, and all the leaders of the community went to meet them outside the camp, saying:

> Anyone who has killed someone or touched someone who was killed must stay outside the camp seven days. On the third and seventh days you must purify yourselves and your captives. Purify every garment as well as everything made of leather, goat hair or wood. On the seventh day, wash your clothes and be clean, and after that you may enter the camp. (Num. 31:19–20)

This ritual acknowledged that being in the presence of death altered a combatant's state, making him unable to engage in social activities and cultic rituals until participating in the ritual. Prior to rejoining the community, that reality had to be acknowledged and addressed. According to Numbers 19:11–13:

> One who touches the corpse of any human being shall be 'unclean' for seven days. [Such persons] shall cleanse themselves on the third day and on the seventh day, and then be clean. Those who touch a corpse, the body of a person who has died, and do not cleanse themselves, defile the Eternal's Tabernacle; such persons shall be cut off from Israel.

The state of "uncleanness" to which the *Tanakh* refers was a state that came from breaching a boundary, resulting in a threat to the integrity of the individual and, by extension, the community (Wiener and Hirschmann 2014, pp. 29–32).

The notion that one's integrity can be threatened or altered undergirds the biblical laws and stories related to another, often invisible, condition. *Tzara'at*, frequently (and erroneously) translated as leprosy, appeared on human skin, the walls of buildings, and fabric. Chapters 13 and 14 of Leviticus provide detailed laws for diagnosing this often-unseen condition as well as the many steps that individuals suffering from it needed to take in order to return to their former state and reenter the community as full participants.

These laws can provide us with an additional Jewish lens for understanding the plight of those with soul wounds. Like *tzara'at*, soul wounds can be accompanied by visible physical wounds, yet their existence is largely invisible to the untrained eye. Moreover, they can remain unrecognized and unseen by those who are experiencing them. (Think of a change in the skin on a person's back or scalp that they, themselves, may never notice.) Although others may see symptoms, they often are unsure of what to make of them. They do not know if the symptoms are noteworthy or in need of treatment. Individuals will only have a chance to heal if they themselves notice or if others can lead them to seek help from a trained professional to assess the situation. Then those who have experienced moral injury will be best served if they can acknowledge the wound that has altered their state of being and their understanding of themselves in the world by naming it and alerting others to the nature of their suffering. They can, figuratively, rend their clothes and let their hair down and claim the time, space, and support they need to restore their inner balance. They can lament and the community can respond (Adler 2006, pp. 16–21).[9] Two other interesting but often overlooked aspects of the biblical presentations of those who suffer from *tzara'at* can be found in narrative portions of the biblical text. We learn that the entire camp remained at a standstill until Miriam returned to the community, healed from *tzara'at* (Num. 12:15). Her condition had an impact on the community at large. The halt in her journey halted everyone else's. Those closest to someone with a soul wound are affected (Nakashima Brock and Lettini 2012, p. 52), but the entire society feels its impact, whether or not it recognizes it (Nakashima Brock and Lettini 2012, p. 130). II Kings 7:3–20 presents four individuals who are outside the camp due to *tzara'at*. Rather than each living in isolation, they found each other, kept each other company, and worked together. They still felt strong bonds with the community from which they were separated, and they were willing to risk their own lives to save the lives of their people when they were threatened. This biblical imagery underscores the importance of

---

[9]The power of the community for support and healing is underscored by the Jewish tradition of community members visiting and praying with mourners in their homes for seven days, thus ensuring that the bereaved are not left alone during this most vulnerable period.

helping those who are suffering from moral injuries to find each other, converse with each other, and through these contacts bolster each other and help each other affirm the deep and enduring ties they retain for their families and communities, despite their sense of separateness (Sippola et al. 2009, pp. 15, 26–27).

Through rituals of atonement and rituals of purification, ancient Israelite society acknowledged and restored balance after being in the presence of death, suffering from *tzara'at*, or committing a sin. The destruction of the Temple and its sacrificial cult produced a vacuum. A *midrash* presents two rabbis walking through the rubble that was once the Temple:

> One says, 'Woe to us. The Temple where we atoned for our sins has been destroyed.' The other responds, 'My son. Don't see it as a bad thing for you, since we have another form of atonement which is comparable—that is, acts of lovingkindness. As it says in Hosea 6:6, "It is lovingkindness I desire, not sacrifice." And he said, 'A world of lovingkindness will be established.' And God is described as saying, "Dearer to me is the kindness that you provide for each other than all the sacrifices you sacrificed completely before me." (*Avot d'Rabbi Natan* 11)

The need to restore balance is eternal. The means to achieve it can change.

The possibility of seeing the world and its rhythms entirely disrupted and destroyed and the accompanying feelings of pain, sadness, and confusion as to how to proceed are age-old problems for individuals and communities. However, the possibility of lamenting the loss and realizing that all of one's values and all of one's commitments need not be lost along with the very real loss that one has suffered is equally if not more powerful. It is the cornerstone of resilience and continued meaning (Boss 2000).

A sampling of medieval rabbinic legal literature: The Mishneh Torah

In the section of the *Mishneh Torah* known as Laws of Murder and Preservation of Life (*Hilchot Rotzeach uShmirat Nefesh*), Maimonides[10] offered a way of thinking about the transgressions that can lead to moral injury from a traditional Jewish perspective, building on and expanding biblical categories of transgression. In another section (*Hilchot Teshuvah*), Maimonides explicated the requirements for

---

[10]Moses ben Maimon—Maimonides— (1135–1204) was a physician, philosopher, and codifier of Jewish law. His *Mishneh Torah* ("Review of the Torah") is considered one of the greatest and most innovative Jewish legal texts of all time.

repentance and atonement. In both, Maimonides's approach to those who had caused a grave injury or mortal harm was an appreciation of nuance and context infused with deep compassion. His recognition of the complexity of being a human being permeates his legal writing. Throughout these sections of the *Mishneh Torah*, Maimonides argued that determining legal (and, we would argue, moral) responsibility for death and the application of appropriate means of repentance can only be determined by a rigorous consideration of all relevant factors. In Laws of Murder and Preservation of Life, for instance, Maimonides delineated three categories of "unintentional" killers: those who kill unintentionally with no awareness of the consequences of their actions; those whose killings are "unintentional" because they were caused by forces beyond their control; and those whose acts, although "willfully perpetrated"—e.g., they involved negligence or care that should have been taken—are still considered to have been "unintentional." He gave this example:

> If a person threw a stone into the public domain, and after the stone left his hand, the victim stuck his head out from a window and was struck by it, the person who threw the stone is not liable. (Laws of Murder and Preservation of Life 6:9)

And this:

> If people would use a garbage dump to relieve themselves at night, but would not use it for this purpose during the daytime, but [this time] a person sat there during the day and was killed by a stone that came from a person tearing down an [adjacent] wall, the person who tore down the wall [is not liable]. (6:8)

However:

> When a person throws a stone into the public domain and it causes death, or one tears down a wall into the public domain and a stone falls and causes death . . . [that person] is considered to be close to having acted intentionally . . . and should have checked the surroundings [first] and then thrown the stone or torn down the wall. (6:6)

People are obligated to take reasonable precautions; they may not be considered liable or judged to be intentional killers if the circumstances under which the incident took place were different than usual or if the victims placed themselves in harm's way after the person's action had already begun.

Maimonides offered a nuanced approach, eschewing simple categories of right and wrong, to responding to a death that results from a perpetrator who intended to inflict harm, but not death. Maimonides taught that along with intent and taking precautions, the weapon is another key factor.

> [We] assess the object with which he was struck and the place where he was struck and determine whether or not it is likely that the murder weapon would cause death when used to give a blow in such a place. (3:1)

If death occurred because of an object that one should reasonably have known was likely to cause mortal injury, the perpetrator bears more responsibility than when death results from an object less likely to cause death.

Similarly, the force of the blow must be taken into consideration:

> . . . we evaluate the force of the hand . . . [one cannot] compare a person who throws a stone at his colleague from a distance of ten cubits to one who throws a stone from a distance of 100 cubits. For over an extended distance, the force of the blow will be diminished. (3:2)

Maimonides taught that the relative power of the killer and the victim must be investigated in determining liability. "Is he large or small? Is he strong or weak? Is he healthy or sickly? . . . all factors involved in the person's death should be assessed" (3:3).

The place on the body where the blow landed and the part of the body used are also relevant:

> One cannot compare a person poking at a colleague with his finger to one who kicks his colleague with all his strength. Nor can one compare a blow given on the heart to a blow given in the groin. Nor can one compare a weak person who strikes a healthy, strong person to a healthy, strong person who strikes a weak or sickly person. (3:5)

Mistaken identity removes culpability. "A person who intended to kill one person and instead killed another is not liable" (4:1).

So does a misplaced blow:

> A killer is not held liable . . . in the following instances. He intended to strike a colleague on his loins, and the utensil was not sufficient to kill if it struck a person on his loins, but it instead struck him on his heart and he died. Or a person intended to strike a colleague on his heart, and the blow was sufficient to kill had it struck him on the heart, but instead it struck the victim on his loins and it was not sufficient to kill an

ordinary person if it struck on his loins, but this person died. In these instances, the killer is not liable. (4:2)

A group's actions are assessed differently from an individual's. "If ten people strike a person with ten different sticks and he dies, they are all not held liable" (4:6). Implied here is that [punishment by death penalty] is not required unless one person alone is entirely accountable for the person's death. Nevertheless, an individual's blow either as part of or following a group attack does result in culpability.

Ten people threw stones at a person one after the other and none of the stones was of sufficient weight to cause death. Afterwards, another person cast a stone that was of sufficient weight to cause death and the victim died. The last person who threw the stone should be executed. If a defendant is then liable, the punishment should be carried out. If he is not liable for execution, he should be released. (4:7)

We read Maimonides's use of the word "released" in both the legal and moral senses. In Jewish law, penalties exist for many categories of wrongdoing, and they should be applied when appropriate. Maimonides could be forceful and emphatic when he believed that the facts justified strict condemnation. The taking of a life is regarded with the utmost seriousness, falling into a category all its own.

Although there are other transgressions that are more serious than murder, they do not present as serious a danger to society as murder does. Even idol worship—and needless to say, incest or the violation of the Sabbath—are not considered as severe as murder. For these transgressions involve man's [sic] relationship with God, while murder also involves man's relationship with his fellow man. (4:9)

In Maimonides's view, the power of *teshuvah* cannot be overstated, "*Teshuvah* atones for all sins. Even a person who was wicked his whole life and repented in his final moments will not be reminded of any aspect of his wickedness" (Laws of Repentance 1:3).

Confession plays a central role in the process. "Their sacrifices will not atone for their sins until they repent and make a verbal confession" (Laws of Repentance 1:1). And, "It is very praiseworthy for a person who repents to confess in public. Anyone who, out of pride, conceals sins and does not reveal them will not achieve complete repentance" (2:5).

In Maimonides's view, Jewish law is not for perfect people living in utopian conditions but rather a normative system to guide real individuals who find themselves in imperfect situations and personal crises. He did not legislate a system of absolutes—right or wrong, innocent or guilty—that might result in paralyzing guilt and shame for a person who has caused the death of another unintentionally. Instead, as this sampling of texts demonstrates, Maimonides advocated an empathic understanding of what it means to be human as well as a profound appreciation of the psychology of those who suffer. Maimonides's insistence on recognizing the multiplicity of variables at work in any given situation lifted a burden of unbearable guilt and shame from one who, having caused great damage, suffered a soul wound, thus paving the way for a more realistic assessment of responsibility.

Jewish liturgy

Jewish prayer is almost always done in community; indeed, traditionally, certain prayers may *only* be recited in the presence of a *minyan,* a quorum of 10 worshipers. Jewish tradition recognizes the ubiquity of human wrongdoing, and opportunities for recovery and repair are built into Jewish liturgy and the calendar. This process begins with the acknowledgement of transgression. In the traditional daily liturgy, for instance, the worshiper might offer prayers of supplication (*Tachanun*), recited with the worshiper in a position of humility and submission known as "falling on the face" (*nefillat apayim*) (Hoffman 2002). Seated and bent over, with the face lowered on the forearm in a sitting position, the worshiper recites:

> And David said to Gad: 'I am very distressed; let us fall into the hand of the Eternal, for God's mercy is great, but let me not fall into the hand of man [*sic*]' (II Samuel 24:14). Merciful and gracious God, I have sinned before you. Adonai, Who are full of compassion, have mercy on me, and accept my supplications. Punish me not in your anger; chastise me not in your wrath. Have pity on me, Adonai, for I languish away. My soul is severely troubled. I am worn out with groaning; every night I flood my bed with tears. God has heard my supplication. (Ps. 6)

Some versions of this prayer begin with *Vidui,* a confessional prayer. No general admission, *Vidui* enumerates a number of specific transgressions, and the heart is symbolically struck with the right fist during the recitation of each sin. It is important to note that almost all of Jewish prayer is in the first-person plural—"we," "our," "us"— underscoring the importance of the collective in worship:

We have become guilty, we have betrayed, we have robbed, we have spoken slander. We have caused perversion, we have caused wickedness, we have sinned willfully, we have extorted, we have accused falsely. We have given evil counsel, we have been deceitful, we have scorned, we have rebelled, we have provoked, we have turned away, we have been perverse, we have acted wantonly, we have persecuted, we have been obstinate. We have been wicked, we have corrupted, we have been abominable, we have strayed.

This is followed by the mention of God's thirteen attributes of mercy to underscore God's compassionate response (Exod. 34:6–7):

And in the daily "Standing Prayer" (The *Amidah*):
Return us to Your Torah and draw us to Your service, and in complete repentance restore us to Your Presence.
Forgive us for we have sinned, pardon us for we have transgressed, for You pardon and forgive.
Take note of our affliction and make our struggles Yours.
Redeem us swiftly for Your Name's sake,
For You are the mighty redeemer.
Blessed are You, Adonai, who redeems Israel.

Each of these daily prayers reflects multiple levels of obligation and responsibility. The worshipers' words reflect awareness that their relationships with both other human beings *and* God have been harmed by their actions. They seek to return to a place of wholeness, pleading with God to note their sincere regret and acknowledging God as the source of righteousness and redemption while admitting their own acts of transgression committed against other human beings and God.

In Laws of Repentance, Maimonides identified six stages of a full process of *teshuvah*: (1) introspection and recognition of one's wrongdoing, (2) confession and acceptance of rebuke, (3) repentance and atonement, (4) rejection of repeated sin, (5) forgiveness of self and others, and (6) renewal and transformation. The average Jew becomes familiar with this program through the repetition of the daily liturgy into which the themes of brokenness and repair are woven.

Perhaps the best-known time for atonement is Yom Kippur, the Day of Atonement, the second most sacred day (after Shabbat) in the Jewish calendar. *Teshuvah* is the main work of the day. On Yom Kippur, Jewish tradition imagines each individual walking on the path of a righteous life but veering off the path regularly. Through highly specific liturgical settings, Jews on Yom Kippur follow Maimonides's program by making a thorough review of the past year, admitting their errors, asking for forgiveness, resolving to get back on the "path" by making direct restitution to those they have wronged, and pledging to refrain from making similar transgressions in the future. Fasting and the denial of other bodily pleasures on Yom Kippur allow the petitioner to engage in this process without distraction or relief. Following is an excerpt of the Yom Kippur confession, "For the transgression" (Al-Cheit):

> For the transgressions we committed before You under duress and willingly.
> For the transgressions we committed before You through having a hard heart.
> For the transgressions we committed before You through things we blurted out with our lips.
> For the transgressions we committed before You through harsh speech.
> For the transgressions we committed before You by exercising power.
> For the transgressions we committed before You against those we know and those we do not know.
> For the transgressions we committed before You through baseless hatred . . .
> **For all these transgressions, God of pardon, pardon us, forgive us, grant us atonement.**

Return, according to *Al-Cheit*, is always possible. In response to the hard work of acknowledgment and sincere repentance, God can forgive even the most grievous sins.

It is important to note that, in contrast to *Tachanun*, the construction of both the *Vidui* and *Al-Cheit* shows that naming specific transgressions—not a generalized or blanket statement of responsibility—is central to the Jewish process of *teshuvah*. The precision demanded by both prayers compels the worshiper to reflect on and acknowledge each error individually and to then formulate a response that is targeted to the specific offense.

The prayer "Let us declare the power" (*Unetaneh Tokef*)—recited on both Rosh Hashanah and Yom Kippur—is one of the most powerful in Jewish liturgy. The prayer asks, Do we have any control at all over our fate, or are we truly helpless?

> . . . On Rosh Hashanah it is inscribed,
> And on Yom Kippur it is sealed.
> How many shall pass away and how many shall be born,
> Who shall live and who shall die,
> Who shall reach the end of one's days and who shall not . . .

But repentance *(teshuvah)*, prayer *(tefilah)* and righteousness *(tzedakah)* avert the severe decree.

Much is beyond our control, but human beings are not completely powerless to determine their destiny. *Unetaneh Tokef* suggests that although *teshuvah, tefilah,* and *tzedakah* cannot change one's fate, they can *ma'avirin et ro'ah ha'gezerah:* "mitigate the harshness, the experienced evil of the decree." That is to say, the consequences of what befalls us can be made less severe if we can engage in acts of repentance, prayer, and righteousness. Dominus (2014) and Miller (2008) note parallels for this in their work on recovery from various forms of moral injury. Another way to understand this teaching is consistent with Shapiro (2003); the ways that we find to retell our stories can alter our understanding and recast them in ways that can lead to healing.

Near the close of Yom Kippur, the liturgical tone shifts from one of contrition to hope and joy, with the awareness that forgiveness is at hand. After almost 25 hours of remorse and repentance, the *Atah Notein Yad* offers the promise of getting right with God:

> You hold out Your hand to those who have rebelled against You; Your right hand is stretched out to receive those who turn back to You. Eternal God, You have taught us to confess all our faults before You so that we may turn away from violence and oppression. In accordance with Your gracious promise, accept our repentance, which we offer to You in all sincerity.

The process is complete. After a day like no other, forgiveness has been granted.

Throughout Yom Kippur, the tension between the themes of justice *(din)* and mercy *(rachamim)* is palpable. God is portrayed as loving *and* demanding, compassionate *and* exacting, and these themes reflect the essential Jewish notion of covenant—a relationship between two parties with reciprocal obligations and responsibilities. To be in a covenantal relationship is to take upon oneself responsibility for one's own actions while simultaneously expecting one's partner to do the same. Thus, a relational feedback loop is established in which each party's choices and behaviors impact the other, paving the way for an ongoing bond based on mutuality, obligation, and responsibility. The great pain of moral injury results, in part, from the inescapable awareness that one's choices have had a profound—perhaps irrevocable—impact on the lives of others. Acknowledging the specificity of those choices and taking responsibility for them to the extent possible are essential components of the Jewish healing process.

Conclusion

> My life was bereft of peace.
> I forgot what happiness was,
> Thought my strength and hope
> Had perished before God.
> To recall my distress and my misery
> Was wormwood and poison;
> Whenever I thought of them,
> I was bowed low.
> But this do I call to mind,
> Therefore, I have hope.
> The kindnesses of Adonai have not ended.
> They are new every morning.
> Therefore, I have hope. (Lam. 3:17–21)

Perhaps the greatest peril for one suffering from moral injury is the extinguishing of hope. When no relief from excruciating guilt and pain can be found or hoped for, when one's core moral foundation can no longer integrate traumatic experiences, then the suffering individual's only choice becomes a lifetime of anguish or the decision to end that life altogether (Nakashima Brock and Lettini 2012, pp. 51–52). Although first identified in combat veterans, the definition of moral injury has extended to those in military non-combat roles and beyond the military as well. Our work has been focused on finding sources within the Jewish textual tradition that give voice to the experience of moral injury, consider and challenge assumptions about blame, responsibility, and guilt and offer a pathway to hope and healing from moral injury, however derived.

One of the most frequently quoted sayings from the Babylonian Talmud is "*O chevruta o mituta*" ("Either companionship or death") (*Ta'anit* 23a). In its original context, it meant that individuals needed to be in relationship with others; absent that, life had no meaning. From a Jewish perspective, the ultimate goal for a person suffering a soul wound is return to the self, to community, and to God. Judaism is neither a monastic nor an ascetic tradition, and it places strict limits on all forms of self-flagellation. In the *Tanakh*, Nazirites would consecrate themselves to God by taking vows of restriction, but these were time-limited (Num. 6:1–21). Judaism forbids individuals whose health would be placed in jeopardy by holy day fasting to do so. Mourners deny themselves a variety of the pleasures of living, but these limitations are lifted gradually over the course of a year. The Jerusalem Talmud teaches that those who decline legitimate pleasures will be called to account (*Kiddushin* 4:12). Judaism is a this-world-oriented faith in which suffering is neither desired nor valorized. As such, a threefold path to repair and wholeness is explicated throughout Jewish literature and is essential to a Jewish understanding of recovery from moral injury. *Teshuvah* restores individual to individual and individual to God through a program of repentance. *Tefilah* connects individuals and communities to each other and to God, the Source of goodness, hope, and mercy. *Tzedakah* draws suffering individuals into community through their contributions to repairing the world. The Jewish principles of repair and reestablishment of relationship are reflected in a spectrum of efforts around the world now known as reconciliation and restorative justice (Lapsley 2012). Judaism has no saints and no martyrs. All of our biblical heroes are profoundly complex and flawed characters. Think, for example, of Sarah, Jacob, Moses, the brothers of Joseph, or King David. Judaism understands that life is an ongoing cycle of brokenness and repair, then brokenness and repair once again. Therefore, transgression need not permanently break us nor claim our full identity. We can be known by many names.

> So Moses turned and went down from the mountain, and the two tablets of the Law were in his hands; the tablets were written on both their sides; on the one side and on the other were they written. The tablets were the work of God, and the writing was the writing of God, engraved upon the tablets. And it came to pass, as soon as Moses came near to the camp, that he saw the calf and the dancing; and Moses' anger burned hot, and he threw the tablets from his hands and broke them beneath the mountain. (Exod. 32:15–16, 19)

> God said to Moses, 'Cut two tablets of stone like the first; and I will write upon those tablets the words that were in the first tablets which you broke.' And Moses cut two tablets of stone like the first. (Exod. 34:1)

What became of the broken pieces? The Torah doesn't tell us. But a *midrash* in the Jerusalem Talmud does (*Shekalim* 6:1, 49c):

> Rabbi Judah bar Lakish taught that two arks journeyed with Israel in the wilderness—one for the whole set of tablets, the Torah, and one for the broken pieces. The ark in which the Torah was placed was kept in the Tent of Meeting, but the one containing the broken pieces would come and go with the people. From this we infer that the broken tablets were even *more* treasured by the people. They took them with them

wherever they traveled, just as all of us take the broken parts of ourselves wherever we go. And then—one day—both sets were brought to the Land of Israel and placed together in the Holy of Holies in the Temple in Jerusalem.

Rabbi Alexandri said, 'If an ordinary person uses a broken vessel, it is shameful. But *Ha Kadosh Baruch Hu*, the Holy Blessed One, uses *only* broken vessels.' (Leviticus *Rabbah* 7:2). *Karov Adonai l'mishberei lev*—God draws close those whose hearts are broken. (Psalm 34:19)

Blessed is our God Who treasures brokenness and Who guides all of us to lives of wholeness and purpose.

References

Adler, R. (2006). For these I weep: A theology of lament. *The Chronicle, 68*, 16–21.

Boss, P. (2000). *Ambiguous loss: Learning to live with unresolved grief.* Cambridge: Harvard University Press.

Boudreau, T. (2010). Truth Commission on Conscience in War Testimonies. https://www.brite.edu/programs/soul-repair/ resources/ #avw.

Brichto, H. (1973). Kin, cult, land and afterlife—A biblical complex. *Hebrew Union College Annual, 44*, 1–54.

Currier, J. M., Drescher, K. D., Holland, J. M., Lisman, R., & Foy, D. W. (2015). Spirituality, forgiveness and quality of life: Testing a mediational model with military veterans with PTSD. *International Journal for the Psychology of Religion, 26*(2), 1–28. https://doi.org/10.1080/10508619.2015.1019793.

Doehring, C. (2015). Resilience as the relational ability to integrate moral stress. *Pastoral Psychology, 64*(5), 635–649. https://doi.org/10.1007/s11089-015-0643-7.

Dominus, S. (2014). Portraits of reconciliation. *New York Times Magazine.* https://www.nytimes. com/interactive/2014/04/06/ magazine/06-pieter-hugo-rwanda-portraits.html.

Hoffman, L. (Ed.). (2002). *My People's prayer book: Traditional prayers, modern commentaries, Vol. 6, Tachanun and Concluding Prayers.* Woodstock: Jewish Lights.

Lapsley, M. (2012). *Redeeming the past: My journey from freedom fighter to healer.* Cape Town: Struik Christian Media.

Litz, B., Stein, N., Delaney, E., Lebowitz, L., Nash, W., Siva, C., & Maguen, S. (2009). Moral injury and moral repair in war veterans:

A preliminary model and intervention strategy. *Clinical Psychology Review, 29*(8), 695–706. https://doi.org/10.1016/j.cpr.2009.07.003.

Miller, J. (2008). Vietnam veterans help returning Iraq soldiers deal with the shocks of war. *Christian Science Monitor.* http://www.csmonitor.com/USA/Military/2008/0130/p20s01-usmi.html.

Nakashima Brock, R., & Lettini, G. (2012). *Soul repair: Recovering from moral injury after war.* Boston: Beacon Press.

Shapiro, R. (2003). Our stories our selves: The Jewish chaplain as midrashic healer. *Journal of Jewish Spiritual Care, 6,* 3–6.

Sippola, J., Blumenshine, A., Tubesing, D., & Yancey, V. (2009). *Welcome them home, help them heal.* Duluth: Whole Person Associates.

Wiener, N., & Hirschmann, J. (2014). *Maps and meaning: Levitical models for contemporary care.* Minneapolis: Fortress Press.

Wolpe, D. (1990). *The healer of shattered hearts: A Jewish view of God.* New York: Penguin Books.

6

Muslims in the U.S. Military: Moral Injury and Eroding Rights

— Shareda Hosein —

Introduction

In the context of the United States' longest war, Operation Enduring Freedom (OEF) and Operation Iraqi Freedom (OIF), "Traumatologists have recently proposed 'moral injury' as a newly alternative model for understanding PTSD among military personnel and veterans" (Bryan et al. 2014, p. 2). Litz et al. (2009) state that moral injury results when an individual is "perpetrating, failing to prevent, bearing witness to, or learning about acts that transgress deeply held moral beliefs and expectations" (p. 700). According to Shay (2012, p. 58), a Veterans Affairs psychiatrist, "PTSD, as officially defined, is rarely what wrecks veterans' lives or crushes them to suicide, but moral injury does both." Shay (1994) was possibly the first to use the term "moral injury," defined as "a betrayal of what's right," and to see the injury as "an essential part of any combat trauma that leads to lifelong psychological injury" (p. 20). Shay's definition of moral injury complements Litz's definition but "differs in the 'who' of the violator" (Antal and Winings 2015, p. 384). His version includes three components: "[1] Betrayal of what's right, [2] by someone who holds legitimate authority (in the military—a leader), or [3] in a high stakes situation" (Shay 2012, p. 59).

Given the small percentage of MMP in the United States military, little attention has been given to the kinds of stressors experienced by MMP that would give rise to or exacerbate military moral injuries, nor has attention been paid to the specialized support they would need. The eleven Muslim chaplains currently on active duty are familiar with moral injury from their training but rarely have the opportunity to meet many MMP at their duty stations to help them deal with the symptoms of moral injury or just talk with them as a reassuring presence who understands them and some of their concerns. Muslims serving in the United States military are in a unique and complicated situation: Islam, which is a religion of peace, is the second largest religion in the world. But today it is viewed as a destructive ideology because of terrorists misappropriating the teachings of the religion and engaging in attacks such as 9/11, thereby tarnishing MMP in the eyes of their military peers and fellow citizens.

Antal and Winings (2015) write that military moral injury "is not a personality disorder but rather a wound suffered by a self-reflective and conscientious moral agent. As such, moral injury is best understood as the inevitable outcome of moral engagement with the harsh reality of war and killing" (p. 384). For MMP, the harsh reality of the longest war in American history has created prejudice, racism, and distrust among non-Muslim military personnel about their fellow MMP, causing additional traumatic stress in the already harsh climate of war because the religion of MMP has become a risk factor. However, for Muslims who rely upon their faith to cope and be resilient, education about moral injury could help them become more reflective upon their war experiences. Spiritual care of MMP requires a more active partnership with family, friends, and a local (faith) community which could offer safe spaces for them to talk about their experiences of religious prejudice, help them to use their spiritual practices intentionally in ways that foster safety, and explore meanings from their religious tradition to help them better understand their military experiences. Rather than carry the burden of the emotional distress, guilt, shame, anger, or frustration that they may experience as Muslims performing their wartime duties, they may be able to experience a sense of spiritual solidarity with each other and the chaplain who supports them. If more MMP were aware of the effects of moral injury they experience as an aspect of this war, could they give themselves permission to seek out the needed support to overcome or forgive themselves for these feelings? If religious and spiritual struggles arise from their experiences as MMP, could spiritual care provide a safe space to explore these struggles?[1] Could MMP come to see themselves as good people who have served their country as well as loyal citizens

---

[1]Abu Raiya et al. (2015) studied religious and spiritual struggles in an Israeli-Palestinian, Muslim sample of 139 using the Religious and Spiritual Struggles Scale (Exline et al. 2014) and found that 1.4 to 40.2% experienced various religious and spiritual struggles, including struggles with God/the Divine, struggles with doubt, struggles with punitive entities, interpersonal religious struggles, moral struggles, and struggles with ultimate meaning. Although findings from this sample cannot be generalized to MMP, this study suggests the need for research on religious and spiritual struggles among MMP.

and good Muslims? What would spiritually integrated care of MMP look like? Given the very small number of Muslim military chaplains, the responsibility for such care will need to be taken up by all military chaplains and behavioral health providers, who will need to be trained in such care. In adapting Pargament's (2007) spiritually integrated psychotherapy for Muslim clients, Abu Raiya and Pargament suggest, that "clinicians assess for religious struggles, normalize them, help clients find satisfying solutions to these struggles and, if appropriate, refer clients who struggle to a Muslim pastoral counselor or religious leader" (Abu Raiya and Pargament 2010, p. 181).

In preparation for this article, I reviewed interviews conducted with MMP available in newspaper articles, books, and scholarly research as well as personal conversations I had with MMP to gain further insight into their wartime experiences. In these documents, MMP relate personal stories of their military experiences regarding how they were treated as Muslims within their units and how they felt fighting against fellow Muslims. I will also share my personal experience and my own reaction as I became aware of the concept of moral injury and in turn became aware of my own feelings of being morally injured.

Social-historical background and population size of Muslim military personnel

The listing of "Muslim" as a religious identity in the military record of Americans began in 1952. Through the service and petition of Muslim Arab Americans who had fought in World War II, Islam was recognized by the military as a legitimate religion in that year. Before that, Muslims had to either select "no religious preference" or were sometimes automatically marked as "Protestant" or "P" on their dog tags. In the past, Muslims were integrated into the military like any other faith group. Although Islam was an official religion in the military, it took some years for the growth of the Muslim population to justify representation by a chaplain.

Recently in the U.S. Armed Forces, 5896 military personnel self-identified as Muslim in their official military records, according to the Office of the Secretary of Defense in December 2015 as reported by Khan and Martinez (2015) from ABC News Network (2015). However, based on his observation of the Muslim Friday or Jumu'ah congregational prayer held on multiple bases during his career, lay leader Chief Master Sergeant Talib Shareef (retired) Air Force told me in 2013 that he estimated that the number is higher and may fluctuate between 10,000 and 15,000 MMP. He based his estimate on his observation that actual body counts at prayer services compared to the rosters provided to him by his command of Muslim personnel assigned to the base were about a three to one ratio. In this current war, the majority of MMP prefer to stay below the radar and just do their jobs without having to defend Islam or Muslims. Their reasons for joining the military are similar to many of their peers, i.e., education, income, adventure, service to country, etc., and all they want to do is serve their country.

MMP represent many ethnically diverse backgrounds, with African Americans being the largest, then Arabs (although some Arabs are Christian), Pakistanis, and many other smaller ethnicities such as Somali, Nigerian, Sudanese, Indian, Bangladeshi, Bosnian, Trinidadian, and many others, along with a small population of White and Latino American converts. Some individuals stay invisible because their physical features, names, and accents do not betray them as Muslims, making it much easier for them to fit into the military without being harassed by peers. However, they might pay a higher price psychologically due to not being able to freely declare their full identity, perhaps in terms of religious struggles generated by not being able to publicly integrate their religious faith into their military service.

In today's wars, many Muslims continue to serve in unique, critical roles in the U.S. Armed Forces as cultural advisors and translators because of their language skills in Arabic, Farsi, Dari, Pashtu, Urdu, Bahasa, and Tagalog along with their knowledge of Islamic practices, cultures, and the regions where there is a U.S. military presence. Given the shortage of these language skills among non-Muslims, there is a demand for Muslims to fill these critical positions.

My introduction to the concept of moral injury

In 2014, I was invited to participate in an interreligious think tank for pastoral theologians sponsored by the Soul Repair Center at Brite Divinity School. The center was established to educate faith leaders and members of faith communities about moral injury and to create resources to help veterans heal from these nonphysical wounds. I was one of those who represented Islam as a Muslim chaplain and who also happened to be a soldier in the U.S. Army Reserves. I was aware of PTSD and other war traumas, but learning about moral injury was life-affirming for me because I now had an explanation for my feelings of anger, fear, shame, sadness, sense of hopelessness, and being totally "off my game." I hadn't shared my feelings out of fear that I would be perceived as being weak as an officer or seen as a traitor because I self-identify as a Muslim and didn't always see the focus of the war the way our government and fellow soldiers do. I felt totally isolated, with only myself for counsel.

However, the compassionate listening and safe space provided by my seasoned peers (faculty, ministers, and rabbis) at Brite Divinity

School gave me hope, and I began to explore moral injury not as a private burden but as a starting point or opportunity to reclaim my life. Having a term to explain my experiences allowed me to let down my guard and trust people, and the process. I felt I was given permission to openly share my fears of being seen as an outsider or possible traitor who cannot be trusted and, even worse, my unvoiced dread that the government could silence me without any due process. The fear of not being able to trust one's government, feeling a sense of insecurity, as an outsider had pushed me into a space of isolation and living at a heightened state of alertness or vigilance. My husband, who feared for my safety, cautioned me against speaking out negatively even in our home for fear it was bugged. The media heightened my anxiety and caused more fear by painting Muslims as a monolithic community identified with the terrorists. Some women wearing the headscarf or hijab took it off for their personal security, but I chose to leave it on to understand what my fellow Muslim sisters were experiencing, despite my husband's request to take it off because of his fears for my safety.

Knowing that I wasn't alone and knowing that moral injury is a part of war gave me hope. I learned that the effects of moral injury are compounded from one experience to the next. My colleagues at Brite Divinity School and my peers in the think tank became lifelines as a starting point to help bring me back to the former self I once knew—a confident person, full of life and the desire to be successful in all that I take on. The process is slow but life-affirming.

I joined the U.S. Army in 1979 right out of high school to travel the world, get money for college, and gain knowledge, just as the advertisements promised. Reflecting upon my past, I will share a few incidents in this article on my journey in the military. Two decades after I joined the military, my first day at Hartford Seminary, where I had enrolled to become a Muslim chaplain in the U.S. Army, was September 11, 2001. It was the biggest shock of my life to learn that Muslim terrorists had attacked my country. I knew immediately it was inevitable that we would go to war. I recalled what had happened to the Japanese Americans after the bombing of Pearl Harbor and wondered if this same fate would befall American Muslims.

In the afternoon on that day, the local imam came to Hartford Seminary and asked to speak to all the Muslim women, especially those who wore the hijab, because he was afraid for our safety as we engaged with the public. He reported that a Sikh man was killed in Arizona while working at his gas station earlier that day. Sadly, he was perceived to be a Muslim due to his cultural garb (Lewin 2001). The local imam offered to do our errands if needed and advised us to stay indoors as much as possible. I felt fearful of my fellow Americans for the first time.

Some Muslims in America were physically detained, and others were monitored through all their communication devices. I heard many horror stories about people in detention; they weren't allowed access to counsel, bank accounts were being frozen—all of which was legal under the Patriot Act. Life was scary and uncertain. Even though I was in the military and had security clearances, I no longer felt safe in my country.

A month after 9/11, my security officer in my Reserve unit pulled me aside and briefly said, "Shareda, I don't know if you thought about this, but you may want to consider that the military personnel may not trust you and your Muslim community also may not trust you because you serve in the U.S. military." I was shocked at his statement. I wondered why my colleagues would distrust me after having known me for many years. How could they imagine that my loyalties wouldn't lie with the nation that I had served for over 20 years? The list of negative experiences from this war were compounding in my mind, causing me great distress. Where could I turn for support and talk freely? The trauma intensified with every new action taken in the war.

My biggest breakthrough—and the path that helped me find healing when I began to understand the concept of moral injury— occurred that first weekend in 2014 at Brite Divinity School when I finally identified the specific incident that had pushed me over the edge: hearing the sad news about the mistreatment of prisoners at Abu Ghraib in Iraq in April 2004. I was stationed in Kuwait that year, assigned to Central Command's headquarters, which was the higher headquarters for the unit assigned to Abu Ghraib prison. I was confronted with this news head-on as I walked into the dining facility for lunch at Camp Arifjan, Kuwait, and saw the degrading pictures of the male Muslim prisoners on a big-screen TV. Standing in a long line waiting to be served, as I listened to the CNN News announcer, I felt much shame and remorse for these men, especially because women were present viewing their almost-naked bodies. That same day, I was interviewed by BBC's *The World* about my petition to the U.S. Army to become the first female Muslim chaplain. I was asked what I thought about the handling of the prisoners. I was embarrassed, repulsed, and ashamed all at the same time but didn't feel I could share those feelings with total strangers. All I could think about was the question, how could I hold my head up high while wearing my military uniform when we had violated the Geneva Convention rules? My response to the interviewer was, "I don't know much about the prison atrocities, but if what is being reported is the truth, then according to the Geneva Convention the commander needs to take action quickly to do damage control and right a wrong."

I am grateful that my response wasn't part of the recorded interview, but they wanted to know my opinion as a major and future chaplain. I succumbed to a sense of hopelessness, felt violated, and couldn't hold my head up high or feel proud as a soldier as I had in the past. Our military personnel had violated the Geneva Convention rules in dealing with prisoners, rules that I held in high regard as a soldier and saw as a marker of integrity in warfare.

I felt that we, as a nation, lost our moral compass or soul that day. I was disturbed and had no one with whom to process my feelings of fear, shame, disgust, and isolation. I didn't feel safe speaking with anyone out of fear of being seen as a Muslim (enemy) sympathizer and disloyal to the military and my country. I kept silent, and I wondered why none of my peers discussed it with me. Were they, too, ashamed or afraid to discuss this topic with me? Not processing this horrendous act with others and not receiving official words from the command's leadership deepened my sense of isolation. I felt violated and as if I had failed to prevent the immoral acts of others (this is an element of moral injury, I found out later). I was numb and felt distant from everyone, including life itself. I was in survival mode, focusing on keeping busy in order not to acknowledge my own thoughts. The rules that help us keep our humanity in check were broken—violated, as I saw it—and I felt I could only trust God.

Chaplain (Captain) James Yee

As documented in his book *For God and Country, Faith and Patriotism under Fire* (2005), West Point graduate and chaplain James "Yusuf" Yee served at Guantanamo Bay as Muslim chaplain to the prisoners with unrestricted access for 10 months. In September 2003, he was secretly and wrongfully arrested for spying and aiding the Taliban and Al Qaeda. He spent 76 days in solitary confinement due to vindictive charges. Eventually all charges were dropped, but Yee's reputation was tarnished. His bright future was taken away, and the trauma he experienced, his moral injury, was the outcome of the U.S. government's violation of his rights and the U.S. Army Chaplain Corps' failure to protect him. His story haunted me that year because it was around the same time I petitioned for, and was denied, approval to become a chaplain in the U.S. Army. I worked with the same endorser as James Yee, and it became demoralizing to hear about the harassment both these men experienced, as later showcased in the media (Debusmann 2007). This incident demoralized me and made me scared of my own government as I pondered how easy it was to arrest James Yee and ruin his life. Many incidents like these put kinks in my moral armor, causing me moral injury.

But everything changed in 2014 when I attended the workshop at the Soul Repair Center. The people there helped me by defining the feelings I had as moral injury. After reading the book assigned by the team leaders, *Soul Repair: Recovering from Moral Injury after War* by Brock and Lettini (2012), I began to awaken from the coma that had begun on 9/11 and continued with all that had transpired since then. Thirteen years after 2001, learning about the feelings associated with moral injury was the beginning of my healing process. A year later, after many years without having such a physiological experience, I became aware of the feeling of joy present in my body. I laughed more in 2015 than I had in any of those earlier years. The healing process is slow, however, because the war still continues in Muslim majority countries. The increased hostilities towards Muslims in the United States complicate and slow the healing process and my ability to move forward.

The combat zone isn't limited to the time military personnel are on the battlefields but follows them in their homes and workplaces and is always around them through the media and during their training cycles for additional deployments if they continue in the military. This war is even more heightened for MMP on and off the battlefield because the negative climate and hostilities directed towards them in the United States from fellow citizens cause MMP to experience a constant, stressful, heightened state of alertness. In essence, they are continuously in the psychological state of war.

Symptoms of moral injury among MMP

What are the psychological or emotional symptoms of moral injury among MMP? I have described my own response, but no studies of incidence or prevalence or analysis of their symptoms have been conducted on this population. In an April 2017 conversation with U.S. Army Muslim Chaplain (Major) Dawud Agbere, he said that he had observed soldiers who "know that they are feeling a bit off but can't seem to have an explanation of what they are experiencing." MMP read and hear negative comments in the media such as "Muslims did it," "All the terrorists were Muslims," and "You can't trust them" (Abu-Ras and Hosein 2015, p. 5). This makes them uncomfortable, angry, and upset because of the added pressures and scrutiny placed on them, yet they continue to serve with loyalty and pride. Some MMP keep their heads down low and don't disclose their religious identity for self-preservation, just wanting to serve their country and be left alone. This lack of disclosure may have a long-term negative effect on them.

Shay, a psychiatrist and the creator of the term moral injury, attributes the high incidence of suicide among veterans to moral injury. In exploring the effects of suicide, which is a religious taboo for Muslims, I wondered if this prohibition might actually provide a measure of spiritual strength to MMP, helping them to cope with harassment and endure the resulting moral injuries they experience. I am aware of only one case of an MMP committing suicide, a Muslim male in the Navy. The suicide label was refuted in a phone conversation I had in 2015 with the man's mother, who said her son would never commit suicide and blamed another person for his death. She reported a phone conversation with her son the night before he died and said "He was happy and spoke about visiting with me soon." It is not known how many suicides there are among military personnel who self-identify as Muslims.

Added pressures placed on Arab Americans

The religious animus in some of the rhetoric at the outset of the Global War on Terror brought Muslim Americans center stage, forcing many into the role of apologists for the actions of extremist groups whose members call themselves Muslim but whom most Muslims in America see as enemies of their religion. Anti-Arab hostilities, discrimination, negative feelings, and Islamophobia (fear and anti-Islamic sentiments and attitudes directed at Muslims and the religion of Islam) (Abu-Ras and Hosein 2015, p. 1) were at a record high once it was known that the 9/11 hijackers were Arab Muslims.

In the context of a new and growing institutional racism, social scientist Dr. Louise Cainkar states, "The general profile of the Arab experiences in the United States in the early part of the twentieth century displayed more social, political, and economic incorporation than that of racially excluded African Americans, Asians, Native Americans and Latinos" (2006, p. 241). The relationship with Arab Americans declined in the past thirty years, however, because of the oil embargo in the 1970s, the attack on the Marines' quarters in Lebanon, in Saudi Arabia, and, finally, 9/11. Cainkar finds "this social distance created and reproduced by institutions of power (external to Arab American communities) is measurable, and is manifested in government policies, mainstream cultural representations, public perceptions and attitudes, discriminatory behaviors, physical insecurity, and social and political exclusion" (p. 241). She continues, "In 1990, when Islamist challenges to American global hegemony became more powerful than Arab nationalism, these constructions were extended more broadly to Muslims and became grander—they became civilizational" (p. 250).

Another decade later, the security of the world changed, causing much chaos and America's longest war. Compounding by prior global attacks against America by Arabs, MMP found themselves defending

Islam from terrorists who sought to hijack the religion but also having to stand up to fellow citizens, politicians, the media, and even fellow service members who misunderstood or flatly rejected the idea of a peaceful Islam that shares the roots of Christianity and Judaism. The first condition causing moral injury among MMP was the loss of trust they experienced even though they had sworn an oath to protect and defend the constitution of the United States and fully intended to remain true to that oath.

> Wahiba Abu-Ras (2009), a social worker, documented that the number of hate crimes against Arab and Muslims and people who look like Arabs, increased 17- fold since September 11, 2001. In addition, the federal government enacted several new immigration policies specifically targeting individuals of Middle Eastern origin. These policies have allowed for the detention of more than 1,200 people of Arab, Muslim, and South Asian heritage. (p. 397)

These policies were similar to the ones that led to the detention of Japanese Americans during World War II. The Abu-Ras et al. study also reports that the many negative effects of these current policies are not limited to mental health assessments ....[H]ate crimes and backlash against Arab and Muslims [leads] to depression and fear and religious-based discrimination and its impact on their mental health . . . suggesting that the type of duration of the discriminatory experience may affect individuals' psychological health differently. (p. 398)

Muslims and Arab Americans have been "raced" as "terrorists," disloyal, and imminently threatening (Saito 2001, p. 12), and have been exposed to derogatory terms aimed at Muslims and Arab American military personnel such as "haji," "camel jockey," and "raghead" (Abu-Ras and Hosein 2015, p. 2). The study also found that these "faith-related stressors put many MMP at additional risk for increased vulnerability to PTSD, psychological distress, other adjustments, and mental health issues" (p. 2).

I describe Cainkar and Abu-Ras's studies here, which focused on Arab Americans and Muslims who were harassed and discriminated against before and after 9/11, to demonstrate the hypervigilance that MMP have experienced while serving in the military and simultaneously navigating life in the civilian sector. Abu-Ras's study notes that this population has been treated similarly to the Japanese Americans during World War II, who were rounded up, placed in camps, and isolated from mainstream populations. Although American Muslims or Arabs haven't been segregated from society into enclosed camps and are permitted freedom of movement, some people would say that current technology creates a cyber-encampment in which their electronic communications are monitored. This produces the feeling of being under a double-edged sword threatening their well-being and sanity.

Fatwa or religious opinion

In the religious sense, Muslims are exhorted in their holy book, the Qur'an, not to fight other Muslims. Being part of the military highlights the importance of this theological construct for MMP, making it necessary to reconcile that edict with one's duty to the nation's defense, as the design of today's modern state dictates. Religious struggles and moral injury are present for some MMP when they interpret the edict literally as meaning that Muslims should not kill Muslims. They may not fully understand what is appropriate or permissible for them, given the oath they have taken to defend their country when invaded or attacked. Some MMP have opted out of the military as conscientious objectors in this war, and others have remained in the military and have somehow found ways to reconcile this contradiction.

The first Muslim chaplain in the U.S. Army, Major Abdul Rasheed Muhammad, felt it necessary to address this religious concern, and in September 2001 he asked the religious scholars at the Fiqh (Juridical) Council in the United States for a fatwa (religious opinion) on the permissibility of Muslims fighting Muslims in Afghanistan and other Muslim countries. Chaplain Muhammad asked about the three points listed below and in particular wanted to specifically know, "Is it permissible for those who can transfer to serve in different capacities other than direct fighting?" (Stark 2011, p. 487). In response, the Fiqh Council took the three points listed below and the permissibility of Muslims not being placed in direct fighting to international senior scholars skilled in Muslim minority issues. Yusuf al-Qaradawi and others in Doha, Qatar, granted a fatwa for the United States to take military action for the following reasons:

> 1) Retaliation against those who are thought to have participated in planning and financing the suicide operation on September 11th, against civilian and military targets; 2) Eliminating the elements that use Afghanistan and elsewhere as safe havens as well as deterring the governments that harbor them, sanction them, or allow them the opportunity for military training in order to achieve their goals around the world; 3) Restoring the veneration and respect for the U.S. as a sole superpower in the world. (Nafi 2004, p. 79)

Al-Qaradawi's fatwa demonstrated that he understood the complexities of the world. He realized that America's sovereignty was violated by Al Qaeda and that the United States was soon going to go to war in Afghanistan and he granted the fatwa as proposed to him by Chaplain Muhammad. He felt that a clear religious opinion would help the MMP with their moral dilemma since many MMP were already serving in the military with some of them in combat unit who would be fighting a co-religionist enemy. It could also help those MMP who were not previously aware of the religious contradiction yet felt troubled by fighting Muslims while feeling a sense of commitment to defending their country. Those MMP who stayed and honored their contracts may be vulnerable to a crisis of conscience as it relates to moral injury as defined by Brock and Lettini: "When soldiers violate their core moral beliefs, and in evaluating their behavior negatively, they feel they no longer live in a reliable, meaningful world and can no longer be regarded as decent human beings" (Brock and Lettini 2012, p. xv). Or does war with its inevitable exposure of a soul to atrocities cause its own trauma of moral injury for anyone, regardless of religion, even if war is labeled permissible and sanctioned?

Some MMP turn to their religion to help them cope with the hardship of returning from war, as shown in a recent study. As one participant in the Abu-Ras and Hosein (2015) study stated, "My coping is just that when I read the *Qu'ran* and I read the *Hadith* [the narration of Muhammad's actions and sayings], I understand that this [life] is a trial" (p. 8). Others said that spirituality and religion were important factors for them in coping with the stressors of this war. However, how do MMP cope with deployment reintegration stress when someone suggests that their religion, the source of comfort for them as they cope with post-deployment stress, was and is the cause of the devastations of this war? Backlash, harassment, and distrust from their colleagues can also make it problematic for some of them to rely on their religion to cope with the stressors of war. MMP are also exposed to negative comments and opinions about their religion repeated by some members of their unit. These experiences contribute to a distinct sense of not belonging in their unit because they aren't sure whom they can trust and at times feel unable to rely on the chain of command. Moral injury results from the violation of one's inner compass through not being able to trust one's leaders or peers, a key component of life in the military. And when that trust erodes, the void and isolation cause much pain.

Major Nidal Hassan

As already confirmed, some Muslims select "no religious preference" when joining the military as a coping strategy to avoid the judgment of peers and superiors. This is only possible provided the individuals do not have distinctive names such as "Muhammad" or "Ali" or "Hassan." Nidal Hassan, the Fort Hood shooter, listed himself in his Army records as having "no religious preference," according to co-workers who reported his devout religious practices (Zakaria Nov 6, 2009b). One could easily wonder if he was experiencing some degree of moral injury, as he was getting ready to deploy to Afghanistan when he fired on his unit's personnel and didn't want to kill fellow co-religionists (the enemy), or "whether he was radicalized to violent Islamic extremism" (Lieberman and Collins 2011, p. 36). The latter would cause immense moral injury for fellow MMP.

According to Hassan's aunt, who was interviewed by the media, "Some people can take it, and some cannot. He had listened to all of that, and he wanted out of the military and they would not let him leave even after he offered to repay for his medical training." She further stated, "He must have snapped. They [the military] ignored him. It was not hard to know when he was upset. He was not a fighter, even as a child and young man. But when he became upset, his face turns red. You can read him in his face" (Zakaria Nov 6, 2009b).

According to news reports, Hassan's anger and struggles were evident to others: "Colonel Terry Lee, a retired officer who worked with him at the military base in Texas, alleged Maj. Hassan had angry confrontations with other officers over his views of the war" (Zakaria Nov 6, 2009b).

The comments of Hassan's aunt and his unit members and my own perception of long-term discrimination indicate that he was morally conflicted about going to war. Is that what pushed him to kill 13 and injure 30 soldiers from his own unit? His action caused massive trauma for many people while making it more difficult for MMP serving in the military and the Muslim American population. Many of his colleagues stated that he was odd and spoke out against the war. So, why wasn't Hassan flagged for his troubled behavior by his behavioral health colleagues? This deadly act of fratricide points to the danger of ignoring poor mental health and the harm it can cause. Would awareness of the fatwa discussed above have helped get Hassan out of the military or assigned him away from the combat zone? There are more questions than answers, but surely this situation demonstrates that there is a need to not treat all problems in the same way but take into consideration that humans differ and may require different treatment to resolve their individual problems.

Coincidentally, I was at another base in Texas near Fort Hood on temporary military duty on the same day that Major Hassan shot his unit members. It was a sharp blow for me as a civilian chaplain and soldier because I saw Major Hassan as a fellow officer, a fellow Muslim, and a fellow healer. In my grief, my thoughts were, how much more can I cope with?

Significantly, my shame was greater than my fear when I met my military colleagues for dinner that evening. We were speaking about the incident when one person avowed, "I told you that it was a terrorist who did it." He quickly looked my way and stopped talking. It was an awkward moment for him and a shameful one for me. After the Fort Hood shooting, my morale spiraled downwards even more than after 9/11 because those who died were fellow soldiers killed by one of our own. I felt my credibility in educating my colleagues about Islam and the global cultural diversity of Muslims in my role as a cultural engagement officer was diminished with some individuals. It became harder for me to serve out of my shame that I might not be trusted by some of my coworkers. I believe the fear and distrust of Muslims in the military increased even more after this incident. After that day, I felt I was walking on eggshells and wondered how I could regain the trust of my coworkers. I believed that many MMP felt that they had to single-handedly defend Islam and American Muslims from the negative backlash as they built bridges of understanding with people of all faiths so that Muslims wouldn't be lumped into the same category of "terrorists" like the attackers on 9/11, Major Hassan, and others.

Another soldier at Fort Hood, Army Specialist Klawonn, who had arrived in 2008, a year before Hassan, said, "I knew people were going to immediately and automatically draw a comparison between us, just due to the fact that we were both Muslim. There was a vibe that people weren't coming around to talk with me, and they really asked me to justify the situation, you know, why he did that" (Blackburn and Aro 2010, April 14). Klawonn had been dealing with prejudice since basic training in 2008 and felt stigmatized by the shooting. In a morning formation during basic training,

> A drill sergeant read aloud a list of religious services, and when he got to the Islamic service sarcastically asked if anyone planned to attend. "I raised my hand, and he was shocked," recalled Klawonn. "Then, he called me out of formation, took me to the front and basically made a mockery of it [Islam]." (Blackburn and Aro 2010)

Klawonn filed a lawsuit against the government for harassment.

The Fort Hood shooting caused some politicians to respond negatively in trying to make the nation feel safe again by marginalizing Muslims and by not recognizing that Muslim Americans have rights as American citizens, especially those who are serving in the military. One such politician, State Representative Rick Womick (R-TN), said,

"Personally, I don't trust one Muslim in our military because they're commanded to lie to us through the term called *Taqiyya* [practicing deception]. And if they truly are a devout Muslim, and follow the *Quran* and the *Sunnah*, then I feel threatened because they're commanded to kill me" (Clifton and Fang 2011). Comments like these from politicians expressing misinformation as facts can trigger fear and frustration and lead many Americans to hold anti-Muslim sentiments. This negative discourse also discourages Muslims from joining the military, even though there is a need for their language and cultural skills. For those who are already serving, these words from a government official may cause more hardship by marginalizing MMP among their fellow military personnel, causing them to feel more isolated and intensifying their feelings and emotions of moral injury.

I felt uplifted when General George Casey, Chief of Staff of the Army, spoke up during an interview with Tabassum Zakaria from Reuters News (Zakaria 2009a, November 8). He said, "I'm concerned that this increased speculation could cause a backlash against some of our Muslim soldiers. And I've asked our Army leaders to be on the lookout for that." NBC's *Meet the Press* host asked the general whether Muslim soldiers are conflicted over fighting wars in Muslim countries like Afghanistan and Iraq. Casey said,

> I think that's something that we have to look at on an individual basis. But I think we as an Army have to be broad enough to bring in people from all walks of life The bottom line is the military benefits from diversity", he said. "Our diversity, not only in our Army, but in our country, is a strength. And as horrific as this tragedy was, if our diversity becomes a casualty, I think that's worse." (Zakaria Nov 8, 2009a).

General Casey's words showed great leadership and care for all his soldiers and gave public support to MMP in uniform.

Testimonials on racism and moral injury

Since the War on Terror is in its eighteenth year as of 2019, with no end in sight, Muslims continue to be under a dark cloud of mistrust, both in society at large and within the military. MMP have had to face racism, prejudice, and hatred from some of their peers,[2] while the media

---

[2]The intersection of religious, racial, and class prejudice toward MMP has yet to be studied. Abu-Ras and Hosein (2015) did find that 6 out of the 20 MMP they interviewed in their qualitative study reported fewer negative experiences due to engaging in Muslim religious practices, "but the differences can be explained by education, rank, and appearance. Six participants who are highly educated, Caucasian, or had a non-Muslim name, reported some positive experiences and fewer negative incidents" (2015, p. 5).

and some politicians exacerbate the burdens of war for this alienated and marginalized population. The dual effects of war and cultural bias may be contributing to moral stress and injury as an experience of "a betrayal of what's right," especially since MMP may not know how to express these feelings (Shay 1994, p. 20).

A number of media networks have showcased the roles of MMP during significant events in American history in the past 16 years. Some of them have been fair and balanced in their reporting on what life is like for MMP as they cope with the war. Even though MMP might still be guarded in speaking with the media, the following two excerpts, which come from the same *Washington Post* article entitled "For Muslims in the U.S. military, a different U.S. than the one they swore to defend" (Gibbons-Neff 2015), demonstrate that it is helpful for the American public to have access to accurate information about life for MMP on active duty.

Hadzic migrated from Bosnia as a refugee and wanted to give back to the country that saved him, so he joined the Marines with the intent to help peacekeepers in his homeland. He was proud to serve, but he feels that America has changed to a more anti-Muslim climate. He said, "We used to be a balanced people. We used to be true to our values, but now we're willing to betray our values because of a sense of fear? That's not American," said Hadzic. "What the hell happened to that America I immigrated to?" (Gibbons-Neff 2015). For Muslims who are former and current members of the armed services, the prejudice and anti-Muslim rhetoric are particularly painful.

Muslims comprise just .027% of both active and reserve components of the military. In many units, they number in the single digits and often find themselves acting as representatives of the religion in their platoons, answering basic questions about the tenets of Islam (Gibbons-Neff 2015). Former Marine Corporal Mansoor Shams said the anti-Muslim rhetoric especially dishonors the memories of American Muslims who have died in uniform. "Every time [anti-Islamic] comments are made, we're pretty much doing a disservice to them, we're not honoring them." Shams is a Pakistani American who left Karachi when he was six years old and joined the Marine Corps in 2000. "They're people that have died for this country, and we're bashing their faith around all the time." Shams watched the 9/11 terrorist attacks unfold from his duty station in North Carolina, and in the days following the attacks he was asked to teach Marines about his religion. As a new Marine lance corporal, "Shams stood up in front of hundreds of his comrades in Camp Lejeune, North Carolina's main theater, and taught the five pillars of Islam" (Gibbons-Neff 2015). Many individuals like Shams, myself included, have taken on the responsibility of educating their peers about Islam to counteract the negative stereotyping that the terrorists created. In fact, this was my official job for the last six years of my military career when I was assigned to U.S. Special Operations Command.

Despite the heightened sense of suspicion over the entire Muslim American community in the United States, some young Muslims are still inspired to join the military. Some feel their language and cultural skills might benefit the military, especially in Afghanistan and Iraq. Many MMP endure harassment from their peers and respond by trying to act as if religious and racist harassment is a joke. But the potential effects of moral stress and injury for these younger MMP could easily manifest as a huge trauma because if they feel "remorse about various behaviors, they will experience guilt; if they blame themselves because of a perceived personal inadequacy and flaw, they will experience shame" (Litz et al. 2009, p. 700). It is not easy to discern their deeper feelings from the interviews quoted above, other than outrage and the desire to show Islam and Muslims in a good light to the rest of their peers, the military, and the American public at large.

Spiritual support for moral stress and injury in MMP

Keshavarzi and Haque (2013) state that Islam plays a central role in the lives of Muslims and call for "more spiritually-oriented methods of approaching psychological treatment with this group" (p. 230). As an example, the traditional five daily prayers could help ground Muslims by building routines and stability in their lives while they sort out their moral injury issues. Similarly, the demands of Islamic rituals motivate Muslims to follow the practice steadily while mastering self-healing.

Shay, who has worked with combat veterans for many decades, acknowledged as early as 2002 that "religious and cultural therapies are not only possible, but may well be superior to what mental health professional conventionally offer" (Shay 2002, p. 152) as a means to heal from the wounds of the War on Terror. To hear Shay speak of spirituality as a vehicle of healing resonates with Muslims because they are already predisposed to the benefits of religious rituals.

Abu-Ras and Hosein (2015) report that "studies suggest that people who practice their religion have higher levels of wellbeing" (p. 3). A Muslim in the military said, "I have friends. They go overseas [on assignments], and they've become much more religious because religion provides a sense of peace and a sense of comfort in a time [of] uncertainty" (p. 12). To help MMP cope with their stressors, manage their lives, and begin to feel joy rather than depression, they must have both discipline and the desire to begin the healing process. MMP "referred to Islam as a habitual part of their daily routine or what many called a way of life" (p. 6). Many MMP who self-identify as Muslims in their military records feel they must defend Islam and be good examples to others. They use their daily religious practices and the support of family as their coping strategies.

Limitations

In describing the moral stress and injury of MMP, I have relied upon information about MMP from the following sources: blogposts, journal articles, interviews of Muslims by the media, documentaries, personal conversations, and my own experiences of service in the military. These resources are limited in terms of not explicitly describing the specifics and nature of moral stress and injury experienced by MMP. There is an absence of in-depth research on the complex experiences of MMP navigating combat, racism, and religious bigotry (or Islamophobia), which, taken together, surely intensify the experience of moral injury common to military service in a time of war.

Further quantitative and qualitative research is needed to obtain a better understanding of Muslim Americans, Islamophobia, and moral injury as it impacts MMP in a war that is fought in Muslim-majority countries against co-religionists. I would also recommend further research analyzing individual responses to war experiences and to serving in the military in general as it relates to religion as a key component in the Global War on Terror. Future research will need to include a large number of participants to get an accurate understanding of the diverse MMP population (diverse in terms of ethnicity, age, rank, branch of service, gender, and duty position) in order to discern to what extent each of these factors affects the experience of moral injury.

Conclusion

This article offers a glimpse into the stress-filled lives of a few MMP, along with more general supporting information about the marginalized Muslim population serving in the United States military. The historical and social data shared in this article may shed some light for readers on the behavior of MMP as they have tried to cope with experiences of moral stress and injury following September 11, 2001. Since then, the fear among non-Muslims has intensified rather than diminished with each new incident involving shooters who identify as Muslim that has occurred in both the civilian and the military sectors: the Fort Hood shooting, the San Bernardino shooting, the Orlando nightclub shooting, along with the ongoing atrocities of ISIS in the Middle East. These events and even those reported in foreign countries continue to feed the prejudices of non-Muslim groups, especially those exposed to what is now known as "fake news." At the same time, the mission of the U.S. military is expanding, with fighting spreading into many more countries with no end in sight. The entire U.S. military needs more education about Islam and cultural diversity in the areas of the world in which we are engaged if we hope to reduce fear, tension, and the prejudice that some feel towards the Muslim population and, more specifically, MMP.

It will also be beneficial for the Muslim civilian community to support MMP as a form of service in giving back to their country and fellow Muslims by providing safe spaces for them to talk about their war experiences and traumas as they relate to being in combat against their co-religionists with imams and Muslim counselors and chaplains who understand how to support them from a spiritual space of healing. This process could be life-affirming for MMP as they reintegrate into their faith communities and the community at large.

The media interviews with MMP that I have shared showcase their service and dedication to their country as they struggled with issues that negatively impact them as they face an enemy who shares a common religion. The information gleaned about MMP's experiences identified some psychological and emotional components of moral injury as they continued to serve their country. In spite of it all, they portrayed optimism in their interviews with the media. They showed courage and willingness to continue living an engaged life rather than secluding themselves. I hope that the majority of the MMP who stay in the background and have experienced some form of moral stress, injury, and trauma from this war will receive assistance, as I did, when they come to recognize the sources of their moral injury, and I hope that this understanding will ultimately be of use to them as they process the trauma of war and seek to become resilient in their lives.

As the war continues, it is clear that the military needs more Muslim chaplains to serve MMP and help meet the diverse religious and spiritual needs of all military personnel as well as provide cultural and religious knowledge and consultation to commanders in the field and military personnel. Having more Muslim chaplains will positively affect the overall mission of the military and help to maintain an environment of good order and discipline for MMP. The increase in Muslim chaplains and the education of non-Muslim chaplains about moral stress and injury could promote more safe spaces for MMP to process their moral injury without fear of being judged or misunderstood.

It would serve the military well to discern how to normalize the presence of MMP so that they are not seen as a threat to their military colleagues but rather as trusted agents and assets. Since there are only a small number of studies on this population of MMP, it is hard to gauge how the overall MMP population is faring. Surely, further studies of this population could benefit their healing process as well as contribute to the greater military population, especially since it appears that the United States will be engaged in Muslim-majority countries for the foreseeable future. Even though the nation is still at war, the healing process can begin any time MMP are ready to engage in the process. As taught in Islam, everything begins with the intention, and then the follow-through will happen with support and practice. Through writing this article, I had the time to reflect and adjust my perspectives as I learned more about myself, and I realized that I am resilient and have used my faith as the vehicle to move me through the process of healing one day at a time. Also, since retiring from the military, I no longer have to stay fully engaged with the war or global conditions for my job and can simply ignore the news and just live my life engaging in actions that bring me joy and peace of mind.

Through this article, I hope to spark the interest of clergy/imams, lay leaders, mental health professionals, military leadership, and chaplains, along with families and community members, in moral injury as it relates to military personnel, along with the additional factor of religious backlash experienced by MMP. Get involved!

References

Abu Raiya, H., & Pargament, K. (2010). Religiously integrated psychotherapy with Muslim clients: From research to practice. *Professional Psychology: Research and Practice, 41*(2), 181–188. https://doi.org/10.1037/a0017988.

Abu Raiya, H., Exline, J. J., Pargament, K., & Agbaria, Q. (2015). Prevalence, predictors, and implications of religious/spiritual struggles among Muslims. *Journal for the Scientific Study of Religion, 54*(4), 631–648. https://doi.org/10.1111/jssr.12230.

Abu-Ras, W., & Hosein, S. (2015). Understanding resiliency through vulnerability: Cultural meaning and religious practice among Muslim military personnel. *Psychology of Religion and Spirituality, 7*, 179–191. https://doi.org/10.1037/rel0000017.

Antal, C., & Winings, K. (2015). Moral injury, soul repair, and creating a place for grace. *Religious Education., 110*(4), 382–394. https://doi.org/10.1080/00344087.2015.1063926.

Blackburn, B., & Aro, M. (2010). Muslim-American soldier claims harassment in the Army. http://abcnews.go.com/WN/army-dis

crimination-muslim-army-specialist-zachari-klawonn-shares/
story?id=10372314. Accessed 17 April 2017.

Brock, R. N., & Lettini, G. (2012). *Soul repair: Recovering from moral injury after war*. Boston: Beacon Press.

Bryan, A. O., Bryan, C. J., Morrow, C. E., Etienne, N., & Ray-Sannerud, B. (2014). Moral injury, suicidal ideation, and suicide attempts in a military sample. *Traumatology, 20*(3), 154–160. https://doi.org/10.1037/h0099852.

Cainkar, L. (2006). The social construction of difference and the Arab American experience. *Journal of American Ethnic History, 25*(2/3), 243–278.

Clifton, E., & Fang, L. (2011). On Veterans Day, State Rep. Rick Womick (R-TN) calls for purging Muslims from the military. *ThinkProgress*. https://thinkprogress.org/on-veterans-day-state-rep-rick-womick-r-tn-calls-for-purging-muslims-from-the-military-ee277e59beb8. Accessed 4 May 2017.

Debusmann, B. (2007). Former Guantanamo chaplain wants U.S. Army apology. *Reuters*. http://www.reuters.com/article/us-usa-muslims-yee-idUSN0644620520070207. Accessed 20 May 2017.

Exline, J. J., Pargament, K., Grubbs, J. B., & Yali, A. M. (2014). The religious and spiritual struggles scale: Development and initial validation. *Psychology of Religion and Spirituality, 6*(3), 208–222. https://doi.org/10.1037/a0036465.supp.

Gibbons-Neff, T. (2015). "For Muslims in the U.S. military, a different U.S. than the one they swore to defend." *The Washington Post*. https://www.washingtonpost.com/news/checkpoint/wp/2015/12/09/for-muslims-in-the-u-s-military-a-different-u-s-than-the-one-they-swore-to-defend/. Accessed 29 April 2017.

Keshavarzi, H., & Haque, A. (2013). Outlining a psychotherapy model for enhancing Muslim mental health within an Islamic context. *International Journal for the Psychology of Religion, 23*(3), 230–249. https://doi.org/10.1080/10508619.2012.712000.

Khan, M., & Martinez, L. (2015), More than 5,000 Muslims serving in US Military, Pentagon Says. *ABC News*. https://abcnews.go.com/US/5000-muslims-serving-us-military-pentagon/story?id=35654904. Accessed 29 April 2017.

Lewin, T. (2001). Sikh owner of gas station is fatally shot in rampage. *New York Times*. http://www.nytimes.com/2001/09/17/us/sikh-owner-of-gas-station-is-fatally-shot-in-rampage.html. Accessed 25 May 2017.

Lieberman, J., & Collins, S. M. (2011). A ticking time bomb: Counter-terrorism lessons from the U.S. Government's failure to prevent the Fort Hood attack. *U.S. Senate Committee on Homeland Security and Government Affairs*, 1–91. https://www.hsgac.senate.gov/imo/media/doc/Fort_Hood/FortHoodReport.pdf. Accessed 17 September 2017.

Litz, B. T., Stein, N., Delaney, E., Lebowitz, L., Nash, W. P., Silva, C., & Maguen, S. (2009). Moral injury and moral repair in war veterans: A preliminary model and intervention strategy. *Clinical Psychological Review, 29*(8), 695–706. https://doi.org/10.1016/j.cpr.2009.07.003.

Nafi, B. M. (2004). Fatwa and war: On the allegiance of the American Muslim soldiers in the aftermath of September 11. *Islamic Law and Society, 11*(1), 78–116.

Pargament, K. (2007). *Spiritually integrated psychotherapy: Understanding and addressing the sacred*. New York: Guilford Press.

Saito, N. T. (2001). Symbolism under siege: Japanese American redress and the racing of Arab Americans as terrorists. *Asian American Law Journal, 8*, 1–29. https://doi.org/10.15779/z38b56v.

Shay, J. (1994). *Achilles in Vietnam*. New York: Atheneum.

Shay, J. (2002). *Odysseus in America: Combat trauma and the trials of homecoming*. New York: Scribner.

Shay, J. (2012). Moral injury. *Intertexts, 16*(1), 57–66. https://doi.org/10.1353/itx.2012.0000.

Stark, H. (2011). Religious citizens after September 11th: The impact of politics on the jurisprudence concerning Muslim American military service. *The Muslim World, 101*(3), 484–493.

Yee, J., & Molloy, A. (2005). *For God and country faith and patriotism under fire*. New York: PublicAffairs.

Zakaria, T. (2009a). General Casey: Diversity shouldn't be a casualty of Fort Hood. *Reuters*. http://blogs.reuters.com/talesfromthetrail/2009/11/08/general-casey-diversity-shouldnt-be-casualty-of-fort-hood/. Accessed 27 April 2017.

Zakaria, T. (2009b). Fort Hood shooting: Profile of Nidal Malik Hasan. *The Telegraph*. http://www.telegraph.co.uk/news/worldnews/northamerica/usa/6511814/Fort-Hood-shooting-profile-of-Nidal-Malik-Hasan.html. Accessed 27 April 2017.

7

"Turn Now, My Vindication Is at Stake": Military Moral Injury and Communities of Faith

— Zachary Moon —

I'm not a natural killer. I'm a trained killer.
— Sgt. Benjamin Peters, United States Marine Corps
(2014, p. 1)

"How could you provide pastoral and spiritual care to a trained killer?" The question may be jarring, but our theological positions and lived experiences greatly influence our answer. Some religious leaders and communities of faith seem to avoid military service members altogether, either recusing themselves due to a lack of cultural connection and knowledge or because certain pacifist theologies discourage such ministries (Moon 2015). Others recast the function of military service by revering it as heroic, therefore making it a patriotic task to serve and support veterans and military families (Schake and Mattis 2016). Still others rationalize the providing of care as supporting those who have been traumatized by military experience, thereby transcending certain potential political and theological challenges with the religious mandate to care for anyone who suffers. Whether people of faith justify such opportunities as caring for "heroes" or as caring for "head cases"—or whether they avoid veterans altogether—this question, simultaneously daunting to personal, political, and theological sensibilities, too often separates us from one another and withholds the full bounty of resources that could be available to veterans and military families in communities of faith. As theologian Shelly Rambo states, "The task of religious people is to cast backward and forward, as we draw from ancient traditions yet reach forward to live faithfully, addressing the moral and spiritual challenges of this century" (Rambo 2013, p. 462).

Authentic and resourceful ministries with veterans and other military personnel cannot minimize the interlocking complexities of providing care to those who have been rebirthed into a warrior culture. This chapter addresses the barriers to providing effective pastoral care in communities of faith and advocates for its crucial role in the reentry and reintegration process post-deployment. The circumstances of moral injuries only intensify the opportunities and need for care and engagement within communities of faith.

Surviving trauma

The utility of the concept of moral injury is that it offers a better understanding of the complexity of the human experiences in the aftermath of traumatic stress (Drescher et al. 2011; Nash and Litz 2013). Broadly speaking, trauma is an embodied experience of having one's normal functioning and connection to meaning (beliefs, values, behaviors, and relationships) overwhelmed in a way not readily accommodated or assimilated, leaving the person grasping for new coping strategies (Beckham et al. 1998; Berg 2011; Herman 1997, 2011; Janoff-Bulman 1992; Kauffman 2002; Park et al. 2012). The diagnostic lens of post-traumatic stress disorder (PTSD) provides a useful characterization of the most common symptoms of post-traumatic stress: intrusive thoughts, memories, and dreams; avoidance of perceived threats and triggers; and the neurophysiological experiences of hypervigilance and hyperarousal (Herman 1997).

These post-traumatic stress symptoms can be generated by different kinds of traumatic experiences. The diagnosis of PTSD accounts for only one kind of causative experiences—actual or perceived life threat, serious injury, or sexual violence. However, the military currently identifies three additional causes for post-traumatic stress symptoms: extreme fatigue, grief, and moral injury. Given the military operational structure since September 11, 2001, under which many military service members are repeatedly deployed, many service members and their families suffer post-traumatic stress symptoms from one or more of these traumas, often compounding their interlocking effects (Litz et al. 2016).

Alleviating post-traumatic stress symptoms is the priority of the medical establishment, often pursued through a combination of pharmacological and therapeutic measures; however, symptoms often persist when the stories that lie beneath are left unheard or are minimized or misunderstood (Kinghorn 2012; Stallinga 2013, p. 14). It is here that religious leaders who provide spiritual care can and must situate ourselves. We must turn toward those who serve in the military and their families, make ourselves available to their fear, exhaustion, grief, and moral anguish, and accompany them on their terms (Stallinga 2013, p. 22).

Working with moral emotions

In instances of moral injuries, moral emotions will be central to those experiences and must therefore be central in the providing of pastoral care (Doehring 2015a, 2015b; Morris 2017). Moral emotions are distinguished from non-moral emotions by their pro-social function in that they serve to preserve social relationships. Moral emotions span a range of feelings from compassion and gratitude at one pole and guilt, shame, disgust, and contempt at the other. Guilt and shame direct their moral evaluations inward. Guilt evaluates a specific action or inaction: "This thing I have done was bad and/or wrong." Shame evaluates in totalized terms: "I am bad and/or wrong." Guilt often allows for more direct reconciliation through responsibility-taking and reparation, whereas shame's totalizing evaluation often leads to further distancing and exile (Bryan et al. 2013, p. 56; Haidt 2003; Herman 1997, p. 263; Kim and Thibodeau 2011, p. 70; Tangney and Dearing 2002).

Moral injuries can also be generated by disgust and contempt, which direct their moral evaluations outward at the actions or inactions of others. With moral injuries, the overwhelming experience is rooted in the transgression and violation of shared moral covenants within a social-relational world. Persons who have been indoctrinated—ritually re-formed—through recruit military training have through that process assumed multiple moral worlds, one corresponding to their civilian identity and one rooted in that military identity (Moon 2019). Such persons embody multiple sites that can be impacted by moral injuries. For instance, a person may be a trauma survivor prior to military service, and that trauma may be re-elicited because of certain circumstances or experiences during military service. "When I was seventeen, I enlisted because it was the quickest, surest, and most legitimate way to run away from home" (Moon 2015, p. 10). Someone else might experience a crisis of meaning between values and beliefs held prior to military service and those instilled during military training and service. Some others may struggle to reconcile the behaviors and beliefs that allowed them to survive in combat contexts with their post-military life in civilian worlds. As one Army veteran shared, "A lot of things really make sense when you're doing them over there. But when you come back, it's just like, 'How did I do that?'" (Brock and Lettini 2012, p. 45). Versions of this same moral dissonance are echoed by many veterans. Another combat veteran put it this way, "Being in a war zone, I did many things in those years that I wasn't proud of, and [when I returned home] my conscience kicked me around quite a bit. I started to suffer from episodes of depression, and I had an overpowering sense of uselessness" (Moon 2015, p. 20).

Both guilt and shame are self-reflective moral emotions critical to the sustainability of well-ordered social life and necessary in "negotiating problems of cooperation, group living, and maintenance of social relationships" (Kim and Thibodeau 2011, p. 69). Judith Herman writes that "shame may serve an adaptive function as a primary mechanism for regulating the individual's relations both to primary attachment figures and to the social group" (Herman 1997, p. 262). Other clinicians have echoed Herman's assertion by stating that "shame is a motivational response to threat to social integration or social standing" (La Bash and Papa 2013, p. 164). A person experiencing traumatic levels of stress-inducing shame might not recognize the pro-social function of shame (Woodyatt and Wenzel 2014, p. 128). The care seeker and care provider may both seek to alleviate shame by avoiding or minimizing its impact, which may increase the shame's life-limiting power and further disconnect the person from shame's adaptive, pro-social function (Woodyatt and Wenzel 2014, p. 133). An engaged response to shame necessitates a concerted effort toward reconnection with the beneficial, restorative functions within shame and supporting actions that reconnect and reconcile with meaningful social-relational worlds (Kim and Thibodeau 2011, p. 72). A Marine Corps veteran recounted,

> When I came home, I attempted to transition right back into "regular life." In fact, most people didn't even acknowledge I was gone, with the exception of a few questions like, "How was it?" to which I answered, "What do you think?" Coming home was a massive challenge. I didn't sleep well for a long time, and I dealt with extreme bouts of anger, which I internalized. (Moon 2015, p. 18)

When experiences that generate guilt and shame are left unacknowledged or are avoided or minimized within meaningful relationships, the guilt and shame often become more entrenched and interpersonally isolating in function. Such responses to another's guilt and shame diminish and neglect the pro-social function of those moral emotions, and the fear of additional anguish caused by further instances of such responses tends to indicate to the veteran that they are both undeserving of compassion and that they will consistently fail to receive compassion from meaningful others.

As with guilt and shame, disgust and contempt are socially learned responses designed to maintain social order and interpersonal balance (Engelhard et al. 2011, p. 58). "The primary function of both moral disgust and contempt [is] to mark individuals whose behavior suggests that they represent a threat and avoid them, thereby reducing the risk of exposure to harm" (Hutcherson and Gross 2011, p. 720). Disgust and contempt, like shame, generate a totalizing negative evaluation that can be violently destructive. As with guilt and shame, disgust and contempt are too often minimized and/or avoided in care encounters that deem these emotional responses to be inappropriate, unhealthy, or dangerous. This manner of interpretation fails to recognize the ways in which disgust and contempt are adaptive and socially learned and that these moral emotions have important self- and social-protective functions, namely, to protect oneself from exposure to harm.

The moral emotions of shame, guilt, disgust, and contempt are not by their nature disordering, but when experienced in a way that enforces a persistent sense of unforgiveability, they can become entrenched and fuel chronic symptoms and unhealthy behaviors (Kinghorn 2012 p. 61; Litz et al. 2009, p. 701). Moral emotions have pro-social and reconciling goals within them, but they begin with the recognition that a violation has occurred within a person's internalized moral code or of shared social moral covenants. Just as pastoral theologians have sought to redeem the positive qualities of anger (Lester 2003), it is critical that we understand the ways in which shame, guilt, disgust, and contempt beckon persons toward compassion and relational health.

Consider military veteran and scholar Michael Yandell's reflections on his own moral injuries.

> Moral injury is more like a chronic illness than an acute one. It is something like the pain of arthritis or an old, bad knee that someone complains about when it rains. The pain manifests itself in strange ways. I have experienced spontaneous tears of rage while driving to the grocery store that seem to bubble up from nowhere. Sometimes I cannot look a family member in the eye after she has thanked me for my service. Sometimes when I see the children in the youth group with which I work, who are surrounded by loving parents and church members, who anticipate lives of opportunity, my mind wanders to the streets of Baghdad and to the children who asked me for candy, who grew up in the midst of war. (Yandell 2015, p. 13)

Scholars from various disciplines who are engaging with moral injuries suffered by military service members all emphasize the importance of communities that can hear and respond to the stories of moral suffering and live together into new possibilities (Brock and Lettini 2012; Graham 2017; Kinghorn 2012; Litz et al. 2016; Shay 1994, 2002; Sherman 2011, 2015). Jonathan Shay calls this "a living community to whom [a veteran's] experience matters" (Shay 1994, p. 198). As Yandell's reflections remind us, when a person's values and beliefs have been breached, that person's suffering may be experienced in bits and pieces, transitory moments of remembrance triggered by seemingly mundane features of daily civilian life. If these experiences "matter," then attention must be paid.

Rebuilding the house

I have used the following metaphor for moral identity, moral injury, and recovery extensively in pastoral counseling and small group facilitation with veterans and military families, as well as in training congregational leaders (Moon 2015). I understand each person's spiritual life, their faith, their moral identity—however one may name this dimension of themselves—as a house. Our house is comprised of our values, beliefs, behaviors, and meaningful relationships. This is the moral meaning structure a person has to protect them from the storms of life. The first house one lives in is largely built by meaningful others: our families of origin, teachers and mentors, and close friends. None of us came up with our moral ideas, theological assertions, or spiritual practices out of thin air. We learned what was good within the conditions of the world we inhabit from those around us (Janoff-Bulman 1992; Park 2005; Rai and Fiske 2011).

In everyday life, persons experience some stressful circumstances, some more severe than others. In most cases, a person's house—their values, beliefs, behaviors, and meaningful relationships—are able to adjust to, accommodate, and assimilate those stressors, challenges, and changes without being overwhelmed. In certain conditions, however, the protective and orienting structure is breached or destabilized, and it crumbles (Yandell 2015). Multiple questions of meaning are raised in the aftermath: Why and how did this happen? Who was responsible? What should I do now? If the structural integrity of someone's moral home has been undermined, are pharmaceutical remedies or an entitlement check suitable? Do I feel better about the devastation with money in my pocket? Do these pills solve the grief, the anger, the fear I feel when I look at my home that is now in ruins?

If I look around and see everybody else's houses still standing and my neighbors averting their eyes and refusing to come to my aid, I may also experience profound social-relational alienation. Here, the moral emotions are animated. This situation becomes subject to negative evaluations: something is wrong with me or something is wrong with my house or something is wrong with my neighborhood. If I am responsible, I may punish myself and withdraw. If the house is to blame, I may not seek out new accommodations or fault the persons or experiences who built that house. If my neighbors are blamed, I may experience rage and contempt for their actions and inaction and may not continue to relate to them.

This is the crisis of moral injury in nonmedicalized terms, and it is here that communities of faith and sincerely committed persons can provide life-giving and redemptive support. At first, this will be a ministry of presence. Do not avert your eyes. Do not shutter your windows. Meet me where I am. As the questions emerge, don't rush to quick fixes and placating answers. Rebuilding is possible, but the next house will need to be stronger than the last. Religious leaders too often fall into savior roles, swooping in and saving the person in danger. In this metaphor, such saving acts would equate to rebuilding the house for the person. This will not serve a person's needs; each of us needs to know that we are owners of our own houses, and each of us should be making our own architectural and design decisions.

There are three central discernment questions in every rebuilding process: What, here in the ruins, needs to be discarded and improved upon? What, here in the ruins, needs to be reclaimed, refashioned, and restored in place in the next house? Who needs to be a part of the rebuilding team? Not everything in the mess is a part of the problem, so it is not necessary to start from scratch. Let go of what needs to be left aside and carry forward what is still life-giving. Each of us needs to be the lead builder, but none of us needs to do everything by ourselves, so discern who are the trustworthy friends who can put in some work along the way. As a pastor, a religious leader, a chaplain, or anyone else who cares for someone in such circumstances, you can support this discernment process while empowering the person's agency and affirming that good labor is sometimes really hard work. The next house will be a stronger and better home in which to live (Pargament et al. 2006).

Moral injury and communities of faith

What inhibits communities of faith from becoming the kind of communities that "are able to embrace thick and particular conceptions of human flourishing and human failing"? (Kinghorn 2012, p. 71). It is crucial that potential pastoral care providers prepare themselves for this ministry (Drescher and Foy 2010). One's own cultural identity and one's capacities and deficiencies in terms of knowledge and engagement must be subjected to sincere self-reflection (Moon 2015). And as Rambo (2013) writes, "Because war remains a theologically charged and polarizing issue, discourse about war places us in this tragic gap . . . [requiring] new means of theological navigation drawn from the richness of our theological traditions" (p. 443). Most of us avoid potential threats to our familiarity and comfort; entering into authentic relationships with military service members and military families may stretch our personal, political, and theological orientations (Rambo 2013).

Particularity matters in communities of faith

Each community of faith is unique; therefore, each needs to know itself in terms of how it sustains its frames of meaning-making through practicing its particular traditions. Certain values, beliefs, practices, and partnerships will be great resources in nurturing authentic relationships and providing effective pastoral care, but others may prove to be stumbling blocks (Moon 2015).

For example, most congregations already have veterans and military families present, offering a great starting place for engagement. Getting to know them better, and inviting all in the community of faith to reflect on their own relationship to military service, will stimulate substantive conversations and illuminate capacities too often left hidden, opening up shared sources of lament (Graham 2017).

There is, and probably should always be, a variety of political perspectives within a community of faith. "Life is fraught with moral dissonance arising from conflicted moral communities, or moral tribes" (Graham 2017 p, 56). Pastoral theologian Larry Graham draws upon moral psychologist Jonathan Haidt's research to unpack conflicting values at the heart of moral dissonance and to invite communities of faith to "open hearts through 'friendly interaction' [in] authentic collaborative engagement as moral equals with curious openness to listen, understand, and discover" (Graham 2017, p. 60). Although there are political dimensions to military moral injury as well as veteran affairs more broadly, politics cannot be the primary lens through which to engage with veterans and military families. Communities of faith have moral and theological resources for radical empathy amidst intense political differences, as Graham (2017, pp. 56–61) notes. Just as communities of faith should not proceed in clinical and medical diagnostic modes of engagement, so, too, they should present more than political ideas and values. They need to be primarily oriented to their respective traditions and theologies, wrestling with issues grounded in those norms. This is the precious uniqueness of religious communities, and it needs to be maintained and brought to bear in this opportunity.

Building trustworthy relationships

Communities of faith need to proactively work against their habitual impulse to avoid conflict. Avoidance is a key coping strategy for many who have been traumatized, so avoidance is sure to be already present in the human spaces we are exploring here. Personal fears speak without words to one another, agreeing all would be better off without confrontation, truth telling, and public grief. Nurturing healthy boundaries is crucial in any social-relational context, but nurturing brave spaces (Arao and Clemens 2013) in which persons relate to each other in authentic ways does not mean breeding "least common denominator" realities. We inhabit brave spaces when we choose alternatives to avoidance, to remain steadfast even when uncomfortable. Religious and spiritual practices offer unique resources for living with the anger, guilt, fear, and sometimes disgust that often energize avoidance (Doehring 2019; see also Geringer and Wiener 2019; Hosein 2019 ; Liebert 2019). Taking care of oneself is not necessarily cowardice, but conflict avoidance for the sake of conflict avoidance should not be allowed to masquerade as necessary safety. Sometimes it is difficult to know the difference, and human beings make mistakes, but such are the terms of doing this work together.

What would trustworthy relationships look like? Just as self-reflection needs to be encouraged within the congregation, so also within each member. As one veteran reflected:

> When I got back, I found a new church family near my duty station in Washington that had a lot of veterans. They were really kind and welcoming. They asked questions about my experiences but didn't push for details. They just gave me a chance to talk if I wanted—that was important. I really needed time to decompress, and I took a couple weeks off and travelled around to see people. It is great when people show a genuine interest in you and your experiences but don't push for details and don't treat you too differently, like you are sick or need help. (Moon 2015)

Veterans often extend more initial trust to other veterans, especially when talking about military experiences (Schake and Mattis 2016). However, what too commonly emerges from that interpersonal pattern is that many civilians rationalize avoidance by saying, "Veterans would rather talk to other veterans," thereby limiting the capacity to build meaningful communities. Members of any subgroups are likely to feel more comfortable with other members of their subgroup, and time and space needs to be created for member-only engagement. However, very few of us would seek to extend that social-relational human instinct to argue for segregation by life experience. Veterans need civilian friends they can trust, and successful reintegration is not possible without those relationships.

Military service members, from their first moments in recruit training, were told that their subgroup of Americans was willing to pursue extraordinary service in the name of their country and its values. They were then taught, in the most intensely reformative ways possible, that each of their lives was contingent on the lives of their unit members. If circumstances warranted, they would give their own lives in protection of these others (Charuvastra and Cloitre 2008). "The process of basic training, and the subsequent welding of the individual into a unit, will have gone some way towards giving the soldier a military identity in which home and family are of diminished importance" (Holmes 1985, p. 79). Civilians should not fault military service members for feeling greater trust with other veterans but instead should recognize the origin of that trust (Litz et al. 2016; Schake and Mattis 2016). Civilians should regard those bonds with respect, without recusing their own potential participation in relationships. If veterans only talk with other veterans, particularly those of this most recent generation where only 1% served in the military, veterans will be interpersonally isolated from virtually all in the civilian world and will be much more susceptible to unresolved suffering.

If shared military experience is not what joins us to each other, what could it be? If we see one another as deserving of compassion and dignity, made in the image of the Holy, and created to contribute and thrive in this lifetime—all these being theological claims that you may resonate with or reject, depending on your context—then we should approach everyone we meet with a strengths-based approach. We are not required to do charity for one another; our humanity and theirs are inextricable.

Working together in service

We need to seek meaningful opportunities to work together. Service is a value that most communities of faith promote. Service is also the value most commonly named by military service members as their motivation for enlisting. The shared value of service is therefore the most sensible place to begin building bridges between communities of faith and veterans.

A useful example for such community service is the veterans' organization The Mission Continues. Founded in 2007, the organization engages veterans in providing opportunities "to find purpose at home through community impact."[1] From their purpose statement:

> We redeploy veterans on new missions in their communities. Our operations in cities across the country deploy veteran volunteers alongside non-profit partners and community leaders to solve some of the most challenging issues facing our communities: improving community education resources, eliminating food deserts, mentoring at-risk youth and more. Through this unique model, veterans build new skills and networks that help them successfully reintegrate to life after the military while making long-term, sustainable transformations in communities.[2]

The choice of language above is distinctly military in its cultural resonances. The purpose statement uses terms such as "redeploy," "deploy," "missions," and "operations" that are framed with a strengths-based tone around meeting challenges, problem-solving, and building new skills. "The Mission Continues is committed to changing the national conversation around veterans. We believe veterans are assets, and through their continued service, they can create better transitions, and build stronger communities."[3] Their vision and language exhibit astute knowledge of military cultural identity, increasing the likelihood that veterans will feel comfortable and engaged in such surroundings.

The nature of their work is simple and powerful: Gather teams of veterans together around a common project. These projects have obvious and immediate value to the participants, i.e., building a house or a school or working with young people. These service experiences provide immediate positive feedback that affirms the veteran's inner sense of goodness and dignity. The central value of service to others connects commitments from a veteran's military service with the well-being of civilian communities back home.

By working side by side with other veterans in a team, participants experience a high level of social-relational connection. They are not being asked to talk about their feelings or relive their worst days in combat. They are instead recognized for what they can offer, through servant leadership, to their communities and are provided with a team environment that is familiar. The Mission Continues facilitates such community service work for veterans exclusively, and for some

---

[1]Our history, *The Mission Continues*, https://www.missioncontinues.org/about/history/. Accessed 5 November 2017.

[2]What we do, *The Mission Continues*, https://www.missioncontinues.org/about/. Accessed 5 November 2017.

[3]Changing the conversation through service, *The Mission Continues*, https://www.missioncontinues.org/buzz/. Accessed 5 November 2017.

veterans this is crucial early on in their reintegration journey. However, this example provides a possible script for collaborative work between veterans and civilians that could be facilitated by communities of faith. Sitting in the office of one's religious leader, or even in one's worshipping community, may not be the most accessible form of reconnection, recovery, and reintegration.

Imagine if religious communities were investing in community service initiatives with veterans and military families in their communities. Some religious communities have been perceived as judgmental, moralistic, and inhospitable to outsiders (Litz et al. 2016, p. 34). Building a house or cleaning up the neighborhood can provide inviting, nonjudgmental, and mutually empowering experiences for all participants. Such projects can also serve to establish trust between persons of different backgrounds without relying too much on verbal communication, while prioritizing the values of teamwork and mission accomplishment in a civilian context.

Congregational ministries

A number of denominations, including the Christian Church (Disciples of Christ),[4] United Methodist Church,[5] and Unitarian Universalists,[6] have provided educational materials in support of congregational ministries to veterans. However, these programs tend to represent the most basic forms of relationship. Many congregations on Veterans Day weekend, for example, ask veterans to stand and be applauded for their military service. Sincere concern and respect are often the motivators for such gestures, but these expressions can appear condescending and/or tokenizing. That impulse can be mobilized more substantively with the life of the congregation and more authentically with veterans and military families.

Here are a few examples of ministries and sacred practices that could address military moral injury:

Outreach ministries to military families Communities of faith can demonstrate their commitment to military families by learning the dynamics of the cycle of military deployments and engaging in the particular care needs in each phase of the cycle. The process of reentry and reintegration can be supported before demobilization, and

---

[4]Care with veterans and their families, Council on Christian Unity, http://councilonchristianunity.org/document/1011/. Accessed 5 November 2017.

[5]Soul Care Initiative: Journeying together as we care for veterans and their families, *JustPeace*, http://justpeaceumc.org/soul-care-initiative-journeying-together-as-we-care-for-our-veterans-and-their-families/. Accessed 5 November 2017.

[6]S. Holland, G. Forsyth-Vail, & M. L. Cummings, Military ministry toolkit for congregations, Unitarian Universalist Association, 2014, http://growinguu.blogs.uua.org/organizational-maturity/military-ministry-serving-wholeness-in-congregations-and-beyond/. Accessed 5 November 2017.

supporting families is a big part of this effort (Moon 2016). Staying connected to the day-to-day lives of military families during all phases of the deployment cycle demonstrates community commitment to that family and nurtures the social-relational connection. Laura, a military spouse of nearly three decades, reflects, "Being there for military families is...complicated. I wish there was an easy answer, and I wish we could tell you what we need. But many times, we are just breathing and stepping forward. Be present and be involved" (Moon 2015, p. 33). What a military family may need, and what a community of faith has to offer, can only be discerned in the context of community.

Rituals and practices All religious traditions have customs, rituals, liturgies, or practices that engage human suffering, loss, and reconnection (Stallinga 2013). In the Catholic Church, the sacrament of reconciliation (formerly known as "confession"), receiving Eucharist, or praying the rosary are practiced to reconnect with God and the church community, unburden oneself, and redevote oneself in faith. In other Christian traditions, the communion table and baptism embody similar themes. The liturgical calendars of different Christian traditions, particularly the seasons of Advent and Lent, highlight many complex human experiences and connect them with religious meaning (Sippola et al. 2009). Across various religious traditions, one will find examples: recognition and remembrance ceremonies, rituals of purification, talking circles, rituals of lamentation, rituals of rebirth and renewal (Liebert 2019; Morris 2017; Stallinga 2013; Verkamp 2006; Wilson 2013, p. 48). These are a sample of the many religious resources that can engage persons' values, beliefs, and behaviors through social-relational embodied practices in rebuilding a morally meaningful world. As pastoral theologian Carrie Doehring (2019, p.16) writes, "Once veterans can experience their bodies and emotions as good, then pastoral caregivers can move to the second strategy of care: sharing the lament of interrogating suffering through exploring values, beliefs, and coping arising from moral injury." Practices that normalize moral emotions for their pro-social function, as well as practices that empower compassion and gratitude intra- and interpersonally, are crucially important in the recovery process in the aftermath of moral injuries.

The suggestions proposed here are possible opportunities for strengthening the ongoing work of meaningful reentry and reintegration post-deployment. As disparate pieces, they are unlikely to succeed, but by organizing such resources into comprehensive reintegration programs, they will provide military service members with the support they need to meet the demands of moving between military and civilian worlds. Such an organized effort will clearly promote: (1) the empowerment provided by continued service and mission in civilian contexts; (2) strengthened social-relational bonds with both military and civilian personnel; (3) embodied forms of reconnection and health-promotion, including ritual and other body-based practices; and (4) the renewal of personal and collective meaning, sense of goodness, and compassion. These efforts will require a higher level of investment and participation from civilian communities, bringing civilians into closer proximity to the experiences of military service. Such bridge-building will benefit all participants and will likely provide opportunities for new conversations about the complexities of military service and war-making, not as defined by political platforms and rhetoric but by the demands of authentic interpersonal relationships.

Although there is much to gain through exposure to clinical source material and related terms and approaches, communities of faith and those seeking authentic and trustworthy relationships with veterans and military families need to develop language that is organic to their context, in constructive deviation from medical assumptions and categories (Stallinga 2013). Communities of faith need to not become pseudo-clinics, where one's suffering is diagnosed with theological and moral judgments and then pacified by shallow religious customs. If this is all they can offer, it would be less harmful to surrender any further attempt and return to business as usual. Instead, if communities of faith can come ready to work, first on themselves and then in meaningful partnerships with others, allowing their cultural patterns and habits to be challenged where they are lacking and to be renewed and re-formed by the needs presented in new relationships, then there is hope. It will require courage, compassion, and creativity, and we will all be transformed because we have something important to offer and we have something important to learn and receive. All of us are a part of a better future for our nation's military service members and their families.

References

Arao, B., & Clemens, K. (2013). From safe spaces to brave spaces: A new way to frame dialogue around diversity and social justice. In L. Landreman (Ed.), *The art of effective facilitation* (pp. 135–150). Sterling: Stylus Publishing.

Beckham, J. C., Feldman, M. E., & Kirby, A. C. (1998). Atrocities exposure in Vietnam combat veterans with chronic posttraumatic stress disorder: Relationship to combat exposure, symptom severity, guilt, and interpersonal violence. *Journal of Traumatic Stress, 11*(4), 777–785. https://doi.org/10.1023/A:1024453618638.

Berg, G. (2011). The relationship between spiritual distress, PTSD and depression in Vietnam combat veterans. *Journal of Pastoral Care and Counseling, 65*(1), 6–7.

Brock, R., & Lettini, G. (2012). *Soul repair: Recovering from moral injury after war.* Boston: Beacon Press.

Bryan, C. J., Morrow, C. E., Etienne, N., & Ray-Sannerud, B. (2013). Guilt, shame, and suicidal ideation in a military outpatient clinical sample. *Depression and Anxiety, 30*, 55–60. https://doi.org/10.1002/da.22002.

Charuvastra, A., & Cloitre, M. (2008). Social bonds and posttraumatic stress disorder. *Annual Review Psychology, 59*, 301–328. https://doi.org/10.1146/annurev.psych.58.110405.085650.

Doehring, C. (2015a). Resilience as the relational ability to spiritually integrate moral stress. *Pastoral Psychology, 64*(5), 635–649. https://doi.org/10.1007/s11089-015-0643-7.

Doehring, C. (2015b). Intercultural spiritual care in the aftermath of trauma. In F. Kelcourse & K. B. Lyon (Eds.), *Transforming wisdom: The practice of psychotherapy in theological perspective* (pp. 148–165). Eugene: Wipf & Stock.

Doehring, C. (2019). Military moral injury: An evidence-based and intercultural approach to spiritual care. *Pastoral Psychology, 68*(1), 15-30. doi.org/10.1007/s11089-018-0813-5.

Drescher, K. D., & Foy, D. W. (2010). When horror and loss intersect: Traumatic experiences and traumatic bereavement. *Pastoral Psychology, 59*, 147–158. https://doi.org/10.1007/s11089-009 -0262-2.

Drescher, K. D., Foy, D. W., Kelly, C., Leshner, A., Schutz, K., & Litz, B. (2011). An exploration of the usefulness of the construct of moral injury in war veterans. *Traumatology, 17*(8), 8–13. https://doi.org/10.1177/1534765610395615.

Engelhard, I. M., Olatunji, B. O., & de Jong, P. J. (2011). Disgust and the development of posttraumatic stress among soldiers deployed to Afghanistan. *Journal of Anxiety Disorders, 25*, 58–63. https://doi.org/10.1016/j.janxdis.2010.08.003.

Geringer, K. S., & Wiener, N. H. (2019). Insights into moral injury and soul repair from classical Jewish texts. *Pastoral Psychology, 68*(1), 59-75. doi.org/10.1007/s11089-018-0848-7.

Graham, L. (2017). *Moral injury: Restoring wounded souls.* Nashville: Abingdon Press.

Haidt, J. (2003). The moral emotions. In R. J. Davidson, K. R. Scherer, & H. H. Goldsmith (Eds.), *Handbook of affective sciences* (pp. 852–870). Oxford: Oxford University Press.

Herman, J. (1997). *Trauma and recovery.* New York: Basic Books.

Herman, J. (2011). Posttraumatic stress disorder as a shame disorder. In R. L. Dearing & J. P. Tangney (Eds.), *Shame in the therapy hour* (pp. 261–275). Washington, DC: American Psychological Association.

Holmes, R. (1985). *Acts of war: The behavior of men in battle.* New York: The Free Press.

Hosein, S. (2019). Muslims in the U.S. military: Eroding rights and moral injury. *Pastoral Psychology, 68*(1),77-92. doi.org/10.1007/s11089-018-0839-8.

Hutcherson, C. A., & Gross, J. J. (2011). The moral emotions: A social-functionalist account of anger, disgust, and contempt. *Journal of Personality and Social Psychology, 100,* 719–737. https://doi.org/10.1037/a0022408.

Janoff-Bulman, R. (1992). *Shattered assumptions: Towards a new psychology of trauma.* New York: The Free Press.

Kauffman, J. (2002). *Loss of the assumptive world.* New York: Brunner-Routledge.

Kim, S., & Thibodeau, R. (2011). Shame, guilt and depressive symptoms: A meta-analytic review. *Psychological Bulletin, 137,* 68–96. https://doi.org/10.1037/a0021466.

Kinghorn, W. (2012). Combat trauma and moral fragmentation: A theological account of moral injury. *Journal of the Society of Christian Ethics, 32*(2), 57–74.

La Bash, H., & Papa, A. (2013). Shame and PTSD symptoms. *Psychological Trauma: Theory, Research, Practice, and Policy, 6*(2), 159–166. https://doi.org/10.1037/a0032637.

Lester, A. (2003). *The angry Christian: A theology for care and counseling.* Louisville: Westminster John Knox Press.

Liebert, E. (2019). Accessible spiritual practices to aid in recovery from moral injury. *Pastoral Psychology, 68*(1), 41-57. doi.org/10.1007/s11089-018-0825-1.

Litz, B., Stein, N., Delaney, E., Lebowitz, L., Nash, W. P., Silva, C., & Maguen, S. (2009). Moral injury and moral repair in war veterans: A preliminary model and intervention strategy. *Clinical Psychological Review, 29*(8), 695–706. https://doi.org/10.1016/j.cpr.2009.07.003.

Litz, B., Lebowitz, L., Gray, M., & Nash, W. (2016). *Adaptive disclosure: A new treatment for military trauma, loss, and moral injury*. New York: Guilford Press.

Moon, Z. (2015). *Coming home: Ministry that matters with veterans and military families*. St. Louis: Chalice Press.

Moon, Z. (2016). Pastoral care and counseling with military families. *Journal of Pastoral Care and Counseling, 70*(2), 128–135.

Moon, Z. (2019). *Warriors between worlds: Moral injury and identities in crisis*. Lanham, MD: Lexington Books.

Morris, J. (2017). The army chaplain as counselor: An exploration of self-reflexivity and denominational particularities. *Reflective Practice: Formation and Supervision in Ministry, 37*, 107–120.

Nash, W. P., & Litz, B. T. (2013). Moral injury: A mechanism for war-related psychological trauma in military family members. *Clinical Child and Family Psychology Review, 16*, 365–337. https://doi.org/10.1007/s10567-013-0146-y.

Pargament, K., Desai, K. M., & McConnell, K. M. (2006). Spirituality: A pathway to posttraumatic growth or decline? In L. G. Calhoun & R. G. Tedeschi (Eds.), *Handbook of posttraumatic growth: Research and practice* (pp. 121–135). Mahwah: Erlbaum.

Park, C. L. (2005). Religion as a meaning-making framework in coping with life stress. *Journal of Social Issues, 61*, 707–729. https://doi.org/10.1111/j.1540-4560.2005.00428.

Park, C. L., Mills, M. A., & Edmondson, D. (2012). PTSD as meaning violation: Testing a cognitive worldview perspective. *Psychological Trauma: Theory, Research, Practice, & Policy, 4*(1), 66–73. https://doi.org/10.1037/a0018792.

Peters, B. J. (2014). *Through all the plain*. Eugene: Cascade Books.

Rai, T. S., & Fiske, A. P. (2011). Moral psychology is relationship regulation: Moral motives for unity, hierarchy, equality, and proportionality. *Psychological Review, 11*, 57–75. https://doi.org/10.1037/a0021867.

Rambo, S. (2013). Changing the conversation: Theologizing war in the 21st century. *Theology Today, 69*(4), 441– 462. https://doi.org/10.1177/0040573612463035.

Schake, K., & Mattis, J. (2016). A great divergence? In K. Schake & J. Mattis (Eds.), *Warriors and civilians: American views of our military* (pp. 1–20). Stanford: Hoover Institution Press.

Shay, J. (1994). *Achilles in Vietnam: Combat trauma and the undoing of character*. New York: Scribner.

Shay, J. (2002). *Odysseus in America: Combat trauma and the trials of homecoming*. New York: Scribner.

Sherman, N. (2011). *The untold war: Inside the hearts, minds, and souls of our soldiers.* New York: W. W. Norton & Co.

Sherman, N. (2015). *Afterwar: Healing the moral wounds of our soldiers.* Oxford: Oxford University Press.

Sippola, J., Blumenshine, A., Tubesing, D., & Yancey, V. (2009). *Welcome them home, help them heal: Pastoral care and ministry with service members returning from war.* Duluth: Whole Person Associates.

Stallinga, B. (2013). What spills blood wounds spirit: Chaplains, spiritual care, and operational stress injury. *Reflective Practice: Formation and Supervision in Ministry, 33,* 13–31.

Tangney, J. P., & Dearing, R. (2002). *Shame and guilt.* New York: Guilford.

Verkamp, B. J. (2006). *The moral treatment of returning warriors in early medieval and modern times.* Scranton: University of Scranton Press.

Wilson, J. (2013). Culture-specific pathways to healing and transformation for war veterans suffering PTSD. In R. M. Scurfield & K. T. Platoni (Eds.), *Healing war trauma: A handbook of creative approaches* (pp. 47– 67). New York: Routledge.

Woodyatt, L., & Wenzel, M. (2014). A needs-based perspective on self-forgiveness: Addressing threat to moral identity as a means of encouraging interpersonal and intrapersonal restoration. *Journal of Experimental Social Psychology, 50,* 125–135. https://doi.org/10.1016/j.jesp.2013.09.012.

Yandell, M. (2015). The war within. *The Christian Century, 132*(1), 12–13.

8

Moral Injury as Loss and Grief with Attention to Ritual Resources for Care

— Nancy J. Ramsay —

Combat is nothing if not existential: It pits an individual against life and its ultimate challenges. It requires seeing the unspeakable and doing the dreaded. It is a role that is immersed and transformative and lingers long after a soldier takes off the uniform. Because of the stressors it involves—unpredictable attack, helplessness in the face of that unpredictability, pervasive and gruesome carnage—it embeds deep.

—Nancy Sherman. *The Untold War* (Sherman 2015, p. 20)

As even ancient cultures observed in sources such as *The Iliad* and *Bhagavad Gita*, participating in war predictably causes grievous existential harm to combatants.[1] Military moral injury is a recent term that describes the ancient insight that, in addition to physical wounds, war wounds the souls of to those who, in combat, transgress otherwise deeply held values related to human life because they kill and maim one another and often innocent civilians. In contrast to the physiological manifestations of post-traumatic stress, moral injury is best described as arising from potentially morally injurious experiences such as *"perpetrating, failing to prevent, or bearing witness to acts that transgress deeply held moral beliefs and expectations . . .* [and may also include] bearing witness to the aftermath of violence and human

---

[1]See, for example, Jonathan Shay's (1994) exploration of *The Iliad* in his exploration of the trauma of combat for Vietnam veterans.

carnage" (Litz et al. 2009, p. 700, emphasis in original). Whatever other consequence moral injury may have, surely loss and grief forever shape the world of those who enter the traumatic vortex of evil and suffering that shapes combat zones (Drescher et al. 2011). Combat support personnel such as nurses and physicians also may return from battle haunted by experiences of medical traumas to civilians of all ages and to combatants (Simmons et al. 2018). Tragically, for some combatants, moral injury arises when they experience religious and racial prejudice from supposed comrades or when they experience no justice after military sexual trauma perpetrated by comrades on whom they must rely in battle. Grief, shame and guilt, anger, loss of meaning and purpose, imaginations burdened by facing a level of radical evil they could not previously have imagined and cradling only tenuous hope— these are indicators of moral injury in the halting stories chaplains and spiritual caregivers hear. War changes lives forever.

How do these soul wounds of war suggest the shape of effective spiritual care? As Larry Kent Graham put it, "Healing from lost innocence is not innocence regained. It is innocence mourned and moral integrity reestablished" (2017, p. 78). This essay proposes resources and describes practices that facilitate grieving such innocence in its guises of human or divine control and supporting a renewed sense of resilience that is born from the struggle to name realistically one's agency in what was lost in the maelstrom of the destructive forces that shape war. Healing from the trauma of dehumanizing evil also entails constructing a framework of meaning that will be adequate for living with a posture of realistic hopefulness after seeing the face of war. The shame and guilt and trauma of moral injury also require a journey of rebuilding a positive sense of self, restoring patterns of relationality, and developing resilience through practices of compassion and resistance to evil that rebuild and sustain a sense of moral integrity.

Specifically, this essay develops a critically constructive correlation of theological and ritual resources shaped by Judaism, Christianity, and Islam explored alongside current methodological and theoretical resources that inform care in relation to grief, particularly when it arises from trauma. Theologically, I address experiences of grief shaped by radical evil and the usefulness of practices of lament found in Abrahamic sources. Experiences of radical evil disclose the vulnerabilities of some constructions of faith as well as the challenges when soldiers have limited faith resources for dealing with the scope of evil war discloses. Ritual practices such as lament illustrate how rituals assist in healing. I recognize the value of drawing on ritual resources and practices that articulate both confessional and ethical or transformative intention.

Ritual practices are essential for human life and life in community. They are especially important in times of transition and crisis. Often when we join ritual practice to shared narratives of faith and ethical life, those rituals empower healing and help restore experiences of belonging. Rituals also have performative power to express, enact, and restore conviction and hope.

Methodologically, I draw particularly on Pauline Boss's (1999, 2006) theory of ambiguous loss. It addresses the distinctive character of loss from moral injury when one returns physically from war, but one's ability to be psychologically present with one's self and relationally is powerfully altered. As Graham (2017) captures, ambiguous loss addresses grief that arises from experiences of innocence lost that cannot be regained. Boss also helps us explore the ambiguities that insinuate historical life and revise any illusion of mastery or control. Boss's theory of ambiguous loss supports the importance of developing resilience and hope informed by the limits of freedom in historical life.

Grief is also particular for each individual and reflects embodied, existential, relational, communal, political, and historical realities that predictably mark and sometimes further complicate moral injury, such as racism, religious bigotry, heterosexism, and sexism. An intersectional analysis helps us be alert to such vulnerability to harm. Persons also bring varied histories, vulnerabilities, and strengths to military service that may influence their experiences of combat. Those who come with earlier experiences of emotional and physical trauma, for example, may be more easily or deeply affected by the trauma of combat. An intersectional analysis reminds us of the simultaneous ways each of us is shaped by power-laden, socially constructed, and sustained experiences of oppression and privilege such as racism and sexism and Christianism (privileging the religious tradition of Christianity). Such experiences also influence a soldier's experiences of vulnerability and violence in combat. The increasing diversity of spiritual and religious worldviews and practices among combatants as well as varied levels of understanding among those who identify with a particular tradition such as Christianity mean that practices of care must be closely responsive to the experience of a veteran. Of course, these same particular, embodied, and contextual factors shape us as caregivers and inform what we notice and how we listen.

Mourning the loss of innocence and choosing to live with a sense of moral integrity are helpful goals for facilitating grief and naming losses that accompany military moral injury. This article focuses on resources and strategies to facilitate veterans and their families in the work of grief and the challenge of rebuilding hope and meaning. The sheer brutality of combat means that moral injury gives rise to an experience of deep spiritual and existential challenge as soldiers come to terms with committing or permitting or witnessing acts of violence they could not have imagined. As a result of military sexual trauma, some in combat and in the "safety" of military bases and their own ships experience moral injury when trusted comrades betray them (Copp 2018; Morral et al. 2018). Practices of care should include supporting survivors of moral injury in their journey to resolve feelings such as guilt, shame, betrayal, and anger so that in time they construct a new sense of integrity. Those who incur moral injury and choose to confront and heal from it bring to mind a familiar story in Abrahamic texts, the story of Jacob wrestling all night at the Jabbok (Gen. 32:24–32) before he faces the brother he deceived and fled from decades before.[2] This story offers a rich frame for those who walk beside veterans who choose to wrestle meaning from their suffering and embrace a new future. To consider that story, I begin with a reflection on how moral injury often silences.

In his essay "Useless Suffering," (1988) Emmanuel Levinas suggests that the evil of suffering lies in the ways it renders those who suffer impotent and isolated and causes them to feel abandoned. Arthur Frank (2013), a medical sociologist who studies the experience of embodied suffering, draws on Levinas's observation to suggest that such suffering disrupts the narratival structure, order, and "voice" of the sufferer's self. He notes, as I will explore later, that such disruption shapes the opening verses of laments such as those in the psalms. Like Levinas, he recognizes that witnessing those whom suffering isolates may offer a "half-opening" or possibility of experiencing the ethical space Levinas describes as the "inter-human" (Frank 2013, p. 177; Levinas 1988, p. 158). Those who recognize suffering through another's "testimony" step into that inter-human space as witnesses who experience the moral agency such suffering bespeaks and evokes in those who will listen. The testimony that "recognizes" the one whom suffering silenced participates in the restoration of the voice of the one who suffers and the ethical possibilities of their story (Frank 2013, p. 150).

Arthur Frank (2013, pp. 181–182) invites us to consider Jacob's wrestling as his struggle with the moral injury he incurred in a series of betrayals that began with his birth family, though we cannot be certain what is being contested that night at the Jabbok. The story suggests that Jacob is wrestling with God in the process of coming to terms with his very sense of self as he confronts the shame and guilt that shape his reflections on his betrayals of relational obligations. Frank poses

---

[2]Captain Beth Stallinga (2013), Chaplain, U.S. Navy, also suggests that Jacob's limp is illustrative of the consequences of moral injury (p. 25).

an important question for those who seek to offer spiritual care: "Is Jacob wrestling a blessing out of the angel or is the angel wrestling the petition for a blessing out of Jacob?" Perhaps both are true. It is certainly the case that the wrestling experience sanctifies the place for Jacob, so he calls it "Peniel," meaning "the face of God" (p. 182). Frank suggests what spiritual care also presumes, that God is present in our struggles to wrest meaning and hope from suffering and blesses such struggles. The struggle was itself wounding for Jacob, and he walked thereafter with a limp but also as new man, Israel. He began a future rich with possibilities for meaning and service. Frank offers a theological insight: "Sanctification is a recursive process. . . to be is to wrestle with God" (p. 182). Indeed, it is difficult to imagine being an effective companion on the journey toward healing if one fails to recognize the power that comes to those who recover a powerful sense of self as they refuse the bonds of silence and give voice to their suffering. As Frank puts it, "The wounded storyteller is a moral witness, reenchanting a disenchanted world" (p. 185).

Indeed, as I will explore in more detail, the ethical importance of bearing witness to the stories of moral injury among soldiers is echoed by veterans such as Michael Yandell (2015, 2019) who remind us that moral injury not only shapes the life stories of those who served in combat, it also has consequences for all civilians on whose behalf these veterans served.

The stories of several veterans and their families

In this section, I present composite fictionalized stories of returning veterans and their families that are representative of moral injury situations that religious leaders and faith communities encounter when we are equipped to recognize moral injury. I have situated these stories in diverse faith communities, and I explore how religious leaders in Jewish, Christian, and Muslim communities might helpfully respond.

Russell Russell is a twenty-three-year-old Army veteran just back from a two-year tour in Afghanistan. Russell, who identifies as an African American, grew up in an African Methodist Episcopal congregation. His father is a Vietnam veteran. His parents own and operate a small business. The entire family has been active in the congregation. Russell received an Eagle Scout award for the community garden he helped initiate at the church. He received a Rotary scholarship when he graduated from high school 4 years ago. He wanted a college education, and after 2 years in junior college, he joined the Army to fulfill his desire to serve his country and contribute to peace and to help fund his last 2 years of college upon his return. Russell was an infantryman like his father before him. He fought in several difficult battles that involved civilian casualties to adults and children as well as deaths and serious injuries to men in his unit. He did not seek assistance in reflecting on these experiences while in the Army, nor did he report being troubled by them at his discharge evaluation.

Russell returned home 8 months ago. Not long after, his parents meet with Russell's pastor to express their deep concern for Russell. They report he has changed in demeanor; he is isolating himself, is anxious, and is no longer sure about the next steps in his life. He had been at the center of family life and energy before he was deployed. Now, it is as if he is only marginally present to them. Russell's mother mentions in passing that there is something about his distance that reminds her of his father's silence about Vietnam. This worries her.

When the pastor calls Russell to get together for coffee, Russell reluctantly agrees, and he shares that he now finds faith in God, a God able to make a difference in the world for good, to be very difficult. He no longer can make sense of the world he saw from the battlefield and bombed-out city streets with too many children's bodies torn by bullets. Further, those images make police violence against innocent African Americans here at home more painful. He cannot justify the way he was ordered to act and cannot recognize himself in memories of his behavior that he knows are true and cannot forget. It is hard to be in church.

Russell is using his VA benefits to attend the local college. He shares an apartment with another veteran from his high school who is attending the same college. Russell describes his classmates as immature. He is focusing on his courses to finish as quickly as he can. He mentioned to his mother that he went to the college health center to talk with a counselor and is taking medication for depression. He only attends church irregularly, but he does come by to chat with the pastor from time to time. He is considering joining the group of veterans in the nearby United Methodist church who meet monthly.

Jim Rachel is married to Jim, who is completing his final one-year tour in Afghanistan as a reservist and should be home in 2 months. Rachel and Jim identify as European Americans. They are the parents of two preschool children, two-year-old Lydia and five-year-old Jimmy. Before they married, Rachel was attracted to Jim's strength and self-confidence in his ability to accomplish his goals and to protect and provide for his family. They married after he completed his service as an enlisted man and began working with an insurance agency. They had not expected his reserve work to result in a tour of duty, but they relied on the additional income to support their family.

While Jim has been in Afghanistan, Rachel has sometimes called on a care team from their Presbyterian congregation to help with the stressors of parenting two preschool children with no grandparents nearby. Rachel has stayed in touch with her pastor from time to time about her communications with Jim. A few weeks ago, she reported that his calls to her had changed in sobering ways. He was recently reassigned from a noncombat position to one that involved patrols in neighborhoods where there had been occasional violence and tense moments, and he and others were ordered to detain civilians for questioning. Now, his calls home have been markedly different. He called distressed by the crossfire deaths of children in a skirmish in which he had participated. The children whose bodies he saw reminded him of their children. In tears, he had asked Rachel if she could still love him and trust him with their children. He said that he was struggling to make any sense of the moral world that had once seemed so orderly to him. He haltingly voiced his fear that he had betrayed the person he had understood himself to be—a good and decent person. Rachel asks her pastor how she can help her husband with his grief and distress and comfort him. Meanwhile, she also worries out loud about who he is becoming. What will happen when he comes home in 2 months? He is clearly not the self-confident, in-control man who had previously only cried at the births of their children. She is anxious about how to support Jim when he returns. She has spoken with a few spouses of veterans and reservists in the congregation who have warned her that re-entry to family life from battle can be very difficult.

Veterans' group A care group for combat veterans gathers monthly.[3] They are members of a United Methodist congregation and of the nearby African Methodist Episcopal congregation Russell attends. The members, all male, include six who served in Vietnam and two who served in the first invasion of Iraq as well as six who have served recently in Iraq and Afghanistan. They meet together at the United Methodist church at the invitation of their pastors. The European American United Methodist pastor is a non-combat veteran. The two pastors each approached veterans in their congregations individually about the possible usefulness of the group and then encouraged them to come and talk about ways they might accompany each other and newly returning veterans. Although the sharing ranges widely, themes of moral injury such as grief due to the loss related to their experiences

---

[3]In developing this vignette, I drew on features of the veterans' group Shelly Rambo describes in *Resurrecting Wounds* (2017). However, the group described here is a fictionalized composite of this and similar groups.

in war and questions about God's love and power and forgiveness are often voiced. They decide to keep their group open to returning veterans such as Russell and Jim. Many of these veterans occasionally share the difficulties of coming home from the war to their spouses and young children. Although the conversation opens their memories in sometimes painfully challenging ways, the group has kept meeting because they find support in exploring memories and feelings, and they appreciate the opportunity to walk with those newly home from war. The veterans from Vietnam and the first Iraq conflict report to their pastor that they wish this had been available to them decades ago. Sometimes they help connect their partners with the spouse of a returning veteran. Occasionally, they also attend together the United Methodist congregation's monthly evening Taizé eucharistic healing and wholeness liturgy. Recently, the pastor reported to the group that the worship committee had expressed their desire to provide a monthly healing and wholeness service shaped especially for the veterans, their families, and other congregants who are friends and supporters of members of the group. He invited the group to explore whether such a service would be helpful.

Frank Frank is a veteran of the Korean War. He was born in 1932 and entered the Korean War when it began in 1950 at the age of 18. Frank is a member of the Jewish (Reform) temple in town. He is now in an assisted living setting with his spouse, and his health is declining. Hospice care is imminent. In the last months, Frank has begun to discuss for the first time with his rabbi his sense of deep grief and remorse about his experiences in combat during the war. He describes participating in combat in the years 1950 to 1952 when he was only a teenager. He mentions scenes of violence against civilians and close combat with enemy forces that have haunted him for more than 60 years. He despairs of ever experiencing peace and forgiveness for some of his actions in those combat situations. Frank's wife also struggles with how to accompany her spouse in his suffering from the memories of this previously undisclosed trauma.

The above four vignettes clarify that moral injury is at once personal, relational, generational, lifelong, and communal in its impact. These veterans and their families, trying to cope with moral injury incurred in combat, will help us to explore resources that may be of use when caring for veterans and their families. Jacob's wrestling match offers us a glimpse into the journey of veterans who travel the challenging, lifelong path toward healing and learn to walk with a "limp." Russell's parents and siblings, Jim's wife and young children, and Frank's wife and adult sons also struggle with the consequences of war for someone they love. These vignettes also remind us that religious leaders and communities of faith can be sources of accompaniment and hope. The worship committee's response to the veterans' participation in the Taizé service discloses that the moral injury that veterans experience poses challenges to any citizen of a country that wages war.

Moral injury and grief shaped by ambiguous loss

Russell, Jim, and Frank and their families help us begin to reflect on what the losses of moral injury look like. Perhaps these stories give us eyes to see and suggest ways we can learn to walk with those who have physically survived a brutal war but are emotionally and spiritually deeply challenged by their experiences. Grief is shaped by the nature of the loss sustained. Moral injury shapes grief in ways that point us toward what Boss (1999, 2006) describes as "ambiguous loss." Ambiguous loss arises when grief is shaped by someone who is physically present but psychologically absent or psychologically present but physically absent. Moral injury meets the first criterion. Veterans are back home, but their experiences may have forever altered them psychologically and spiritually. Boss notes that ambiguous loss stresses family systems and inevitably includes relational losses. This concept is useful in communities of faith where care includes relational networks.

The vignettes demonstrate that the ambiguities shaping the stress of moral injury are not just psychological. Moral injury incorporates spiritual and moral losses. The veterans in these vignettes illustrate what Arthur Frank (2013) calls "narrative wreckage" (p. 68). That is, their ability to imagine themselves as good persons acting in a world ordered by a divine agency that limits destructive evil is in tatters. Russell's spiritual worldview no longer makes sense in light of war's savagery. He seems to be experiencing what Yandell (2015) described as the loss of a "world that makes moral sense." What sort of God lets this happen? Jim also no longer has his earlier confidence in the goodness of the world as he knew and trusted it to be. He fears he may be beyond God's love as well as his wife's love. Frank has quietly lived for seven decades with the anguish that he too is beyond God's forgiveness. The parents, siblings, spouses, and children of these veterans have their own journeys with this ambiguous but very real loss and its consequences for intimacy and care.

Resilience is the goal of care shaped by an understanding of ambiguous loss. Resilience describes the ability to temper expectations of mastering the inescapable tensions of historical life while encouraging a hopeful posture about the ways one can exercise freedom and live with hope, meaning, and love. Agency is limited but real and significant. Boss emphasizes that coming to such a position includes developing more adequate practices and structures that provide for sustaining a sense of meaning, which may include belief systems and spirituality. It includes helping revise and strengthen the connections and organization of family systems and developing patterns of communication that are open and adequate for problem-solving (2006). Developing resilience includes taking responsibility for one's behavior when warranted and externalizing shame and blame when those emotions arise from unwarranted assumptions of responsibility or control. Resilience emerges when veterans can reconstruct a hopeful posture based on recognizing that even in the ambiguities of their experiences, they can exercise their agency in life-giving ways.

In the context of spiritual care, Boss's use of the term 'resilience' reminds us that how we make sense of our world and find meaning in our lives are especially vulnerable in relation to the adequacy of our imagination about hope. Do our imaginations about the nature of meaning and the value of human agency foster a hopefulness that is resilient in the face of our limited ability to control human history? Can we foster hope that is realistic about our accountability for harm, and can we externalize accountability when the causes of the harm are beyond our control? In the context of ambiguous loss, Boss encourages strengthening capacities for hope that recognize the limits of control and ultimately relying on trust in a larger frame of meaning.

Trauma figures prominently in the ambiguous loss that veterans experience. It requires spiritual care practices that take into account veterans' embodiment and witnessing of levels of violence and a scope of evil that shatter their meaning and faith systems. Often, they feared for their lives and the lives of comrades. The very chemistry of their brains is often altered by such sustained trauma. The losses they seek to address in the context of spiritual care are deeply personal, embodied, and imprinted in their memories. The immediacy and acuity of their memories shape practices of care for them and their journey to recover a meaning that is hopeful and life-sustaining. Accompanying veterans in reclaiming meaning or a belief system that provides hopeful resilience in reclaiming a positive experience of agency will likely include a process that begins with safety in sharing through providing "sanctuary" (Herman 2015, pp. 155–174). Eventually, such a place of safety may foster veterans' ability to share and mourn their memories and likely their own behaviors that haunt them. Finally, the goal is to support veterans in reconnecting with people who value them and with whom they may give and receive love that is reciprocally life-giving (Herman 2015).

Spiritual care with veterans and their families affected by moral injury aligns with Boss's (2006) encouragement to employ ritual practices that contribute to experiences of meaning and resilience (p. 75). For millennia, human communities have relied on ritual practices to express needs for order, communal ties and commitments, and transformation in our personal and communal narratives. Ritual practices are particularly helpful in times of transition and crisis such as military moral injury. Ordinarily, the narrative frames that structure each of our lives include a balance of mythic or reconciling themes and parabolic or dissonant themes (Anderson and Foley 1998, pp. 33–34). War throws that balance awry in ways that render connection and hope vulnerable. Trauma such as battle has three interrelated effects. It shatters world and soul, prompts survival mechanisms, and leads survivors to press for recovery and rebuilding (Graham 2017, p. 138). Ritual practices are useful in spiritual care with veterans because ritual offers individual and communal opportunities for reasserting our personal and communal trust in a social and cosmic order that is stronger than the horizon of destructive violence war discloses. Rituals augment practices of care by helping veterans recover their trust in the mythic dimensions of their faith experience. Ritual action is performative. Engaging in ritual practice asserts that ritual reality as available and true, both personally and communally. This performative power of ritual practice assists those isolated by shame and guilt to recover access to communal and relational ties.

Rituals include confessional and ethical modes that help us enact personal and communal awareness of our need and relation to the holy and mark how that relation to the holy creates ethical obligations to God and one another (Driver 1991, p. 107). This confessional and ethical interrelation also reminds us that ritual honesty includes acknowledging the narratival balance of the mythic and parabolic in our personal and communal lives. Ritual practices help individuals and communities experience forgiveness and hope and express sorrow and joy, anger and protest, and they help us perform commitments that facilitate healing and constructive action (Graham 2017, p. 138).

As spiritual caregivers, we have access not only to ritual practices familiar to veterans and their families, such as confession and Eucharist. We also have opportunities to create ritual experiences with veterans that are uniquely responsive to the parabolic dimensions of their moral injury. In providing spiritual care, it is essential to guide established and creative ritual experience in ways that honor the symbolic power inherent in the liminality of its performative character so that the ritual experience deepens participants' experience of the holy in ways that authentically reflect love, justice, and hope (Ramshaw 1987, pp. 19–20). Careful conversation precedes the use of ritual in practices of care to ensure that those engaging in the ritual are prepared and willing to do so.

As we explore possible responses to several veterans and their families described in the above vignettes, we will also consider ritual practices that may support their healing and strengthen faith. We will explore familiar and creative ritual practices that may assist veterans and their families in reclaiming the transformative power of hope and in constructing more adequate frames of meaning and that provide deeper access to resources for resisting the isolation of shame and guilt and strengthening familial and communal support.

As we explore practices of care and ritual resources for responding to veterans' loss and grief, we would do well to remember the words of Chaplain Beth Stallinga (2013), U.S. Navy: "Our faith communities are in need of rites and rituals which openly acknowledge the corporate reality and accountability of war. In a democracy, because a warrior is deployed at the bequest of leaders elected by the populace, an entire country goes to war" (p. 28). The next section not only explores ritual practices to support the process of grief of veterans and their families but also considers practices that may open the way for faith communities to name and confess our complicity in the moral injury of those who went to war on our behalf.

Resources for spiritual care in the context of ambiguous loss

Combat is predictably a world-shattering experience for the belief systems of veterans who cannot easily resume civilian life, haunted by memories of evil and violence and likely their own behavior or lack of it. As Chaplain Beth Stallinga (2013) puts it, a veteran's questions will not be about war, "They will be about God" (p. 22). Theologically, this means that spiritual care should be particularly sensitive to the veteran's journey to make sense of evil, the scope of which had been previously unimagined; God's agency in a world where such evil occurs; and their own vulnerability and moral agency in such a world.[4]

Spiritual care first requires creating a space safe enough to voice the unspeakable. It also requires the ability to provide a space safe enough for voicing and exploring whether there is a credible meaning or belief system that can sustain the veteran going forward. Is hope a viable option? Given what the veteran did or allowed or witnessed, is

---

[4]Two recent theological explorations of theodicy may be useful in walking beside veterans whose questions are shaped by their questions about evil as encountered in war: Farley (1990) and Nelson (2003).

forgiveness available to them? Is their humanity redeemable? These questions are hard to voice. "Hearing to speech" (Morton 1985) is itself the beginning of a more resilient hope.

An adequate experience of "sanctuary" provides the possibility for entering a relationship in which care provides a safe enough space for remembrance and for mourning the experience of war and the moral injury to which it gives rise. Skillful listening includes paying attention to clues about the character of a veteran's earlier imagination about who God is, how God exercises agency in the world, and the character of God's agency. It means listening for their earlier confidence in their own moral agency. Given the decreasing affiliation with faith communities that provide a frame for such reflection and often instruction for youth, ours is a context in which more veterans face combat with a "thin" or absent belief system for imagining who God is and how God is at work in the world. For others, such as Russell described above, the framework they imagined as solidly in place proves inadequate. The God in whom Russell trusted proved inadequate in the face of the evil he encountered. Perhaps this signals a different vulnerability for those whose frame of meaning is so certain that deep ambiguity is shattering. Although Russell acknowledges guilt regarding his actions in war, the aspect of moral injury that seems strongest lies in the deep challenge to his earlier confident faith in God's agency over against evil. His experience recalls Yandell's description of the world-shattering experience of military moral injury in which "the spiritual and emotional foundations of the world disappeared and made it impossible for me to sleep the sleep of the just" (2015, p. 12).

The pain that Russell dares to voice with his pastor and that Yandell (2015) describes is similar to the pain found in the practice of lament so common in Jewish and Christian scriptures such as Psalms and Lamentations. As Billman and Migliore (1999) remind us, laments are the language of pain that opens a way for healing by helping hope to re-emerge, though the path is not simple (pp. 16, 104–5). Laments articulate a piety of protest (p. 31). They are acts of political imagination (Brueggemann 1986) and make space for justice to be born (O'Connor 2002, p. 128). In her commentary on Lamentations, which most believe describe the shattering grief of Babylon's destruction of Jerusalem and the temple around 587 BCE, Kathleen O'Connor describes laments as "truth-filled and faithful prayers" that demonstrate a way to stand before God "angry and tear-drenched" and seek God's intervention (p. 124). In Jewish and Christian scriptures, laments are an "appropriate response to the radical evil that threatens God's purposes for human life and the whole creation and that only God is capable of overcoming" (Billman and Migliore 1999, p. 30).

Critical for practices of spiritual care is recognizing that voicing lament is a "form of truth- telling poetry" that is an "act of survival and testimony" (O'Connor 2002, p. 5). Shawn Fawson (2019) explores the value of such poetry in contemporary laments described as the genre of "witness poetry." Although such poetry may not reference a faith-based political protest, it does offer a complaint against radical and dehumanizing evil, and it is proving useful for some veterans.

O'Connor (2002) helpfully points to the role of witness and testimony in laments that are voiced by persons who, like Russell in the vignette and Yandell (2015) in his experience in war, experience the "wreckage" (Frank 2013) of their assumptive narrative faith and personal agency that had previously offered a hopeful posture in the world (O'Connor, pp. 7–8, 98). In Lamentations, beginning in the first poem or chapter, the Daughter of Zion shares her tears of grief and complains that she has no comforter, by which she means no one to witness and confirm her and validate her pain (O'Connor, p. 98). In the second poem, O'Connor points to what happens to the narrator who does bear witness to the pain and thus validates the humanity of the Daughter of Zion. O'Connor is careful to note that the narrator's recognition of the pain of the Daughter of Jerusalem is effective precisely because it does not reduce or explain away that pain (p. 100). The empathic witness of seeing the pain "turns the spirit" of the narrator (p. 100). This in itself is clearly a powerful reminder of the importance of empathy in spiritual care as we seek to "bear witness" to the devastation a veteran has witnessed in a manner that recognizes the world-shattering and dehumanizing depth of the evil that has injured them.

Levinas (1988) has observed that witnessing radical suffering creates a possibility or "half- opening" for the witness also to be deeply shaped by such suffering and for the humanity of the one voicing the lament to be empowered by the validation of the witness. Perhaps this is the humanizing power of lament as protest. The one whose radical suffering is validated finds the power to recover a sense of the moral necessity of their complaint, and thus their protest reclaims meaning and purpose and hope. O'Connor (2002) also notes that the absence of God's voice in Lamentations emphasizes the importance of the suffering of the witness in Lamentations and points out the book's "theology of witness" that invites our attention for the practice of spiritual care (p. 107). The witness recognized the sacred dimensions of another's pain, and through that attentiveness the narrator discovered a window onto their own pain. The effectiveness of the witness lies in the acknowledgment that the Daughter of Zion and the witness share a common human vulnerability. Our witness in spiritual care must be similarly honest. O'Connor suggests this points to a "spirituality of attentiveness" (p. 108). Both Levinas and O'Connor encourage us to recognize that validating another's suffering discloses not only the sacred quality of that person's human suffering but offers a window onto our own. Together, we weep for a wounded world; together, we may resist the oppressive sources of such pain.

The absence of God's voice in Lamentations underscores the depth of suffering. O'Connor also points out that the voice of another witness in the third poem, verse 33, speaks the one thread of hope inserted in Lamentations by suggesting an alternative way to imagine God's presence in suffering, asserting that God "does not willingly afflict or grieve anyone" (p. 122). Here, O'Connor lifts up the way in which spiritual caregivers not only bear witness to dehumanizing suffering but may also wrestle alongside veterans such as Russell in their search for understanding differently the experience of God's absence or powerlessness. Our practice of care may allow us to recognize that here too is one whom God loves and in whom we see our own vulnerability (Ramsay 1998). Such compassion empowers veterans' abilities to resist the dehumanizing and isolating effects of war.

Spiritual care in the context of moral injury cannot dodge the looming presence of theodicy. Russell's dilemma includes the logical trap of his assumption that God's love is in the service of God's control or power over all that happens. Here, theologians such as Wendy Farley (1990) are helpful for amplifying the insight of Lamentations 3:33 alluding to God's compassion: "God does not will our affliction." War bears witness to the destructive possibilities of the abuse of human freedom, not to God's absence, indifference, or anger. In his discussion of God's trustworthy and empowering compassion in Psalm 23, Patrick Miller (1986, pp. 112, 119) suggests such a theology of suffering. Miller notes that although contemporary readers domesticate the image of the shepherd, for the original audience, it resonated with deliverance from Egypt and survival. It evokes both radical suffering and God's provision and protection (Ramsay 1998, p. 220). Miller suggests that Psalms 22 and 23 are intentionally paired. Psalm 22 voices profound suffering and the wrenching complaint of God's abandonment. Psalm 23 responds with the image of God's protection and the provision of all we need, even when we are surrounded by our enemies. Love does not prevent the presence of enemies and peril, but its fierce tenderness is never absent and will prevail. This image discloses hope as empowering practices of resistance (Ramsay 1998, p. 223). Farley suggests that, "hope in the redemptive power of God's love relies on the incarnation of resistance in the midst of suffering (1990, p. 127). In this way, spiritual care alongside veterans such as Russell seeks to embody a theology of witness found in Lamentations—a compassionate resistance that will mitigate and help heal the effects of radical suffering. This theology of witness also points to an alternative, more hopeful and empowering theological frame by incarnating the love to which it bears witness (Ramsay 1998, p. 223).

Care for Russell is at least initially shaped by the urgency of his sense of alienation from a faith and world and image of himself that once provided an orientation for his faith and life but no longer make sense. Those who offer spiritual care have the privilege of walking with persons such as Russell. Russell's pastor is fortunate to have known Russell for more than a decade, and he also knows Russell's parents. As he listens quietly to the halting story of pain, the theme of lament is clear, and so is the importance of compassionate resistance as a witness to Russell's isolating pain in the collapse of a world that made sense. Russell also quietly mentions his own behavior that he cannot forget. There are multiple possibilities for spiritual care with Russell. One of the pastor's concerns is Russell's relative isolation from his family and his knowledge that he is experiencing depression. This prioritizes his seeking a way to begin reducing Russell's isolation.

Russell's father is also a combat veteran and a former infantryman in Vietnam. The pastor remembers Russell's mother quietly mentioning that Russell's behavior reminds her of her husband when he returned from Vietnam. Perhaps the pastor might wonder out loud whether Russell knows if his experience is anything like his father's in Vietnam. That too was a brutal war for infantrymen. It is likely the case that there has been no such conversation, but what might happen if there were? The pastor might ask Russell what he would want to ask his father. Maybe Russell would learn something important. This possibility of conversation may be especially helpful for Russell and for the family because it appears that Russell's father has not spoken of the ways Vietnam taught him the horrors of war. We only know Russell's mother sees the similarities, and perhaps she could be an ally in bridging this conversation. It is quite possible that the father has much to share and that moral injury has shaped his silence about such a formative time. Here may be an opportunity for intimacy and a chance for healing for two generations. It is also quite possible that Russell's father will understand Russell's recognition of how race and racism shaped his military experience. Both men fought racialized others and began to recognize the political and economic factors that put them in harm's way. Both men now feel the reverberations of war in the racist violence within their community and between police and African Americans. The wound of war has a deeper significance for them that shapes their grief. Moral injury is influenced by cultural and historical contexts such as racism.

Remembering Russell's familiarity with scriptures, the pastor might suggest that Russell read and reflect on Psalm 22 and maybe mention that it might be useful also to know that Psalm 23 seems to be a response to the previous psalm. Perhaps Russell would be willing to take some time each day simply to read and think about Psalm 22. If so, perhaps they could talk about how it speaks to his pain. This, of course, is not unlike the ritual practice of *lectio divina* (Liebert 2019). If reading this lament proves helpful to Russell, maybe he would consider writing his own lament—his own witness poetry (Fawson 2019).

Zachary Moon, a reserve military chaplain and professor, reminds us that moral injury does not eclipse all that a veteran is (2015, 2019). Rather, Moon lifts up the competencies and leadership skills of veterans. At some point in the journey with Russell, the pastor may recall for Russell the importance of the community garden he helped to start that continues to make fresh vegetables available in the urban area. What might happen if Russell chose to return to that project and support it? Perhaps that garden and the story it tells of Russell's commitment to others would provide a hopeful opening. If so, in time Russell and his dad or Russell and his pastor might choose to mark a positive turn in Russell's journey and develop a ritual practice that allows Russell or father and son to name the pain of war and mark a new step into a future in which they will contribute life-giving energy to meeting needs in their community. Such creative rituals, of course, must "fit" the experience of the participants and be shaped in conversation with them (Anderson and Foley 1998, pp. 128–131). For example, Russell might choose to bury spent ammunition casings at the base of a tree that helps shade a portion of the garden. He might wrap them in his own witness poem evoked by Psalm 22.

All of these ritualized strategies augment and extend the possibilities for care with Russell. They provide a context in which Russell can explore alternative ways of imagining who God is and God's care for him and his world. At some point, they will likely open conversation about his guilt related to his own behavior in war. The themes of loss and grief are deep in his young life and will accompany him across decades. But he will come to that reflection on guilt having re-imagined a more compassionate God, which will allow him to imagine forgiveness differently. He has begun a journey that, like Jacob's, will always include a limp, but it will also open up a new sense of himself and of faith and of possibilities for sharing his abundant gifts.

In the experience of Jim and Rachel, moral injury is foregrounded by Jim's grief, and it echoes Larry Graham's reminder that "innocence mourned is not innocence regained" (p. 78). For Jim, the impossibility of forgiveness is front and center, while in the background is the loss of a world that makes moral sense. Now he recognizes that the world is not as he had imagined. But, primary for him is the guilt he feels and perhaps the shame he feels before his wife. Can she love him? Can she trust him with their children since he participated in the killing of children like theirs? Can he trust himself with them? From Rachel's description, Jim went to war as one who enjoyed experiencing control over his life and his ability to protect his family. This strength was part of her attraction to him and apparently part of what it meant to him to be a good husband and father. In his absence, she has had to find and practice strengths she did not need when they shared parenting. But she had hoped to experience his protective strength and confidence again soon. Both wife and husband are affected by moral injury. We can also assume that their children, especially five-year-old Jimmy, will also experience his father differently.

Let's imagine that Jim has returned home and that he and Rachel came to see you, their pastor, at Rachel's insistence. Here, seeking to help them develop practices that give each of them resilience and supporting them as a couple loom large. Other professional colleagues in the community will be important allies in healing. War and moral injury in combat render Jim especially vulnerable because his expectations for mastery loom large in his own life and in his marriage and likely in his sense of himself as a man, husband, and father. He is coming to terms with the realization that the goal of mastery shaping the masculinity into which he was inducted was an illusion. Grace is suddenly important but longing for it is unfamiliar territory for him personally and spiritually.

In this early period of return, coping with ambiguous loss and beginning to develop patterns of resilience prioritize the creation of focused opportunities for Jim to explore the immediacy of his emotional and spiritual challenges and perhaps engage in the kinds of mindfulness therapies and embodied practices that Carrie Doehring (2019) describes. He and Rachel might benefit from the help of a family therapist to suggest some strategies for the immediate need to identify ways Jim can be present to Lydia and especially Jimmy in the interim. And they will need practices for caring for their marriage as they prioritize intensive support for Jim. Because the base is relatively close by, Rachel has opportunities to participate in a support group for spouses like herself. In time, as Boss (2006) suggests, Jim may also find it helpful to join the group of veterans described in another vignette because such established groups extend the web of care and belonging when veterans return from war and are finding their way into a new future.

However, as the couple together and individually steps into this important period of gaining clarity about the cost of war for Jim and for their marriage, their spiritual care is important. As with Russell, a number of responses could be of use for supporting Jim in his grief. With the deep longing for forgiveness voiced so prominently by Jim, and his profound loss of confidence in his earlier sense of himself now altered by shame, Jim and his pastor will want to engage in conversations that focus on assisting him in trusting that God's grace accompanies him on this journey. As the film *Almost Sunrise* (2017) describes, it is often helpful for veterans troubled in ways similar to Jim to engage in reflective conversations with an identified religious leader to assist them in the processes of confession and reimagining grace and experiences of forgiveness. In these conversations, as with formal therapy, it is possible not only to confess and acknowledge grief for behaviors in which Jim engaged but also to explore ways in which Jim's shame and guilt reflect his immersion in a conflict in which his options were shaped by factors beyond his control. He may need assistance in externalizing some of the blame that burdens him while accepting guilt that is rightly his. One ritual possibility that may be helpful is the encouragement to come to the monthly eucharistic Taizé services for healing and wholeness that include the option of anointing. Here, in the company of others longing for a reminder of God's healing and forgiving love, Jim and Rachel may find comfort, and the haunting melodies of the chants in the liturgy will likely also be a comfort to both. Further, Jim may also choose to be anointed with oil during the service, which is also an ancient physical reminder of God's gracious presence. This anointing, of course, is echoed in Psalm 23. As Jim's pastor, you might invite Jim to read Psalm 23 daily alongside Romans 8:38–39 or early verses in Isaiah 43. These passages and many others have significance not only in relation to forgiveness but because they assert God's compassionate resistance alongside forces that deform and destroy human life.

As Tom Driver (1991) suggests, ritual practices include not only a confessional mode but also transformational or ethical dimensions (p. 108). In time, as Jim's pastor, you may invite him to imagine how to symbolize his newly revised understanding of God's grace and forgiveness. One strategy could include renewing his baptismal vows as a way to affirm his stepping anew into God's journey with him and his family and making a commitment that bears witness to the transforming freedom of forgiveness by contributing his time and talents to supporting the futures of children in his city who are at risk. He cannot bring back those he saw die in war, but he can offer love to other vulnerable children. He and Jimmy can share in that work together. As we noted regarding Russell's journey, Moon (2015) reminds us that alongside the journey of recovery from moral injury, veterans benefit from opportunities to share the competencies and the commitments that led them to serve and that were honed in their military training.

For Rachel's spiritual care journey, it is also important to walk with her as she lives with the awareness that moral injury is a relational loss and works with Jim to help protect their children from its generational legacy. She, like Jim, will need ritual practices that offer her strength and renew her confidence that she and Jim do not walk alone. She may discover that although she had learned to rely on Jim's confidence and strength, she always had those resources in her own life. As he comes to terms with his need for grace, she too may find that her strengths are more extensive than she had realized.

In time, through your spiritual care accompaniment, a moment may come when Rachel and Jim choose to renew their commitment as husband and wife and parents. They may invite you to help them ritualize that new imagination for their life together. Like Jim, we can hope Rachel will also emerge from this journey with strengths she has discovered or reclaimed and developed for living differently into the future she and Jim are seeking to reclaim.

As Arthur Frank (2013) reminds us in reflecting on Jacob's long night at the Jabbok, the new life Jim and Rachel seek for themselves, their marriage, and their children will require wrestling with painful and life-threatening challenges. They will be forever marked by that wrestling match, but spiritual care providers have the opportunity to assist in helping them imagine they will be met by grace that will not let them go.

Frank's heartbreaking story of six decades of silence about his memories of engaging in the brutal combat that shaped the war in Korea underscores the importance of spiritual care that invites reflections when we encounter veterans. Perhaps an earlier invitation to share might have created an opening that could have spared him such long imprisonment in the grip of shame and guilt. But Frank's decision to turn to his rabbi now because he knows his death is approaching reminds us that the opportunities to listen for the costs of war last as long as a veteran lives. This situation now includes the shock that his wife and adult sons also experience. Frank's story points to the relational and generational aspects of moral injury. The priority for Frank's rabbi is Frank's own journey to experience and trust promises of forgiveness and to face the end of life with a sense of peace that has eluded him for six decades. However, the rabbi can also help Frank's wife and sons understand how moral injury shaped Frank's life alongside the love he had for each of them. As the rabbi begins her conversations with Frank, she will also be able to help his family to understand the power of the shame and guilt that created this distance; even as Frank entered into marriage and later parented his children, he carried this pain. She can also help them to let go of their possible guilt for not understanding or recognizing this distance when and if they felt it.

Frank and his rabbi have valuable resources for "holding" these sacred conversations during these last weeks or months of his life. Though these conversations do not occur in the High Holy Days marked by Rosh Hashanah and Yom Kippur, they can turn to the prayers of Yom Kippur, where God's forgiveness is explicit. Frank knows these prayers well. But somehow, only now can the full reach of God's forgiveness be explored in relation to the deep pain he has long carried. The prayers promise forgiveness for sin against God, but they command Frank's action toward those he harmed. In the absence of that possibility, the rabbi has the opportunity to assist Frank in recognizing that the violence he committed was in the context of a war in which he and his colleagues were defending innocent civilians. His confession is not about his choice to initiate violence but his participation in war. Portions of the final evening prayers of Yom Kippur on the Day of Atonement are familiar to Frank from decades of reciting them. Their very familiarity is helpful to Frank as he joins the rabbi in saying the words:

> You hold out Your hand to those who have rebelled against You; Your right hand is stretched out to receive those who turn back to You. Eternal God, You have taught us to confess all our faults before You, so that we may turn away from violence and oppression. In accordance with Your gracious promise, accept our repentance, which we offer to You in all sincerity. . . .
>
> And in Your love, O gracious God, You have given us this Day of Atonement, that our sins may cease and be forgiven, and that, turning away from violence and oppression, we may turn back to You and do Your will with a perfect heart. The day is fading; the sun is setting; the silence and peace of night descend upon the earth. Give rest now, O Author of peace, to our troubled hearts; lift up the spirit oppressed by guilt. Turn, O Loved One, to Your children; turn to every broken heart and every burdened soul. Let us at this hour be sure of Your forgiveness.

And still another dwelling-place have You destined for us, O Source of life, an eternal home to which we shall go when our brief day on earth has passed. Open for us then the gates of everlasting peace and keep alive in those who follow us the truths, the visions, and the hopes we have struggled to make real. (Liturgy Committee of the Central Conference of American Rabbis 1978, pp. 514–15, 519)

Christians and Muslims will realize that their traditions also have liturgical sources, especially in Lenten services and in the prayers of Ramadan, in which repentance and the assurance of Allah's mercy are foregrounded.

Frank's rabbi may also draw on the Vidui, the prayer of confession that is offered as the end of life approaches. There is no inhibition to sharing this prayer multiple times when the rabbi and Frank and possibly Frank's wife engage in conversation while Frank struggles to receive forgiveness and experience freedom from the burden of guilt carried across six decades. Different versions of this prayer vary in length, but the opening verses include the following request to Adonai: "So let it be your will, Adonai our God and our ancestors' God, that You forgive all our sins, pardon all our iniquities, and absolve all our misdeeds" (Hoffman 2012, p. 98).

It seems plausible that the rabbi accompanying Frank in this journey toward forgiveness may well find the story of Jacob at the Jabbok useful to share with this man who, like Jacob, has carried awareness of his sins for decades and, on the eve of what may be his death, confronts the one with whom he wrestles for a blessing that comes to him, in Jacob's case with a new name and the awareness that this blessing is from God. Frank may still limp toward his final days, but he can do so without carrying a burden of guilt that belongs with a war not of his making.

The remaining vignette of the veterans' group at the United Methodist church where a noncombat veteran serves as pastor also invites us to imagine ways to offer care that is responsive to veterans and that may respond to Chaplain Beth Stallinga's (2013) chilling reminder that civilians need to acknowledge their corporate responsibility and accountability when their country wages war. Civilians also need to acknowledge their own complicity in the destructive violence of war and explore how moral injury shapes their lives, whether acknowledged or avoided. The presence of this group of veterans may present this congregation with an opportunity to explore a wider appreciation for the reach of moral injury. Our consideration of care with this group of veterans will include this possibility.

First, of course, we affirm the pastor's initiative in going to veterans he recognized in the congregation, hearing their story, and wondering with them about the value of such a group. This is excellent spiritual care in itself, for he conveys informed concern and readiness to walk beside them, and sure enough, many of those invited come in search of care and to provide support to others that they know they too have needed. As Rambo describes in her conversations with a similar group, (2017, pp. 109–143), informal ritual actions help to mark the boundaries of belonging and the time for sharing and support. Intimacy and deeper willingness to risk admitting the need for support are met with care and not judgment. The group also stands ready to welcome others such as Russell and maybe his father. The presence of a pastor who is a veteran in a community of faith offers the opportunity to reflect on how moral injury shapes experiences of faith and struggles with faith. Also present is the growing band of new group members who are welcomed in an outer circle. We could imagine the group members as "bearing witness," the term used by Lamentations and Levinas. They hear the pain and validate its truth. And, somehow, many of the veterans decide to go together to a monthly eucharistic service of healing and wholeness. They are now more public about their journey with the "afterlife" (Rambo 2017) of war. Forgiveness and renewal are unfolding as they face their pain and claim a new way of stepping into the future with a hard-earned limp.

Then comes the opening that may prove to the veterans that their deeper pain is heard—the opportunity to engage with civilian congregants and talk about how such a service could be shaped in ways that are even closer to the veterans' needs. Here, the pastor and congregational leaders have an opportunity to think more honestly about what their role may be in the pain that they are witnessing. The "half-opening" this veterans' group represents invites the civilians to enter into the wider implications of the wounds of war and to recognize the veterans' wounds as the civilians' as well.

We responded to the other vignettes by sometimes drawing on traditional or familiar ritual practices and sometimes, as with Russell and Jim and Rachel, creating ritual responses that are faithful to the traditions of the congregants and to responsible practices, including honoring the effort to open congregants to God's healing presence. Here too may be such an opportunity for the congregation, who thus far has failed to engage with how war changes each of us when our country sends combatants on our behalf. However, as Anderson and Foley (1998) caution, great care must shape any construction of a ritual practice (pp. 128–130). Veterans should be part of the process of exploring the readiness of congregants and helping to shape the liturgy. Then, interpretation of the practice and clarity about how it will unfold help all to enter with trust into what becomes holy space. In the case of the invitation to explore a eucharistic service responsive to the veterans, the opening may come to widen that invitation as the worship committee discusses this invitation with the pastor and some of the veterans. A wider invitation and explanation may then go out to the congregation, along with programmatic opportunities for the pastor and some of the veterans to foster a conversation about moral injury that invites the civilians to reimagine the reach of war and its harm. Bit by bit, an openness to this wider way of imagining moral injury may grow. That particular recurring service of healing and wholeness may pave the way for a special congregational service on Memorial Day or Veteran's Day that many in the congregation embrace as an opportunity for them to offer their own lament and share a broader confession of sin. We have located this possibility in a Christian congregation, but nothing prevents a rabbi from leading similar process with a Jewish congregation or an imam from exploring how the prayers of Ramadan could reframe an understanding of wider accountability for engaging in war.

As Driver (1991) reminded us, such ritual practice includes the opportunity to experience not only the confessional mode of ritual but the path such confession creates for entering into the transformational possibilities of recovery of the freedom to live differently by exercising agency no longer confined by guilt or avoidance of accountability. Perhaps then, as with Russell and Jim, such a service will include a new individual commitment or a new commitment by the community to embrace the opportunity to bear witness to their accountability for war and its destructive consequences. This possibility widens further Levinas' (1988) recognition that in seeing the suffering of another, we may choose to step toward rather than away and in so doing find new healing for our own humanity.

Conclusion

War changes all in its path, especially those who experience its destructive power in their spirits, hearts, and bodies. In this article, I have explored particularly how practices of spiritual care provide opportunities to respond to the particular ways grief emerges and hampers the lives of those who survive war's violence but live with the profound effects of its emotional as well as physical wounds. Moral injury points to the ambiguous losses of the "afterlife" of war (Rambo 2017). In its various forms, spiritual care offers religious leaders and faith communities an opportunity to accompany those affected by moral injury, both veterans and their families. Such care is enhanced by a readiness to deepen opportunities for healing and reconnecting with wider communities through ritual practices familiar in those communities, such as Eucharist and Seder and Lenten observances, the High Holy Days of Rosh Hashanah and Yom Kippur, and Ramadan. Spiritual care in response to moral injury also includes the freedom carefully to shape ritual practices that deepen and widen recognition of the need for confession, the availability of grace, and the possibility of a new life shaped by recommitment and signaled by a limp.

References

Anderson, H., & Foley, E. (1998). *Mighty stories, dangerous rituals*. San Francisco: Jossey Bass.

Billman, K. D., & Migliore, D. L. (1999). *Rachel's cry: Prayer of lament and rebirth of hope*. Cleveland: United Church Press.

Boss, P. (1999). *Ambiguous loss: Learning to live with unresolved grief*. Cambridge: Harvard University Press.

Boss, P. (2006). *Loss, trauma, and resilience: Therapeutic work with ambiguous loss*. New York: W. W. Norton.

Brueggemann, W. (1986). *Hopeful imagination: Prophetic voices in exile*. Minneapolis: Fortress Press.

Collins, M., & Syjuco, M. (Directors). (2017). *Almost sunrise* [Motion Picture]. United States: Veterans Trek Production.

Copp, T. (2018). Sexual assault: Here are the bases where troops are most at risk. *Military Times*. https://www. militarytimes.com/news/your-military/2018/09/21/sexual-assault-here-are-the-bases-where-troops-are-most-at-risk/. Accessed 14 Oct 2018.

Doehring, C. (2019). Military moral injury: An evidence-based and intercultural approach to spiritual care. *Pastoral Psychology, 68*(1), 15-30. doi.org/10.1007/s11089-018-0813-5.

Drescher, K. D., Foy, D. W., Kelly, C., Leshner, A., Schutz, K., & Litz, B. (2011). An exploration of the usefulness of the construct of moral injury in war veterans. *Traumatology, 17*(1), 8–13. doi.org/10.1177/1534765610395615

Driver, T. F. (1991). *The magic of ritual*. San Francisco: Harper.

Farley, W. (1990). *Tragic vision and divine compassion: A contemporary theodicy*. Louisville: Westminster/John Knox Press.

Fawson, S. (2019). Sustaining lamentation for military moral injury: Witness poetry that bears the traces of extremity. *Pastoral Psychology, 68*(1), 31-40. doi.org/10.1007/s11089-018-0855-8.

Frank, A. W. (2013). *The wounded storyteller: Body, illness, and ethics.* Chicago: University of Chicago Press.

Graham, L. K. (2017). *Moral injury: Healing wounded souls.* Nashville: Abingdon.

Herman, J. (2015). *Trauma and recovery with a new epilogue.* New York: Basic Books.

Hoffman, L. (2012). *We have sinned.* Woodstock: Jewish Lights.

Levinas, E. (1988). Useless suffering. In R. Bernasconi & D. Wood (Eds.), *The provocation of Levinas: Rethinking the other* (R. Cohen, Trans., pp. 156–167). New York: Routledge.

Liebert, E. (2019). Accessible spiritual practices to aid in recovery from moral injury. *Pastoral Psychology, 68*(1), 41-57. doi.org/10.1007/s11089-018-0825-1.

Liturgy Committee of the Central Conference of American Rabbis. (1978). *Gates of repentance: The new union prayerbook for the days of awe* (C. Stern, Ed.). New York: Central Conference of American Rabbis.

Litz, B. T., Stein, N., Delaney, E., Lebowitz, L., Nash, W. P., Silva, C., & Maguen, S. (2009). Moral injury and moral repair in war veterans: A preliminary model and intervention strategy. *Clinical Psychology Review, 29*(8), 695–706. doi.org/10.1016/j.cpr.2009.07.003.

Miller, P. D. (1986). *Interpreting the psalms.* Philadelphia: Westminster.

Moon, Z. (2015). *Coming home: Ministry that matters with veterans and military families.* St. Louis: Chalice Press.

Moon, Z. (2019). "Turn now, my vindication is at stake": Military moral injury and communities of faith. *Pastoral Psychology, 68*(1), 93-105. doi.org/10.1007/s11089–017–0795–8.

Morral, A., Schell, T., Cefalu, M., Hwang, J., & Gelman, A. (2018). *Sexual assault and sexual harassment in the U.S. military, vol. 5: Estimates for installation- and command-level risk of sexual assault and sexual harassment from the 2014 RAND military workplace study.* Santa Monica: Rand Corporation. https://www.rand.org/pubs/research_reports/RR870z7.html. Accessed 14 Oct 2018.

Morton, N. (1985). *The journey is home.* Boston: Beacon.

Nelson, S. L. (2003). Facing evil: Evil's many faces: Five paradigms for understanding evil. *Interpretation, 57*(4), 399–413.

O'Connor, K. (2002). *Lamentations: The tears of the world.* Mary Knoll: Orbis.

Rambo, S. (2017). *Resurrecting wounds: Living with the afterlife of trauma.* Waco: Baylor University Press.

Ramsay, N. (1998). Compassionate resistance: An ethic for pastoral care and counseling. *The Journal of Pastoral Care and Counseling, 52*(3), 217–226.

Ramshaw, E. (1987). *Ritual and pastoral care*. Philadelphia: Westminster Press.

Shay, J. (1994). *Achilles in Vietnam: Combat trauma and the undoing of character*. New York: Scribner.

Sherman, N. (2015). *Afterwar: Healing the moral wounds of our soldiers*. New York: Oxford University Press.

Simmons, A., Rivers, F., Gordon, S., & Yoder, L. (2018). The role of spirituality among military en route care nurses: Source of strength or moral injury? *Critical Care Nurse, 38*(2), 61–68. doi.org/10.4037/ccn2018674.

Stallinga, B. (2013). What spills blood wounds spirit: Chaplains, spiritual care, and operational stress. *Reflective Practice: Formation and Supervision for Ministry, 33*, 13–31.

Yandell, M. (2015). The war within. *Christian Century, 132*(1), 12–13.

Yandell, M. (2019). Moral injury and human relationship: A conversation. *Pastoral Psychology, 68*(1), 3-14. doi.org/10.1007/s11089-018-0800-x.